EYES TOO DRY

echo
PUBLISHING

A DIVISION OF BONNIER PUBLISHING AUSTRALIA
534 CHURCH ST, RICHMOND
VICTORIA AUSTRALIA 3121
www.echopublishing.com.au
eyestoodry@gmail.com

PREVIOUSLY PUBLISHED BY THE AUTHORS IN 2017. THIS EDITION FIRST PUBLISHED BY ECHO 2017.

PRINTED IN AUSTRALIA

COVER AND PAGE DESIGN BY ALICE CHIPKIN, EMMA JENSEN AND JESSICA TAVASSOLI
EDITING AND LAY OUT BY EMMA JENSEN.

NATIONAL LIBRARY OF AUSTRALIA CATALOGUING-IN-PUBLICATION ENTRY:
CREATOR: CHIPKIN, ALICE, AUTHOR, ILLUSTRATOR.
TITLE: EYES TOO DRY / ALICE CHIPKIN AND JESSICA TAVASSOLI, CO-AUTHORS & ILLUSTRATORS
ISBN: 9781760680039 (PAPER BACK)
ISBN: 9781760680046 (EPUB)
ISBN: 9781760680053 (MOBI)

SUBJECTS: MENTALLY ILL — SOCIAL CONDITIONS. DEPRESSED PERSONS — SOCIAL CONDITIONS. CAREGIVERS. MENTALLY ILL — FAMILY RELATIONSHIPS. FRIENDSHIP. ART THERAPY. GRAPHIC NOVELS.

 @BONNIERAU

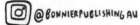 @BONNIERPUBLISHINGAU

 @BONNIERPUBLISHINGAU

AUTHOR NOTES

THIS BOOK WAS CREATED ON THE STOLEN LANDS OF THE WURUNDJERI PEOPLE OF THE KULIN NATION, THE GADIGAL PEOPLE OF THE EORA NATION AND THE TSAWWASSEN FIRST NATION. WE PAY OUR DEEP RESPECTS TO THOSE ELDERS, PAST, PRESENT AND EMERGING, AND ACKNOWLEDGE THAT SOVEREIGNTY WAS NEVER CEDED. WE OFFER OUR RESPECTS TO ALL TRADITIONAL OWNERS OF COUNTRY INTO WHICH THIS BOOK MAY FIND ITS WAY.

CONTENT WARNING

THIS BOOK CONTAINS REFERENCES TO DEPRESSION AND SUICIDE. SOME READERS MAY FIND THIS CONFRONTING AND ARE ADVISED TO TAKE CARE WHILE READING.

CONTENTS

OPENINGS

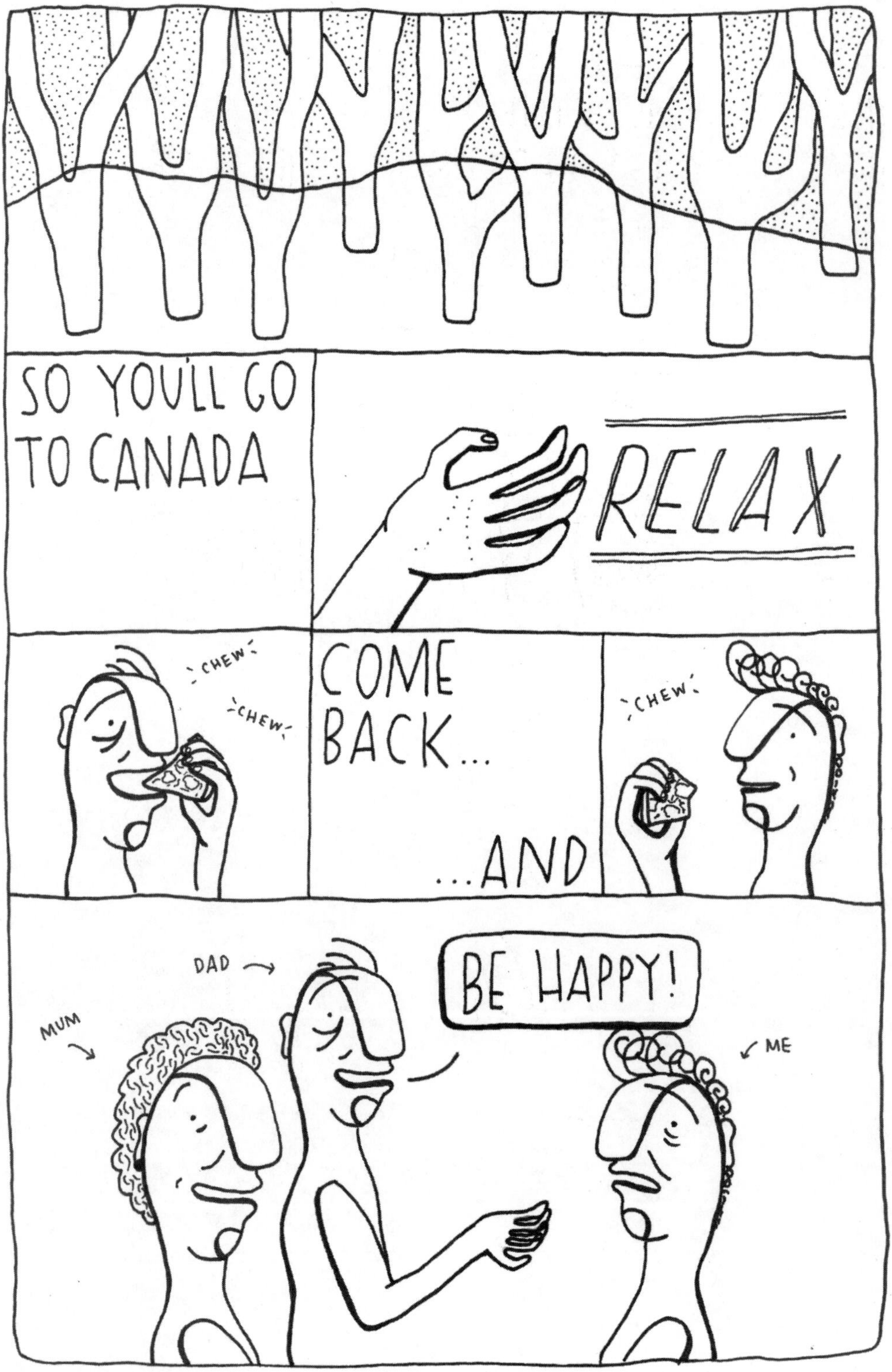

SO YOU'LL GO TO CANADA
RELAX
CHEW
CHEW
COME BACK...
...AND
CHEW
DAD
MUM
BE HAPPY!
ME

WE WERE AT THE SAME RESTAURANT WHERE A FEW MONTHS EARLIER I HAD TOLD THEM I WAS TAKING ANTIDEPRESSANTS
Pizza Espr
by Nicolini
WOULD YOU LIKE SOME WINE?
Ahhh... NO THANKS
WHY NOT? ARE YOU ON MEDICATION OR SOMETHING?
ACTUALLY YES, I'M...

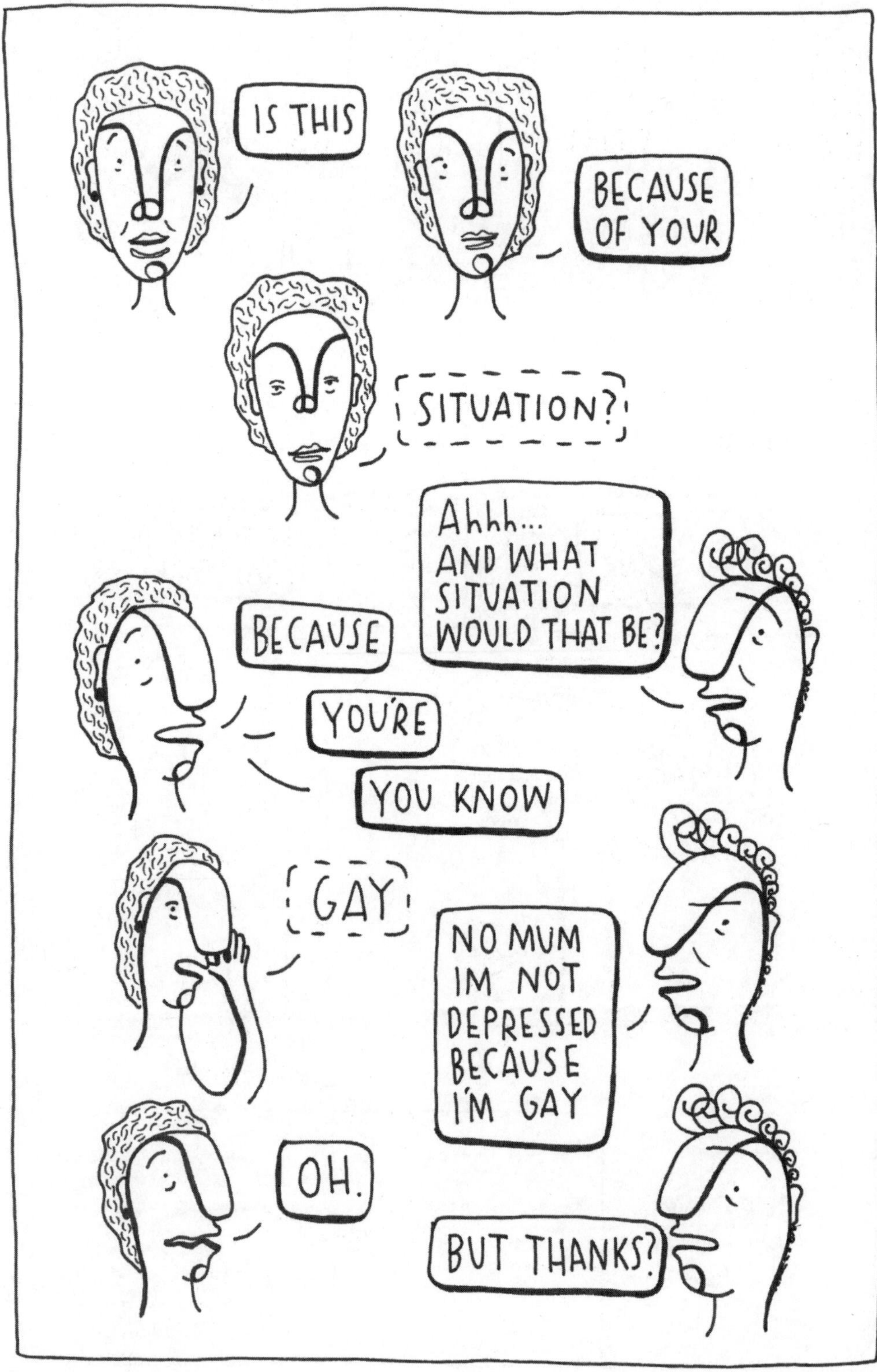
IS THIS
BECAUSE OF YOUR
SITUATION?
Ahhh... AND WHAT SITUATION WOULD THAT BE?
BECAUSE
YOU'RE
YOU KNOW
GAY
NO MUM IM NOT DEPRESSED BECAUSE I'M GAY
OH.
BUT THANKS?

IT'S HARD TO SAY EXACTLY WHEN THIS ALL STARTED
I HAVE BEEN WRESTLING WITH MY FEELINGS FOR THE PAST SIX YEARS

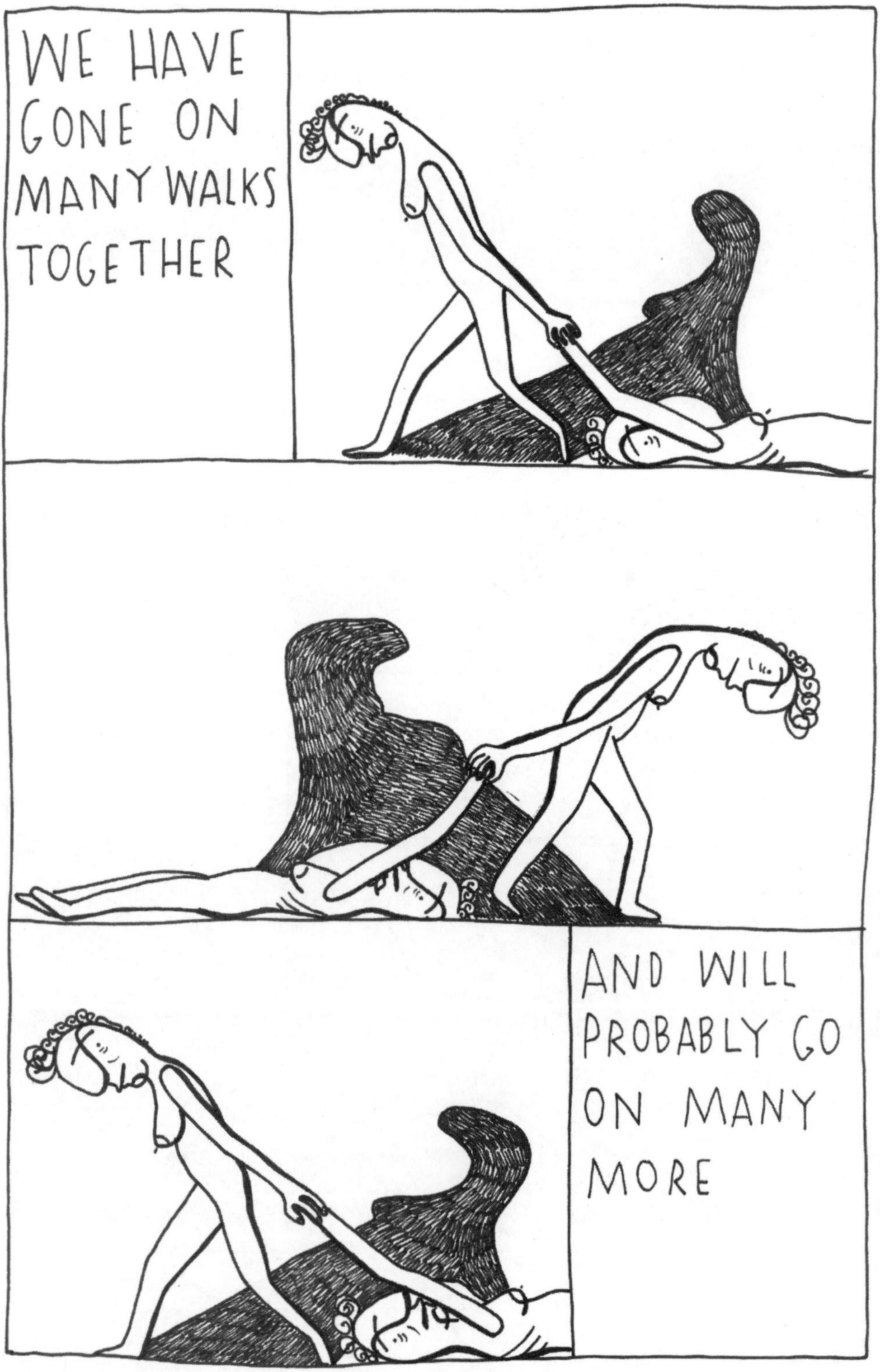
WE HAVE GONE ON MANY WALKS TOGETHER
AND WILL PROBABLY GO ON MANY MORE

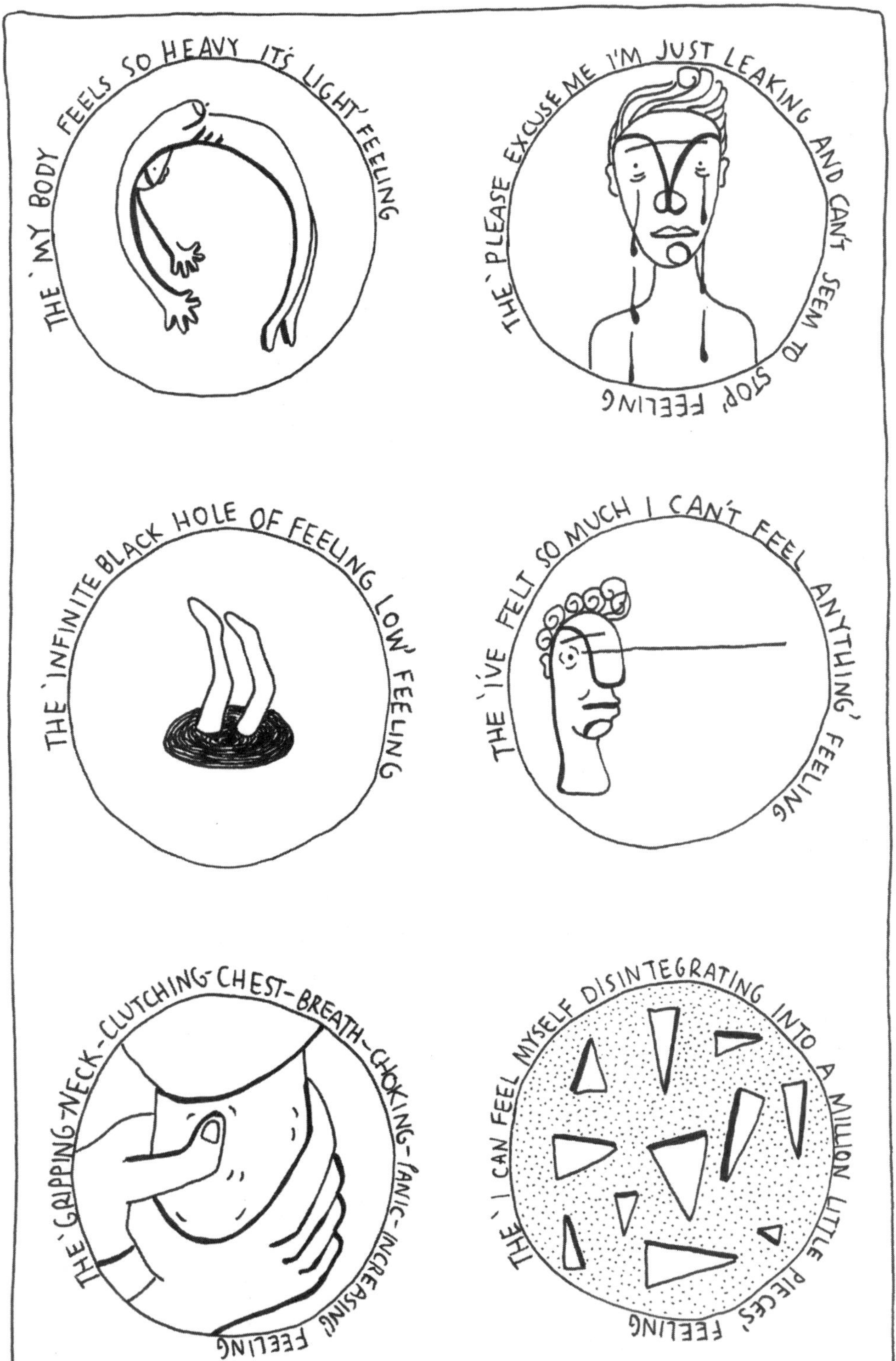
THE 'MY BODY FEELS SO HEAVY IT'S LIGHT' FEELING
THE 'PLEASE EXCUSE ME I'M JUST LEAKING AND CAN'T SEEM TO STOP' FEELING
THE 'INFINITE BLACK HOLE OF FEELING LOW' FEELING
THE 'I'VE FELT SO MUCH I CAN'T FEEL ANYTHING' FEELING
THE 'GRIPPING-NECK-CLUTCHING-CHEST-BREATH-CHOKING-PANIC-INCREASING' FEELING
THE 'I CAN FEEL MYSELF DISINTEGRATING INTO A MILLION LITTLE PIECES' FEELING

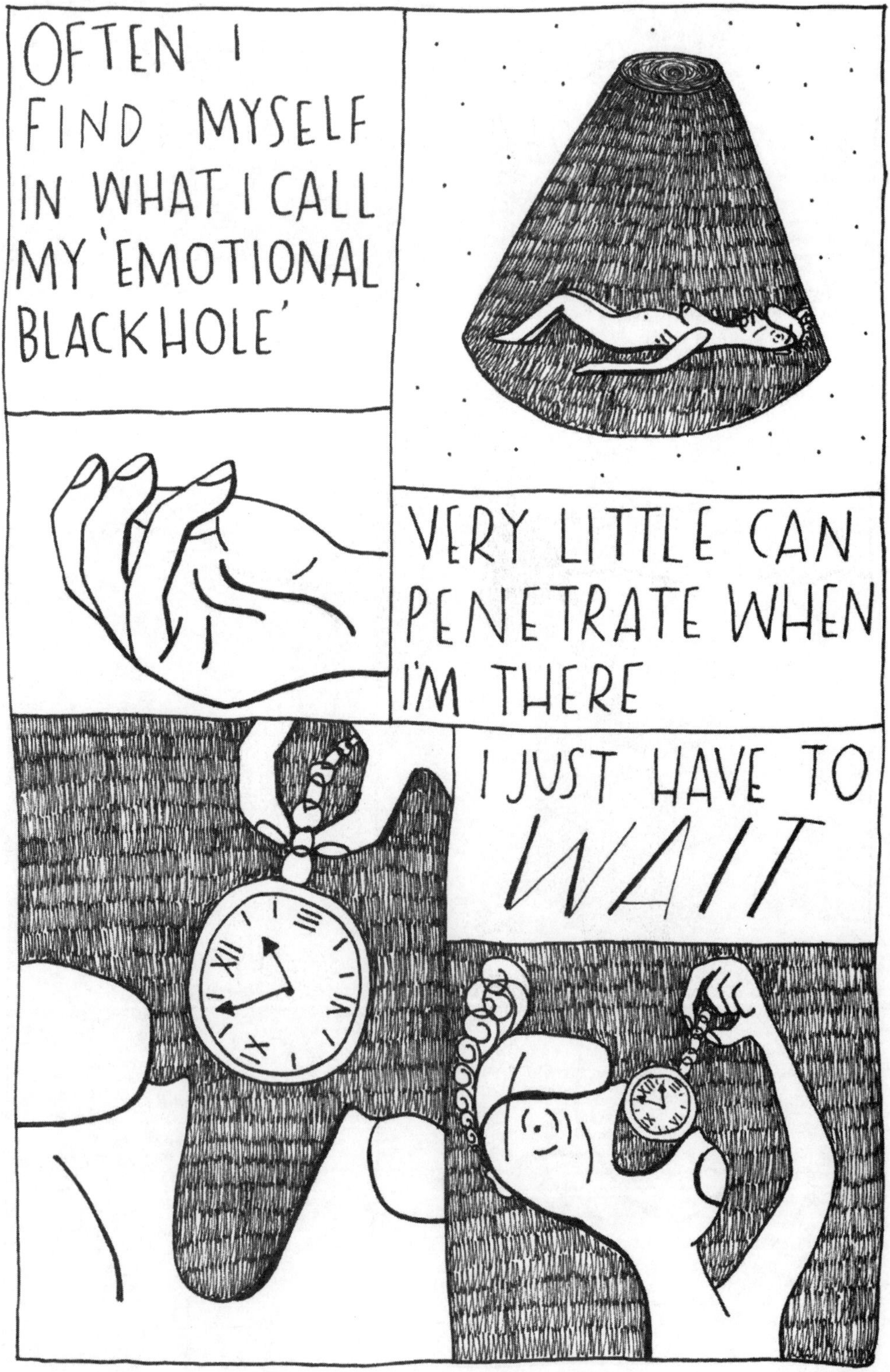
OFTEN I FIND MYSELF IN WHAT I CALL MY 'EMOTIONAL BLACKHOLE'
VERY LITTLE CAN PENETRATE WHEN I'M THERE
I JUST HAVE TO WAIT

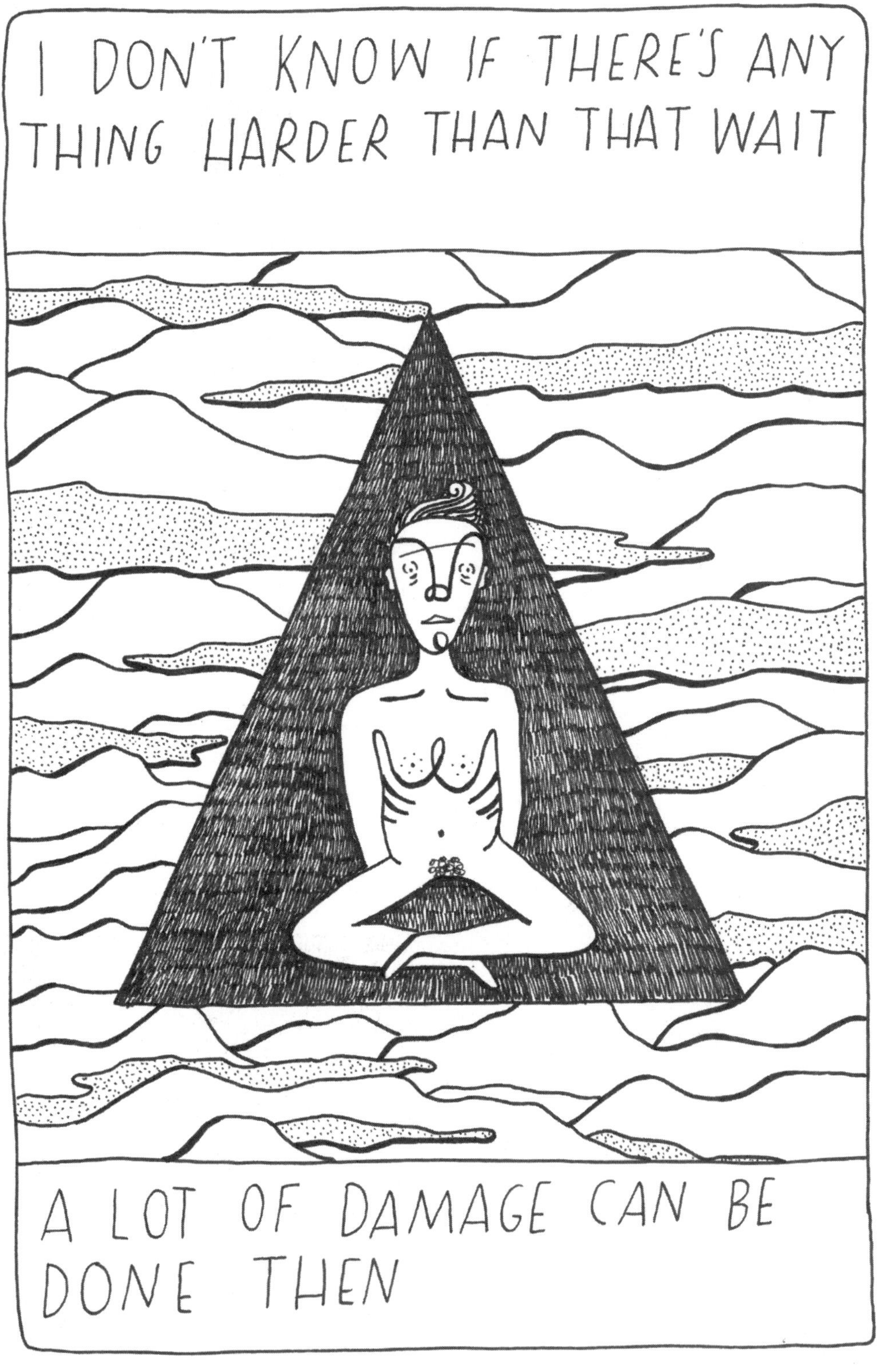
I DON'T KNOW IF THERE'S ANY THING HARDER THAN THAT WAIT
A LOT OF DAMAGE CAN BE DONE THEN

FALLINGS

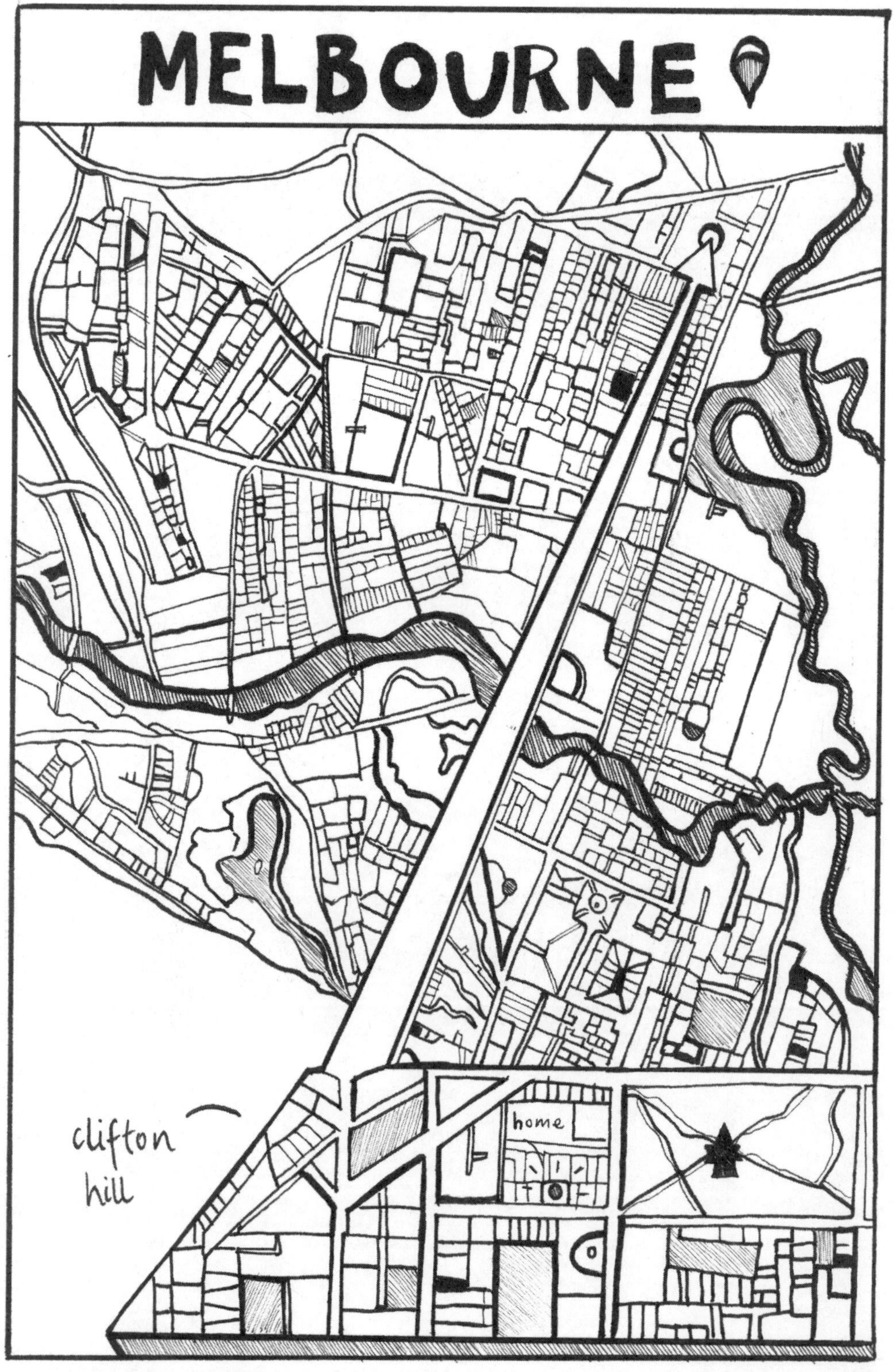
MELBOURNE
home
clifton hill

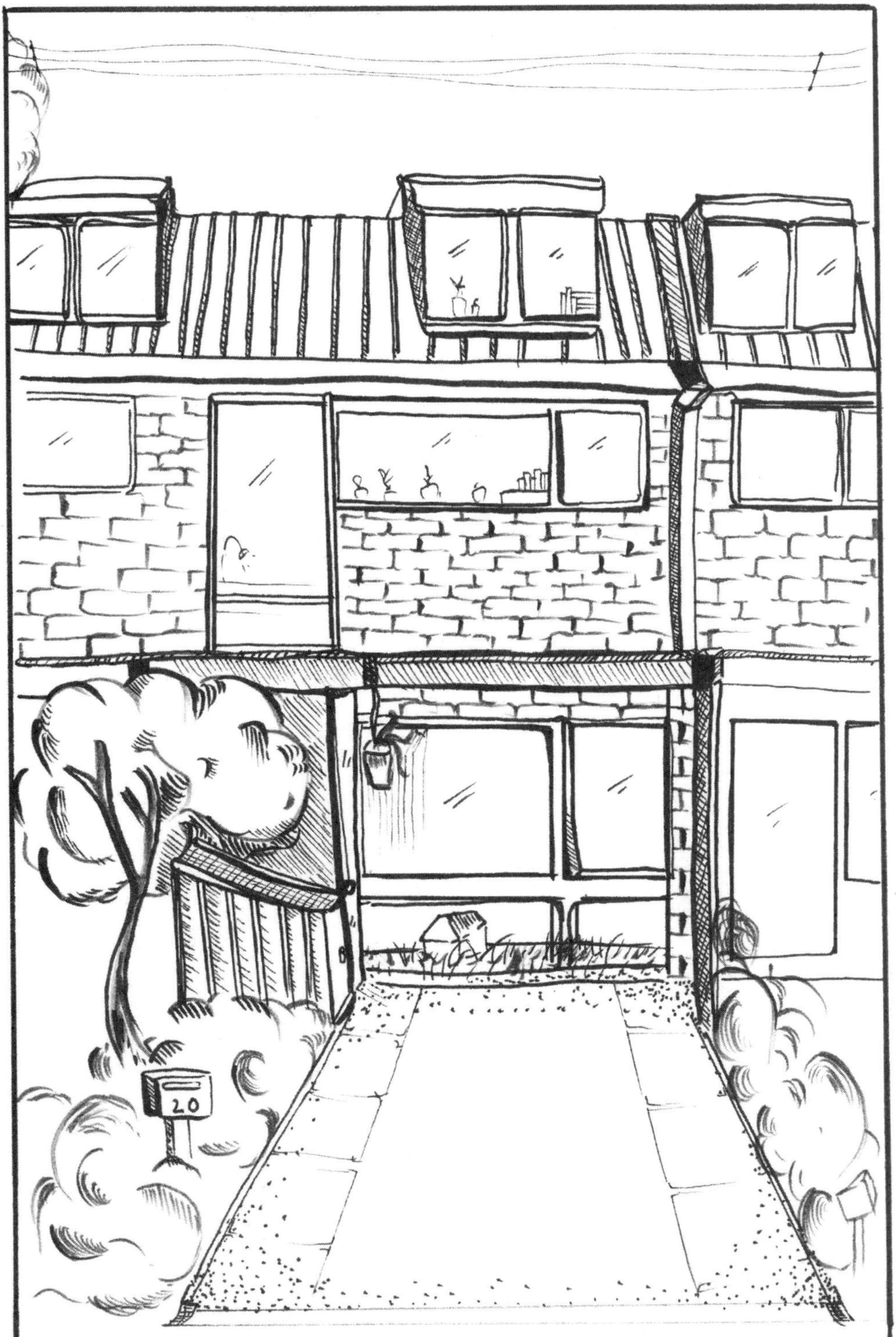
20

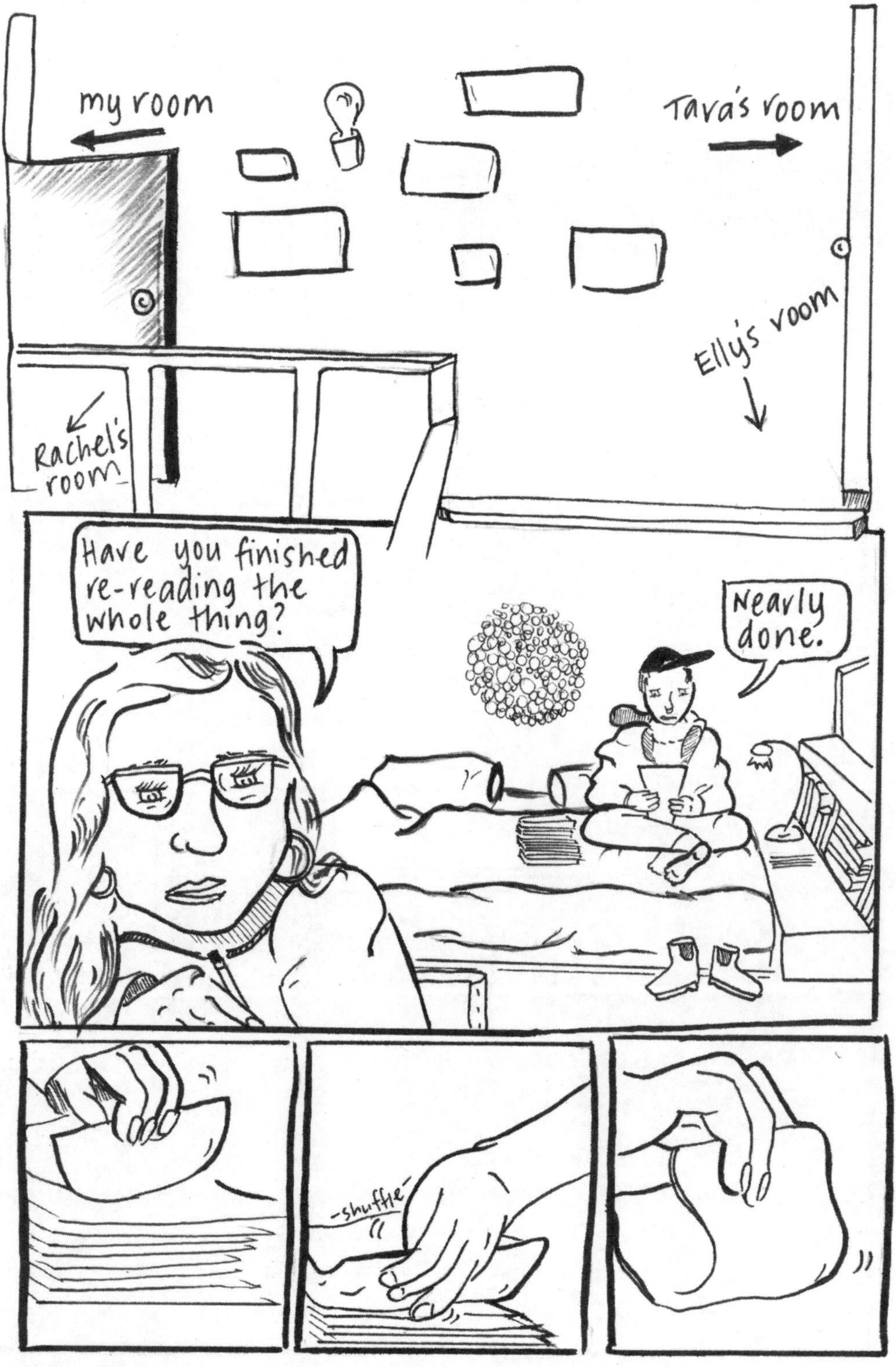

my room
Tara's room
Elly's room
Rachel's room
Have you finished re-reading the whole thing?
Nearly done.
-shuffle-

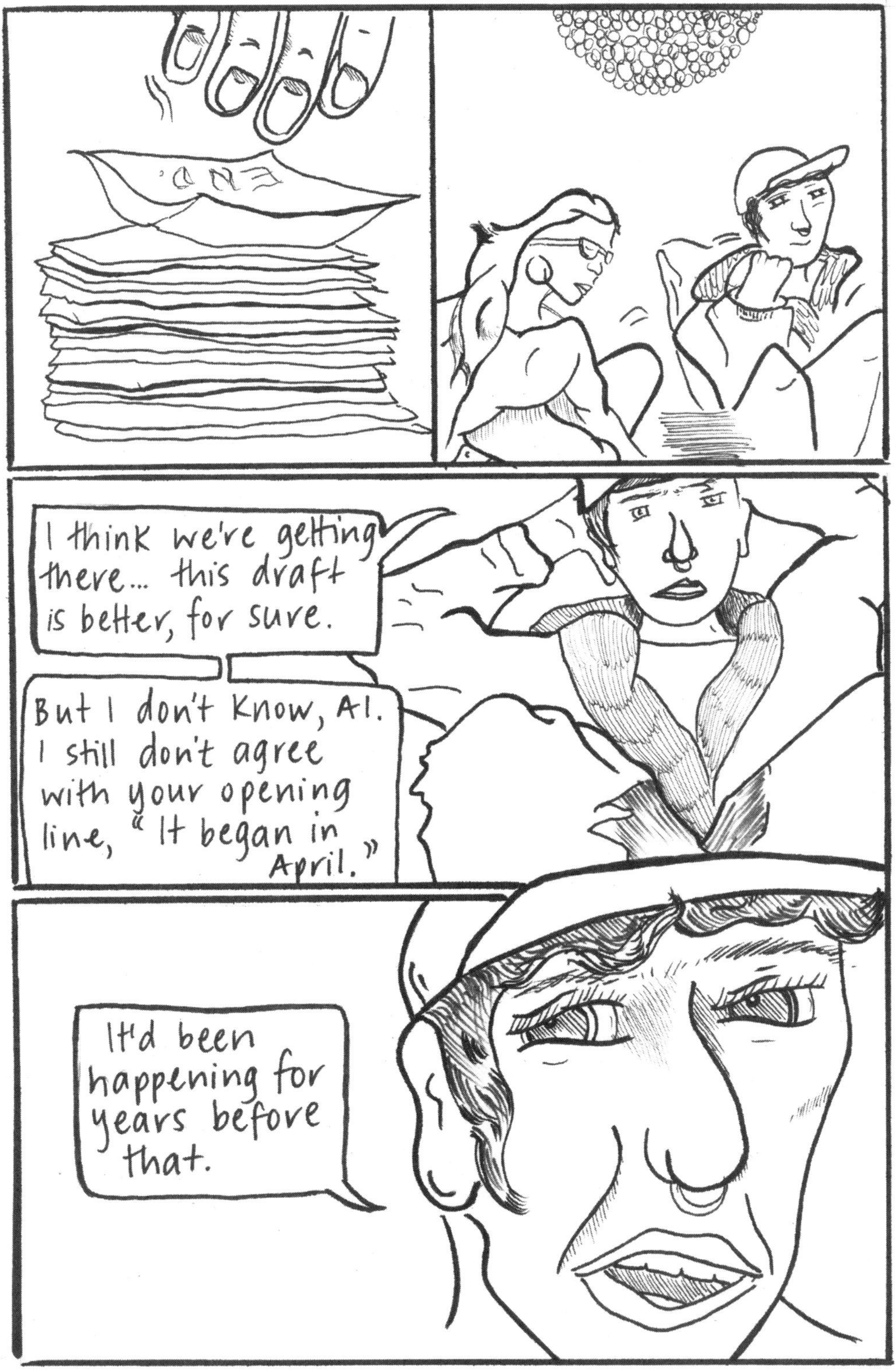

I think we're getting there... this draft is better, for sure.
But I don't know, Al. I still don't agree with your opening line, "It began in April."
It'd been happening for years before that.

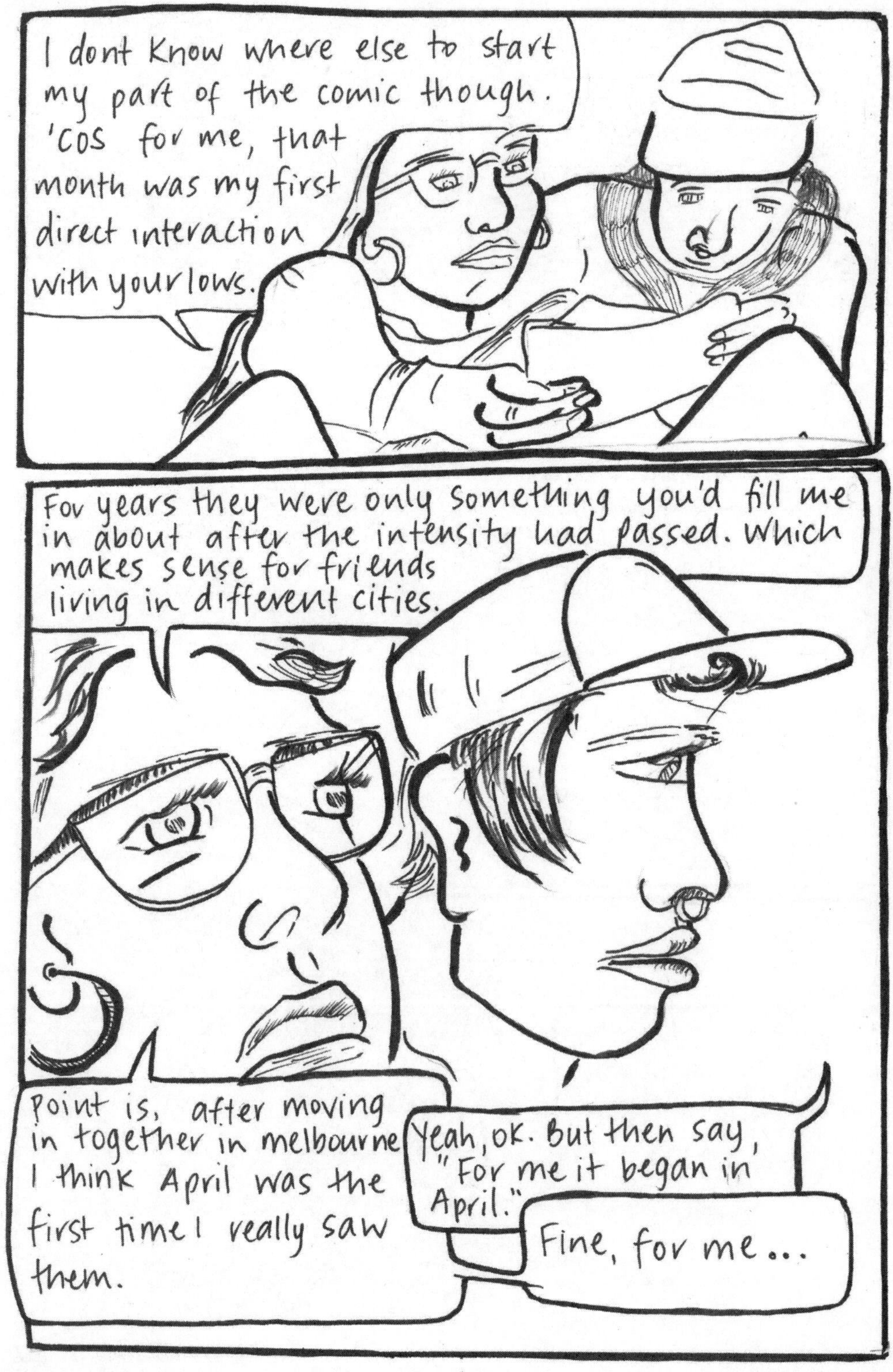
I dont know where else to start my part of the comic though. 'cos for me, that month was my first direct interaction with your lows.
For years they were only something you'd fill me in about after the intensity had passed. Which makes sense for friends living in different cities.
Point is, after moving in together in melbourne I think April was the first time I really saw them.
Yeah, ok. But then say, "For me it began in April."
Fine, for me...

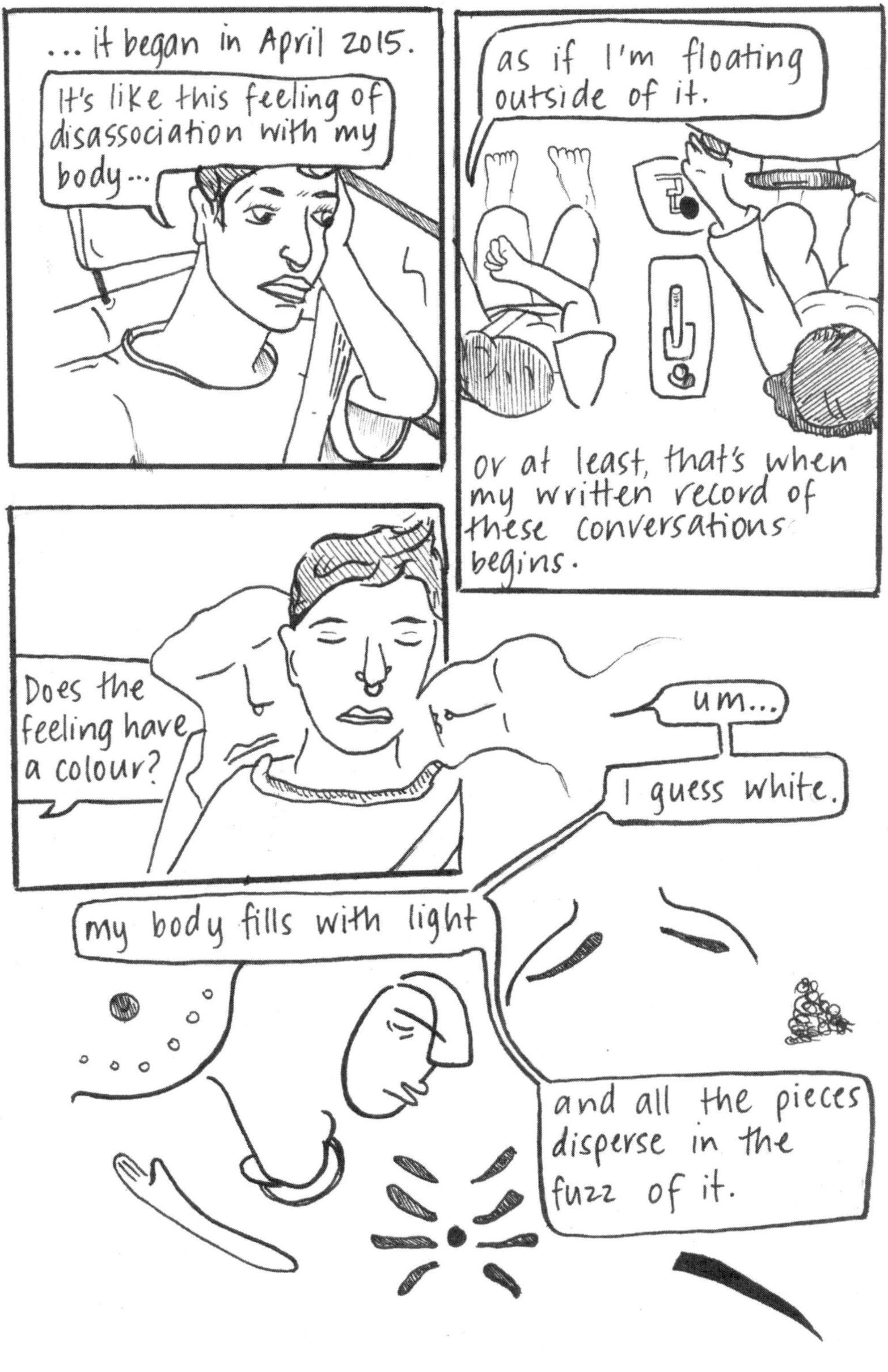
... it began in April 2015.
It's like this feeling of disassociation with my body...
as if I'm floating outside of it.
or at least, that's when my written record of these conversations begins.
Does the feeling have a colour?
um...
I guess white.
my body fills with light
and all the pieces disperse in the fuzz of it.

Hey!
hey.
FTSHUK
miso soup?
I got good at reading you.
yes, please.
The shift was physical.
Pop!
Jar: 0.39
Code: #41
miso paste

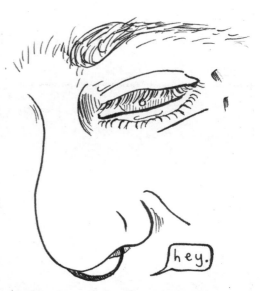

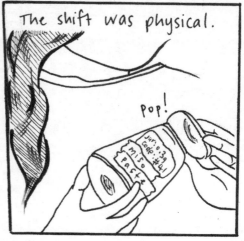

we had a four-step ritual for those nights.

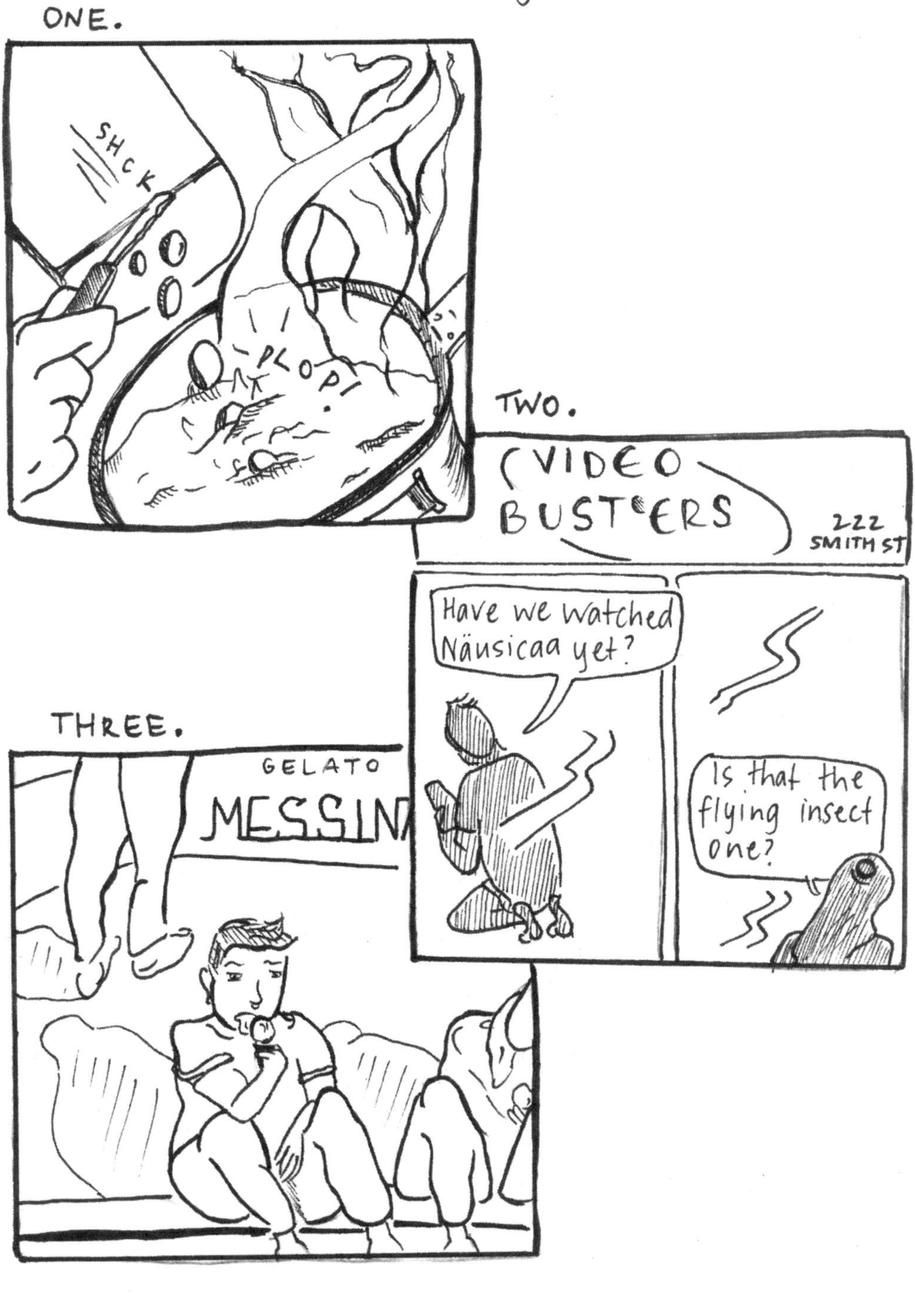
ONE.
SHCK
PLOP!
TWO.
VIDEO BUSTERS
222 SMITH ST
Have we watched Näusicaa yet?
Is that the flying insect one?
THREE.
GELATO
MESSIN

FOUR.

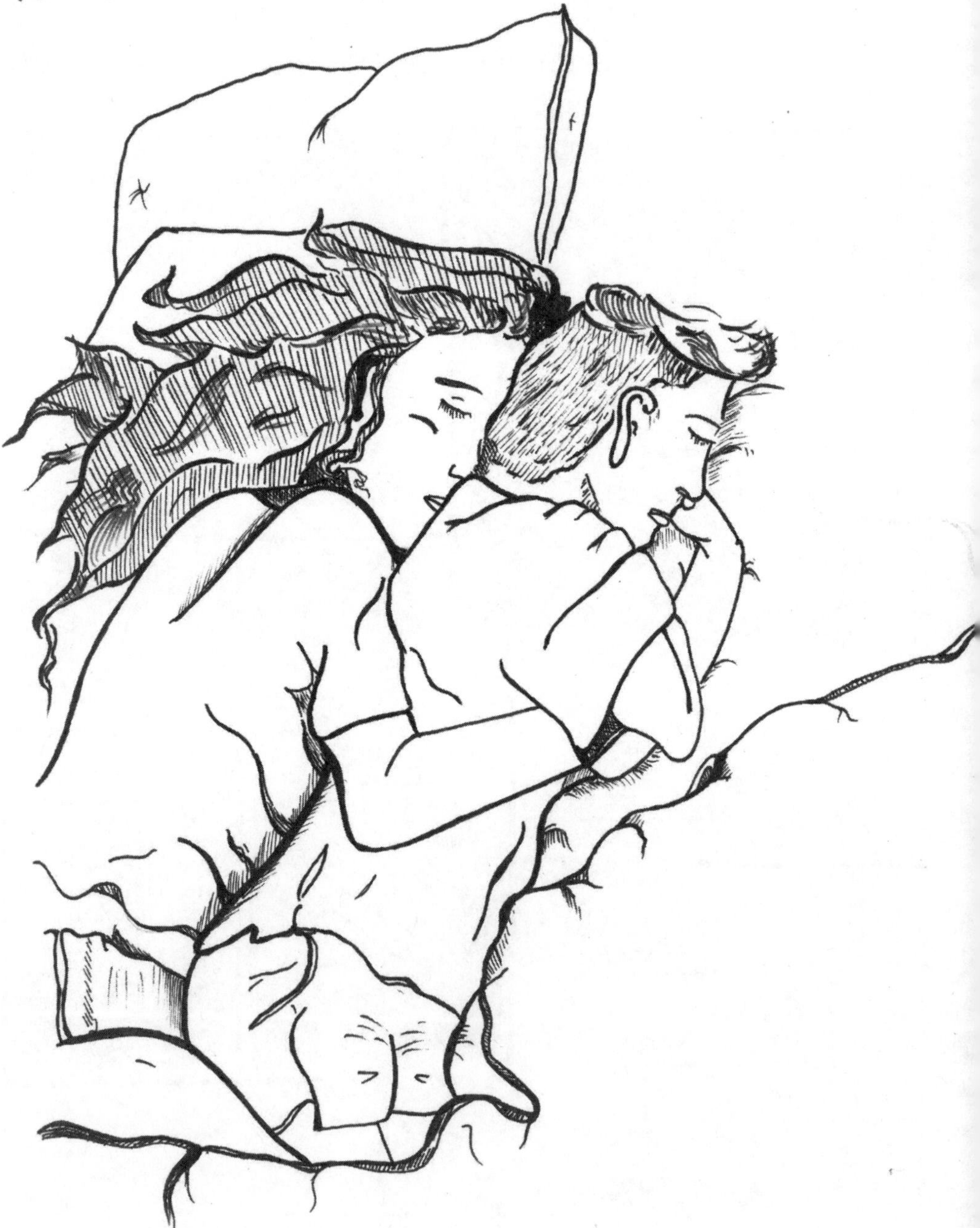

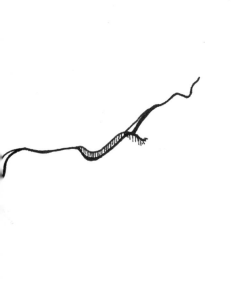

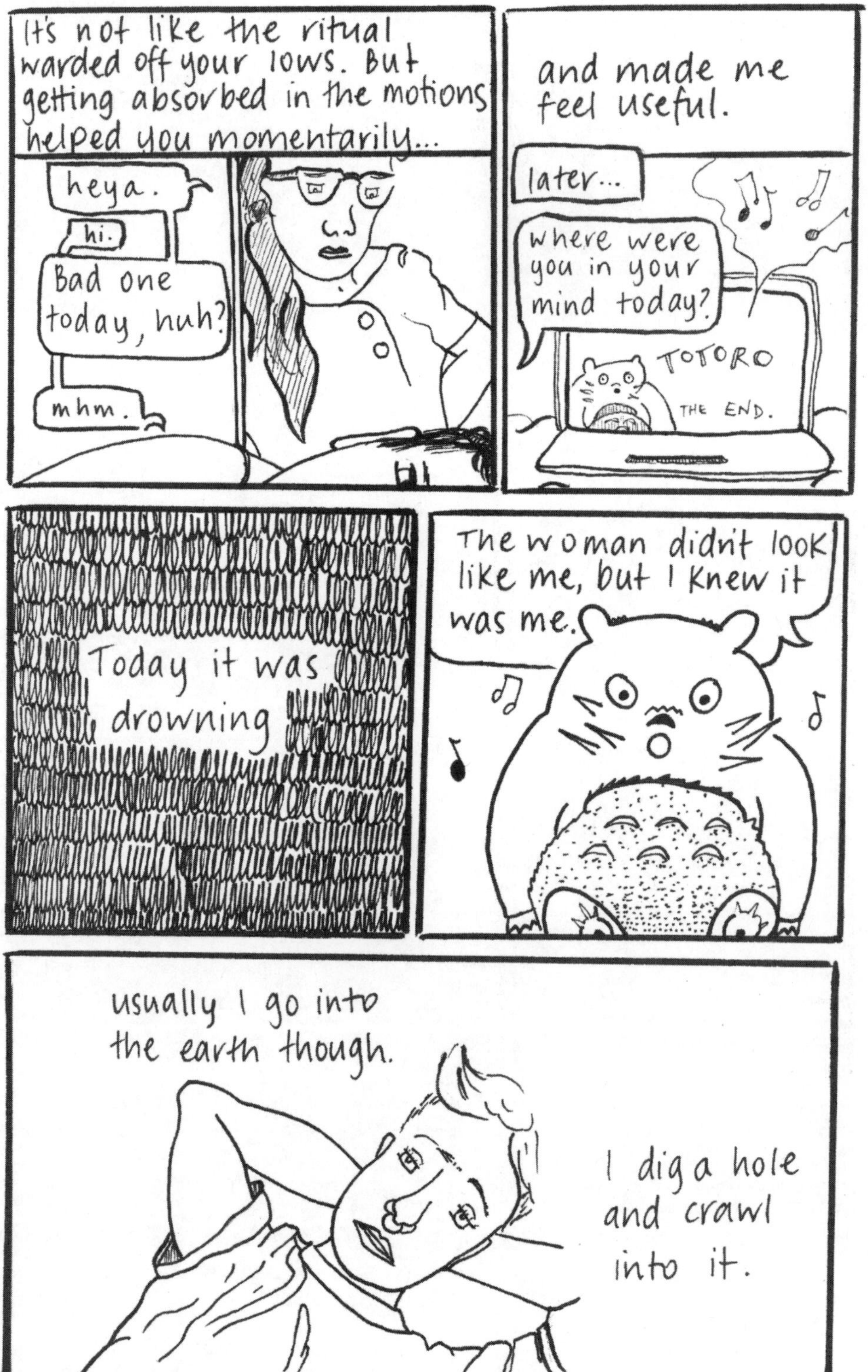
It's not like the ritual warded off your lows. But getting absorbed in the motions helped you momentarily...
and made me feel useful.
heya.
hi.
Bad one today, huh?
mhm.
later...
where were you in your mind today?
TOTORO
THE END.
Today it was drowning
The woman didn't look like me, but I knew it was me.
usually I go into the earth though.
I dig a hole and crawl into it.

what kind of earth is it?

Soil.

Not really wet. But not dry either.

Is it cold there?

Nah. Just comfortable.

Is it, like, a grave? Do you get covered up?

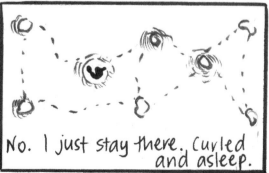
No. I just stay there. Curled and asleep.

As someone who doesn't truly know what depression feels like, I've always doubted my ability to be there for you.

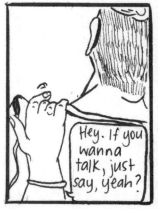

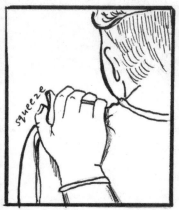

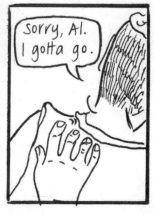

Hey. If you wanna talk, just say, yeah?
squeeze
Sorry, Al. I gotta go.
I started worrying you'd give up on me for support.
Fucking idiot! You never say the right thing!
I also didn't know how to process what was happening.
so I tried asking more questions
TAVA
click
soil convo
drowning
parents
letter 25 Dec
studio ghibli
letters Austin
and began archiving the answers.

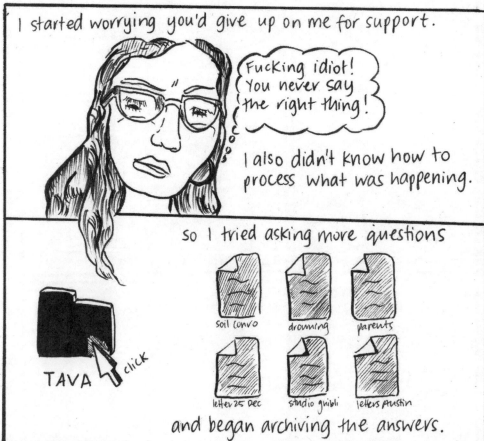

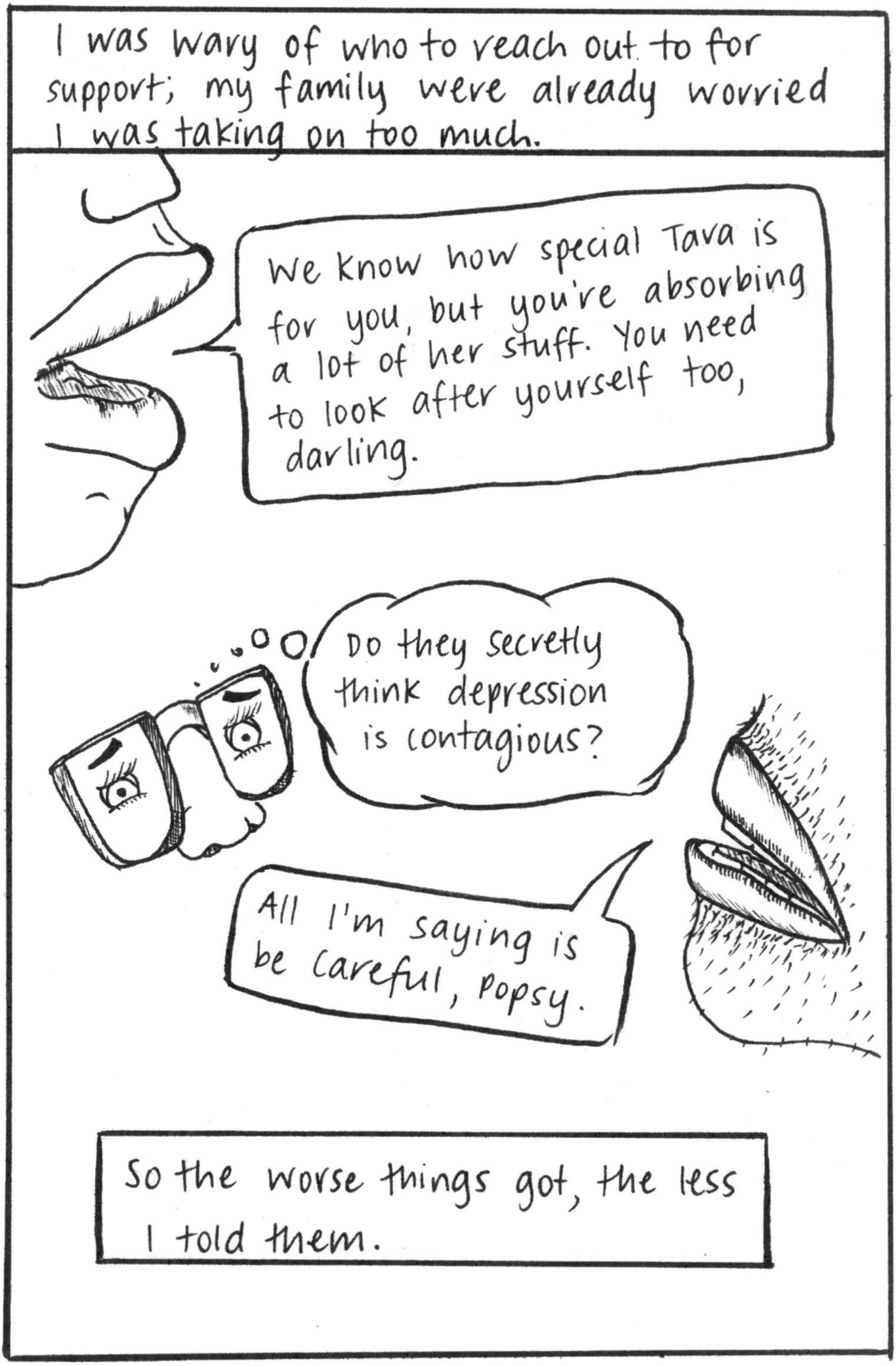
I was wary of who to reach out to for support; my family were already worried I was taking on too much.
We know how special Tara is for you, but you're absorbing a lot of her stuff. You need to look after yourself too, darling.
Do they secretly think depression is contagious?
All I'm saying is be careful, Popsy.
So the worse things got, the less I told them.

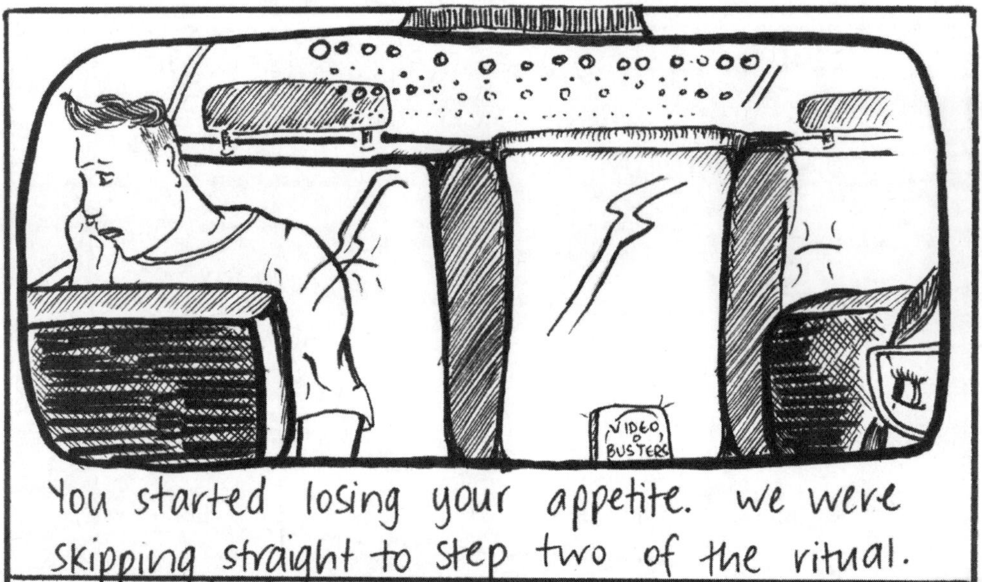
VIDEO BUSTERS
You started losing your appetite. We were skipping straight to step two of the ritual.

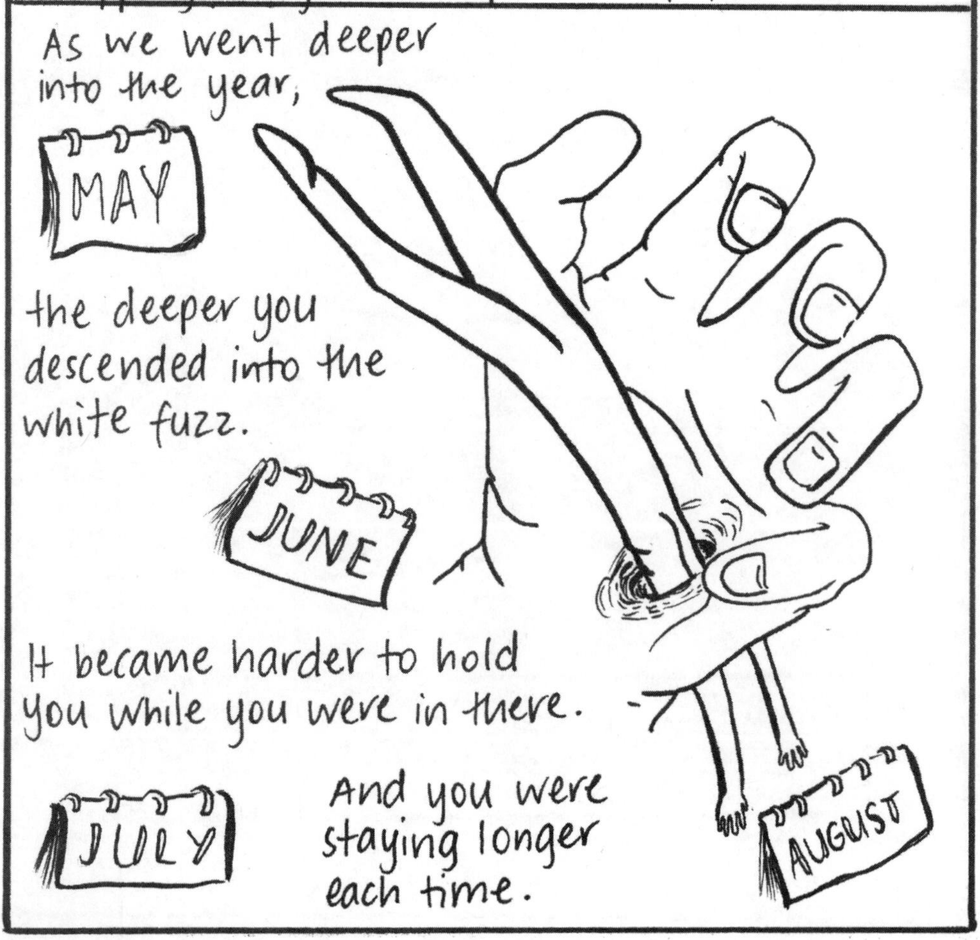
As we went deeper into the year,
MAY
the deeper you descended into the white fuzz.
JUNE
It became harder to hold you while you were in there.
JULY
And you were staying longer each time.
AUGUST

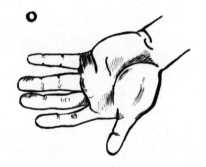

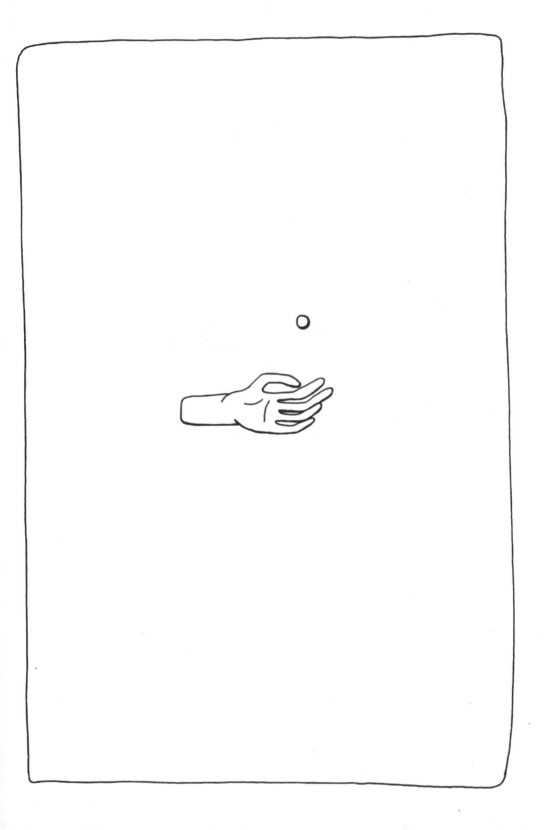

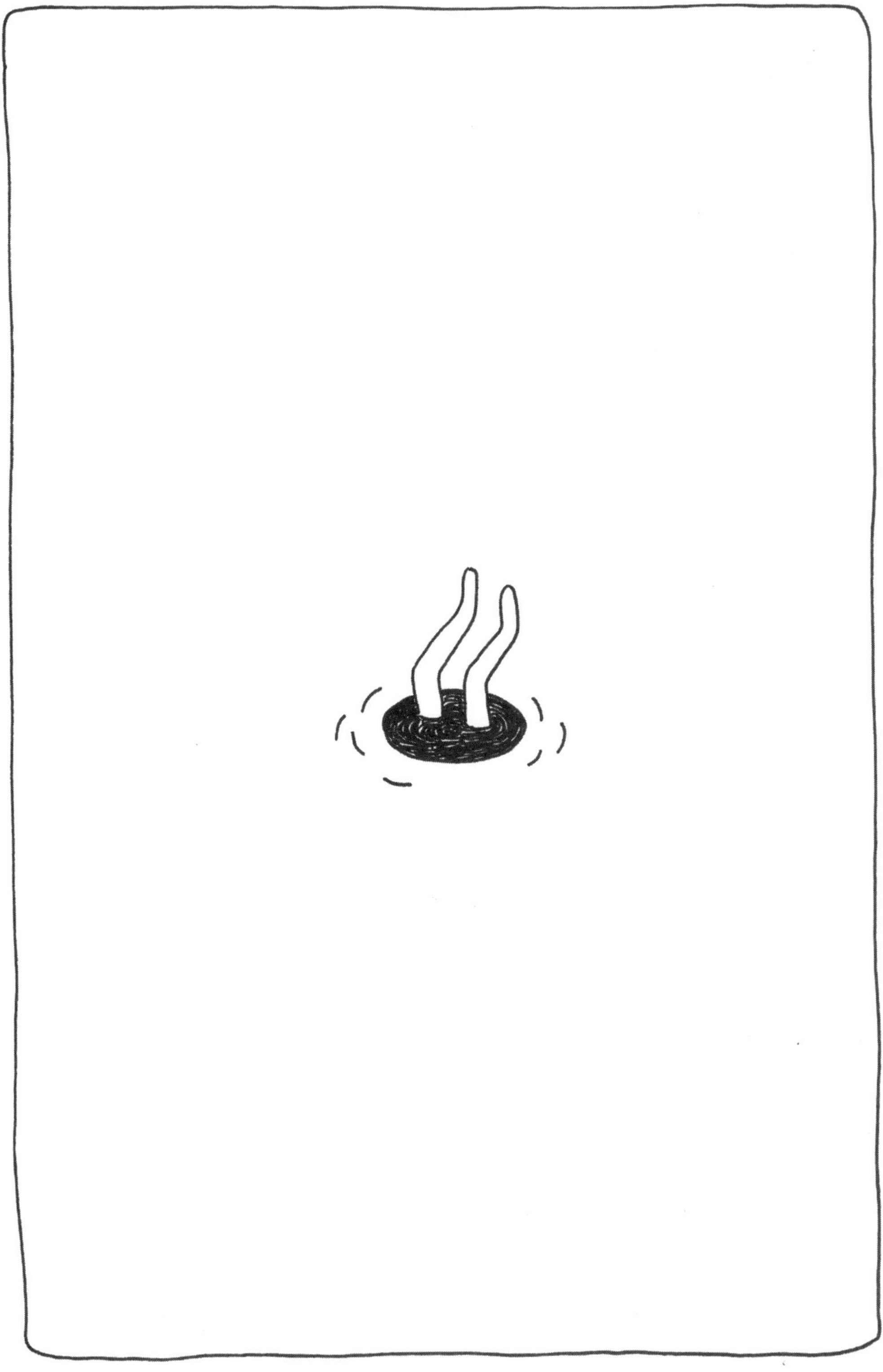

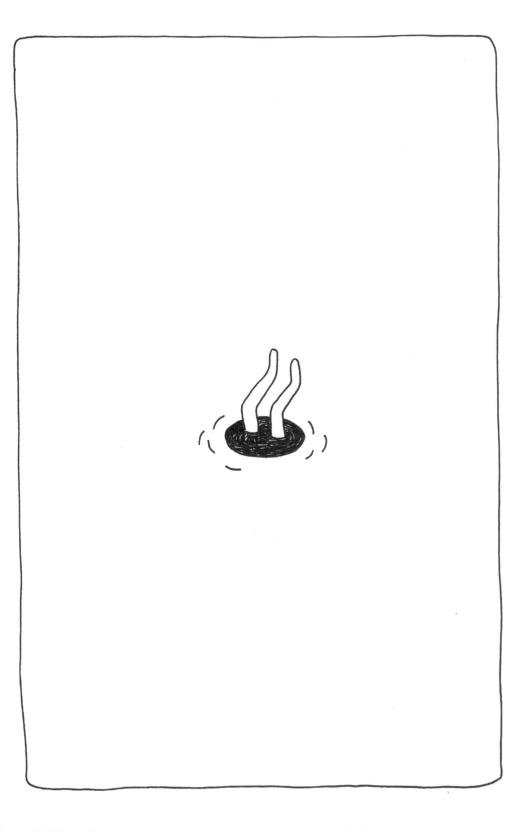

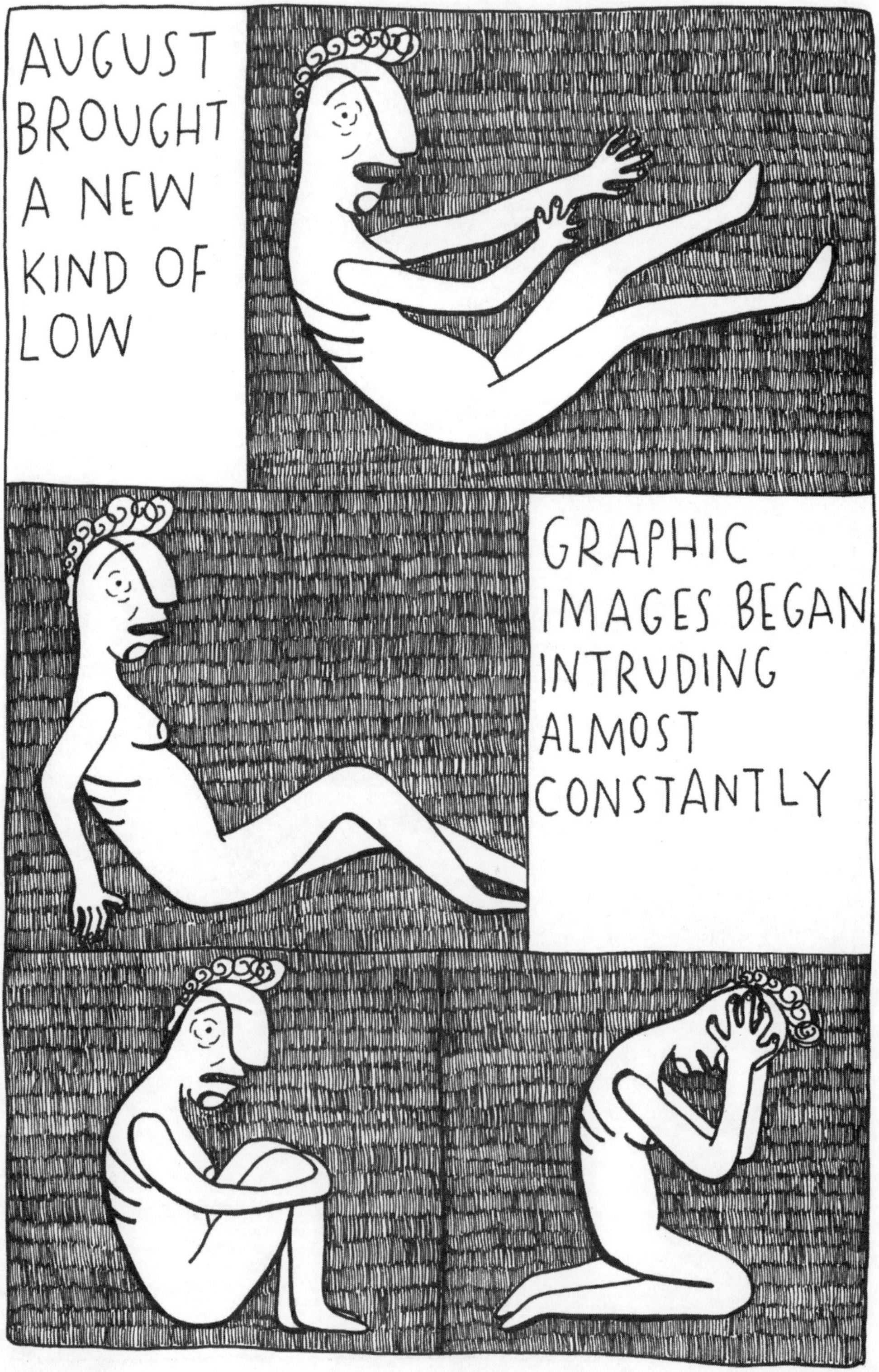
AUGUST BROUGHT A NEW KIND OF LOW
GRAPHIC IMAGES BEGAN INTRUDING ALMOST CONSTANTLY

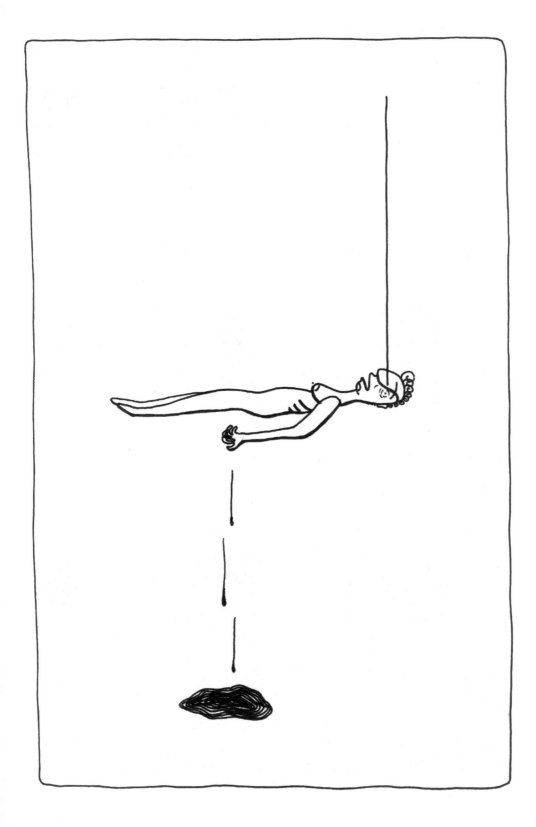

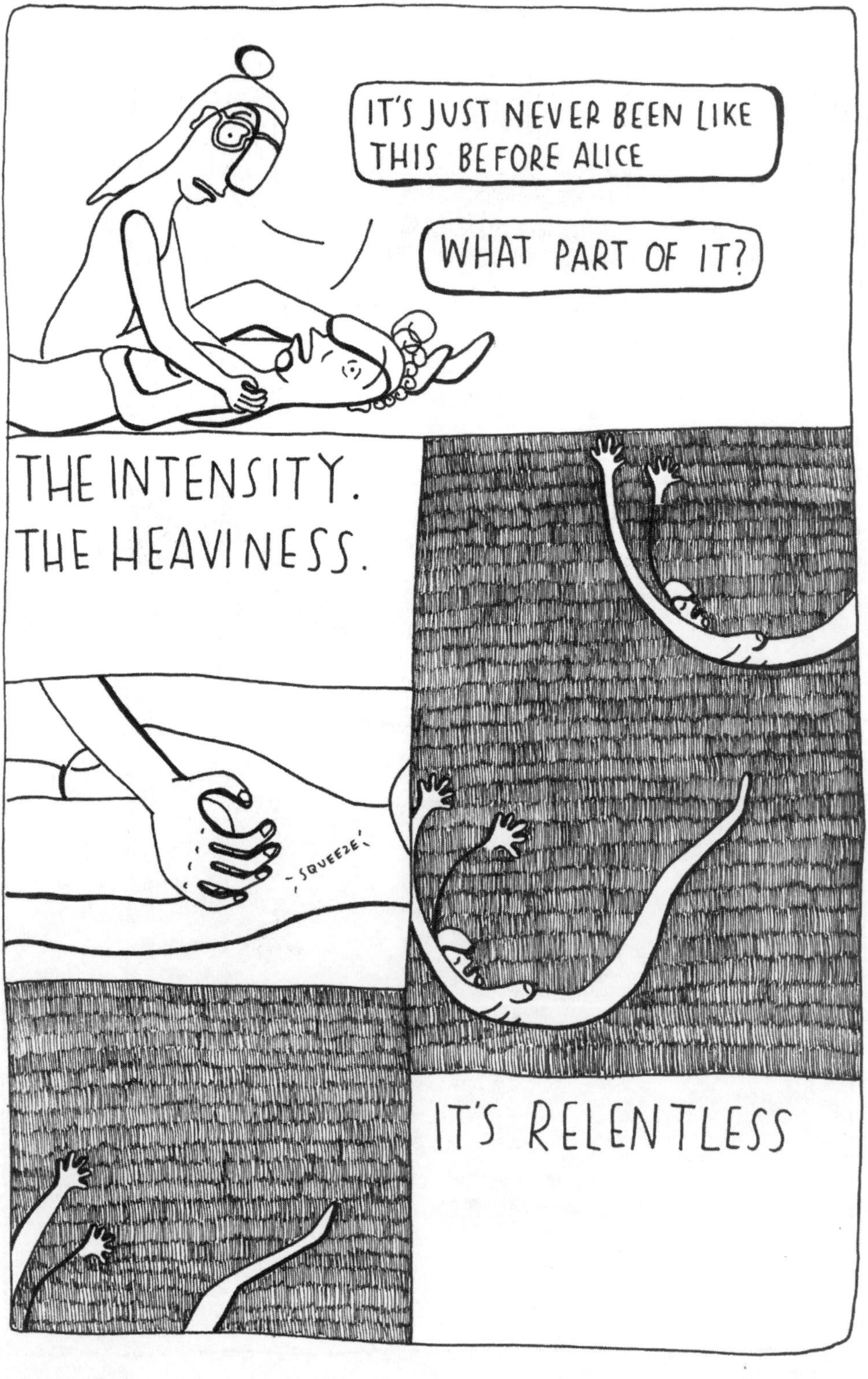
IT'S JUST NEVER BEEN LIKE THIS BEFORE ALICE
WHAT PART OF IT?
THE INTENSITY. THE HEAVINESS.
SQUEEZE
IT'S RELENTLESS

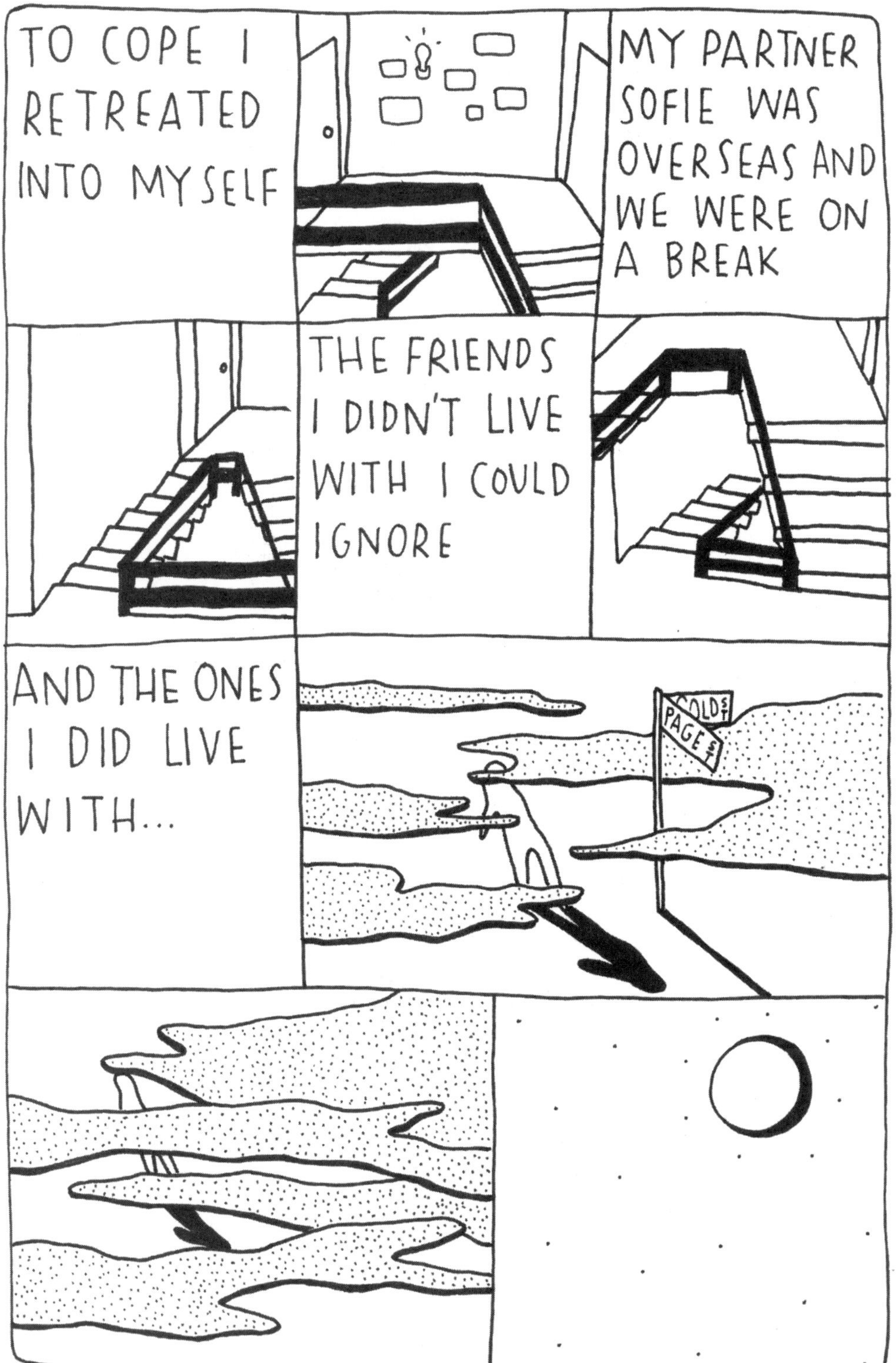
TO COPE I RETREATED INTO MYSELF
MY PARTNER SOFIE WAS OVERSEAS AND WE WERE ON A BREAK
THE FRIENDS I DIDN'T LIVE WITH I COULD IGNORE
AND THE ONES I DID LIVE WITH...
COLD ST
PAGE ST

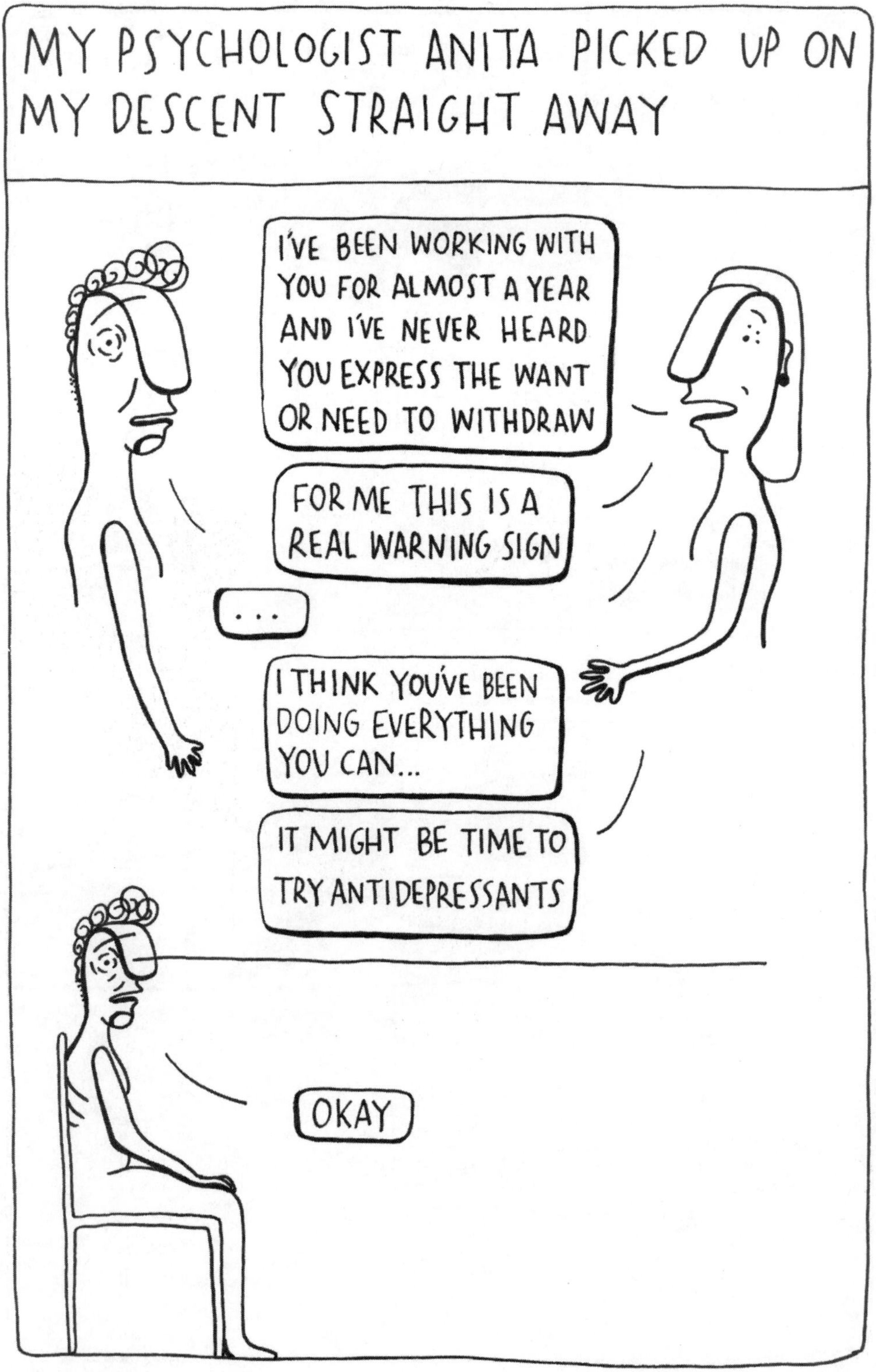
MY PSYCHOLOGIST ANITA PICKED UP ON MY DESCENT STRAIGHT AWAY
I'VE BEEN WORKING WITH YOU FOR ALMOST A YEAR AND I'VE NEVER HEARD YOU EXPRESS THE WANT OR NEED TO WITHDRAW
FOR ME THIS IS A REAL WARNING SIGN
...
I THINK YOU'VE BEEN DOING EVERYTHING YOU CAN...
IT MIGHT BE TIME TO TRY ANTIDEPRESSANTS
OKAY

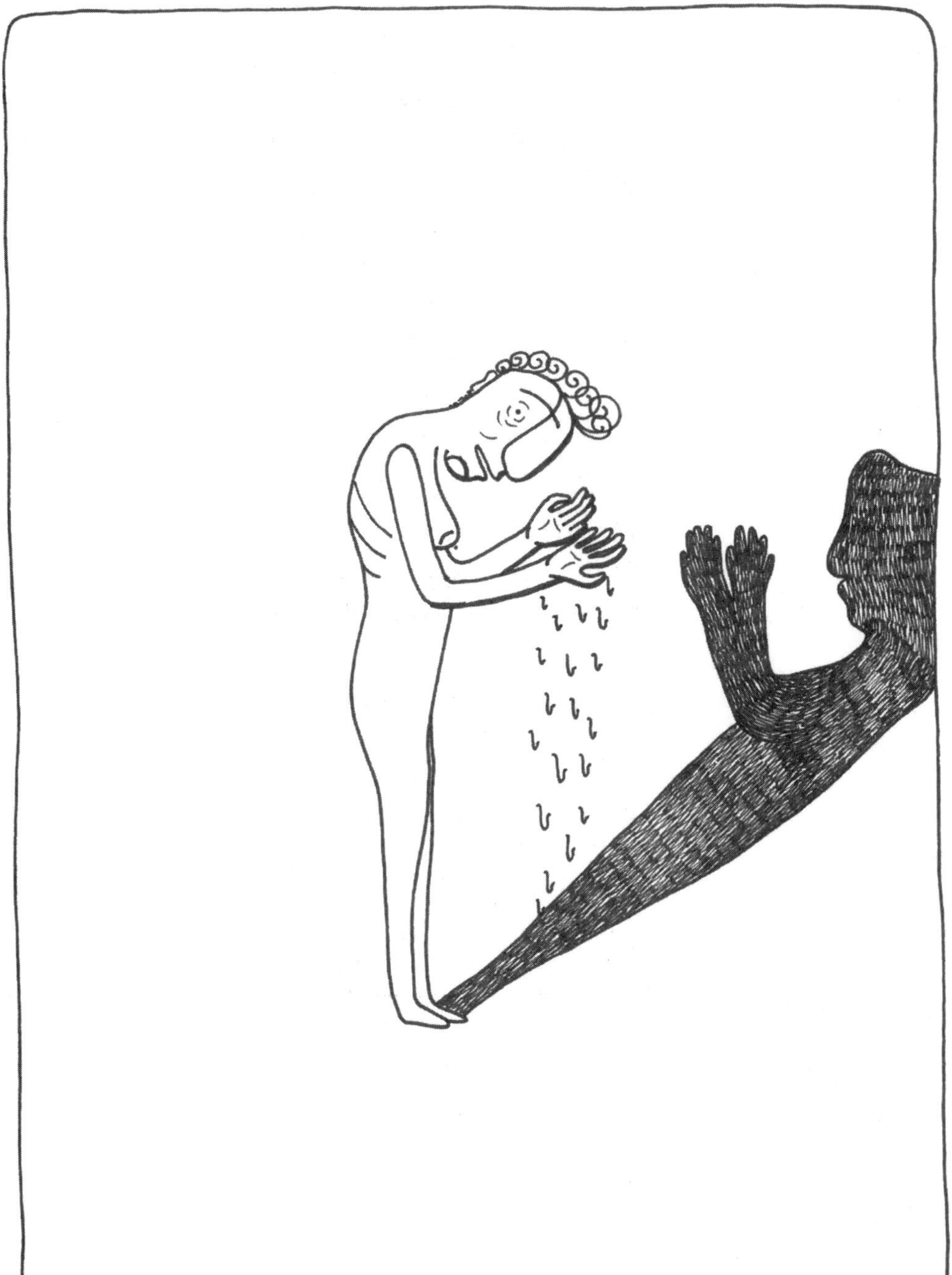

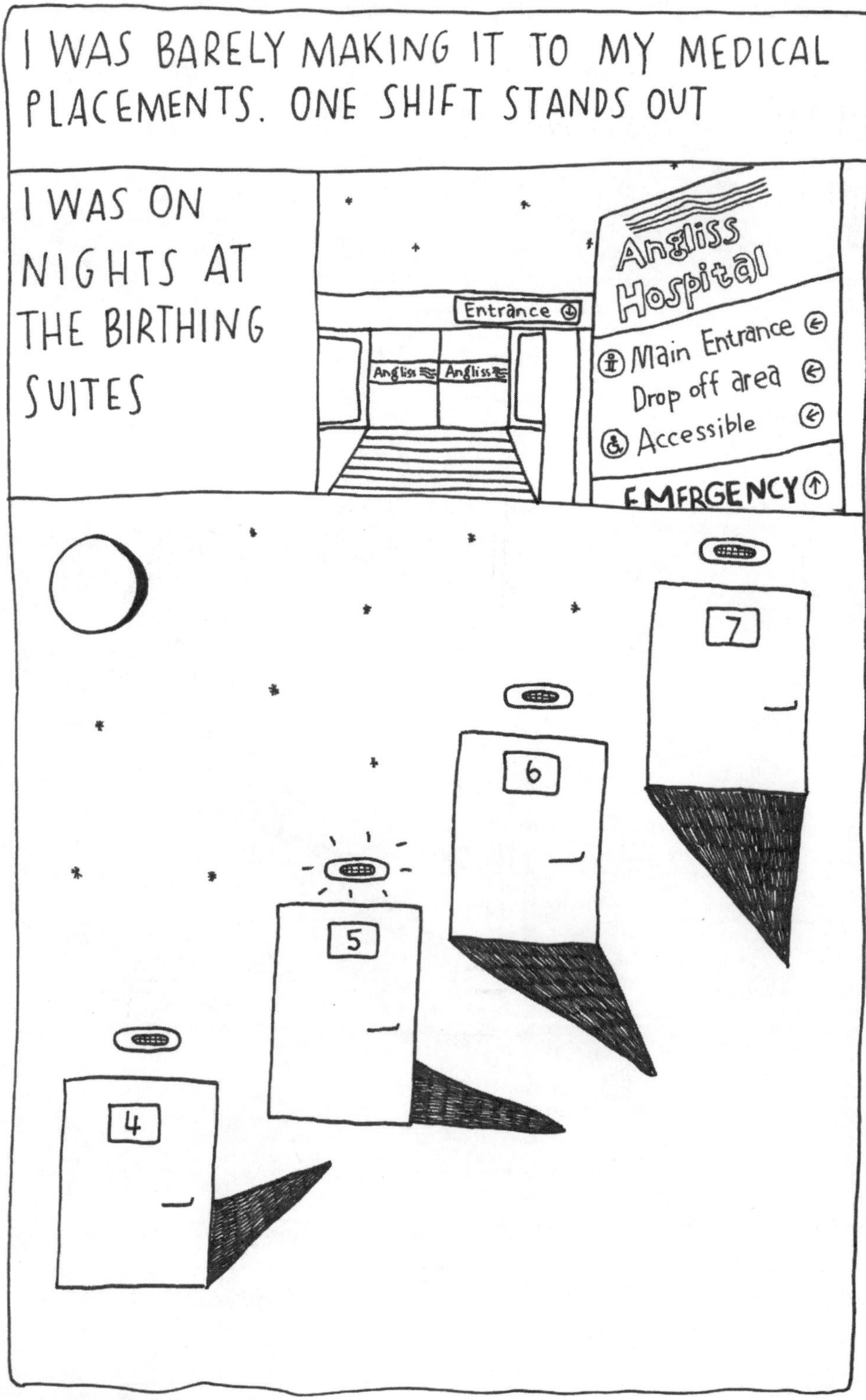
I WAS BARELY MAKING IT TO MY MEDICAL PLACEMENTS. ONE SHIFT STANDS OUT
I WAS ON NIGHTS AT THE BIRTHING SUITES
Entrance
Angliss
Angliss
Angliss Hospital
Main Entrance
Drop off area
Accessible
EMERGENCY
7
6
5
4

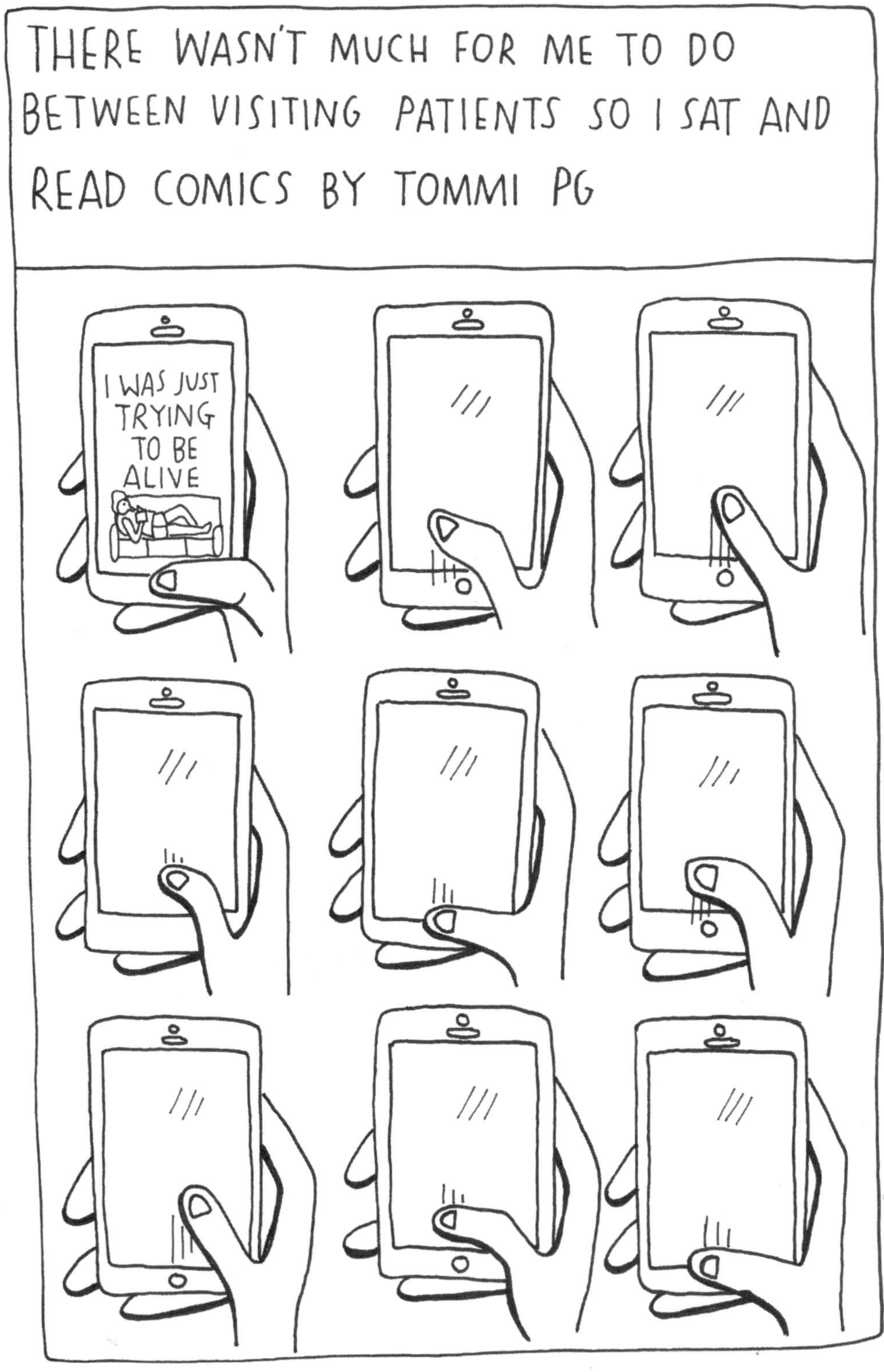
THERE WASN'T MUCH FOR ME TO DO BETWEEN VISITING PATIENTS SO I SAT AND READ COMICS BY TOMMI PG
I WAS JUST TRYING TO BE ALIVE

IT'S HARD TO DESCRIBE THE BEWILDERING EXPERIENCE OF WITNESSING BIRTH

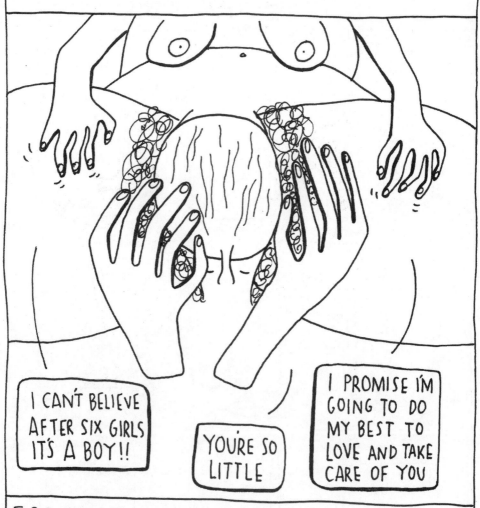

I CAN'T BELIEVE AFTER SIX GIRLS IT'S A BOY!!

YOU'RE SO LITTLE

I PROMISE I'M GOING TO DO MY BEST TO LOVE AND TAKE CARE OF YOU

ESPECIALLY WHEN YOU'RE FEELING NUMB TO YOUR OWN LIFE

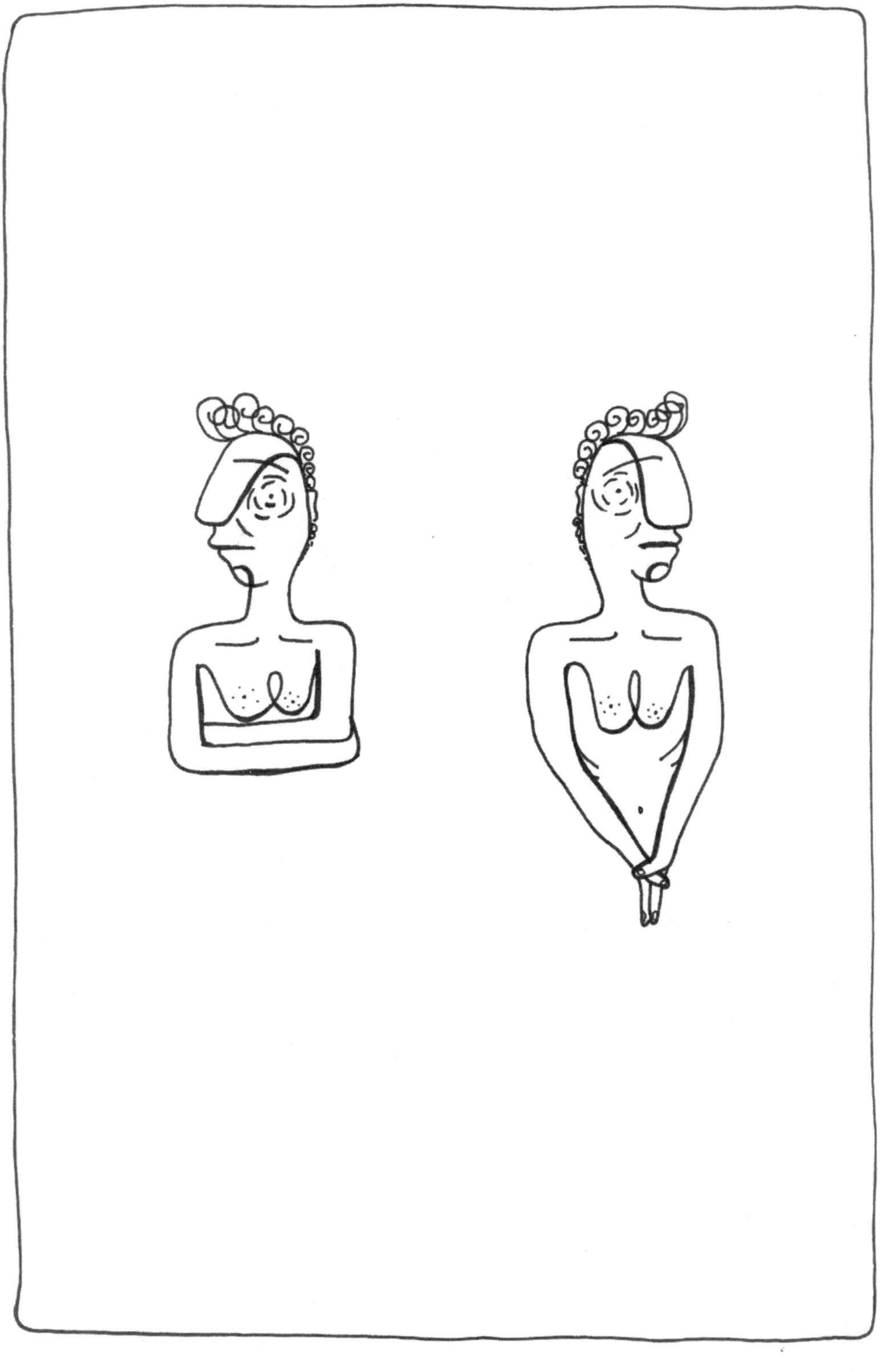

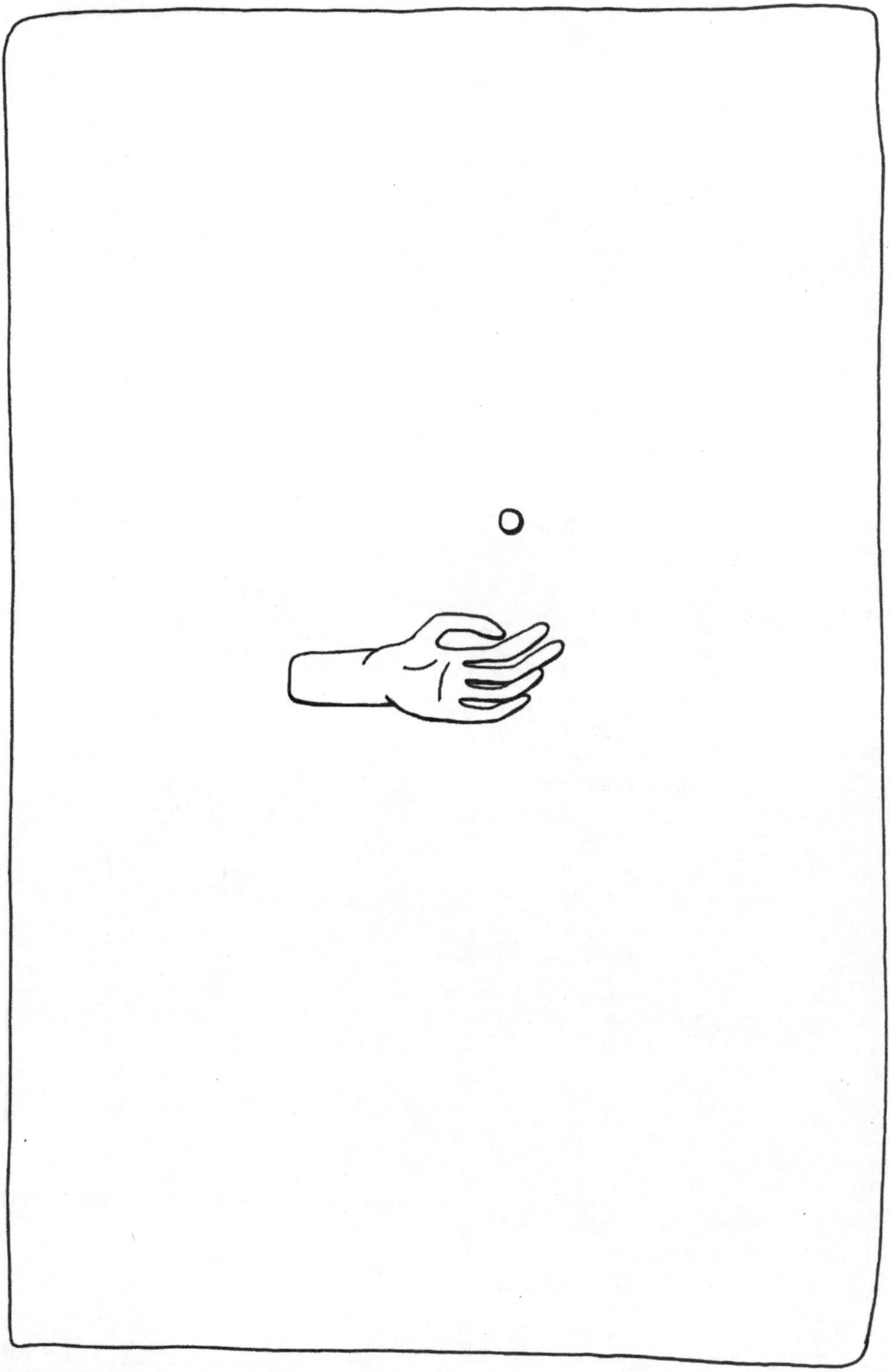

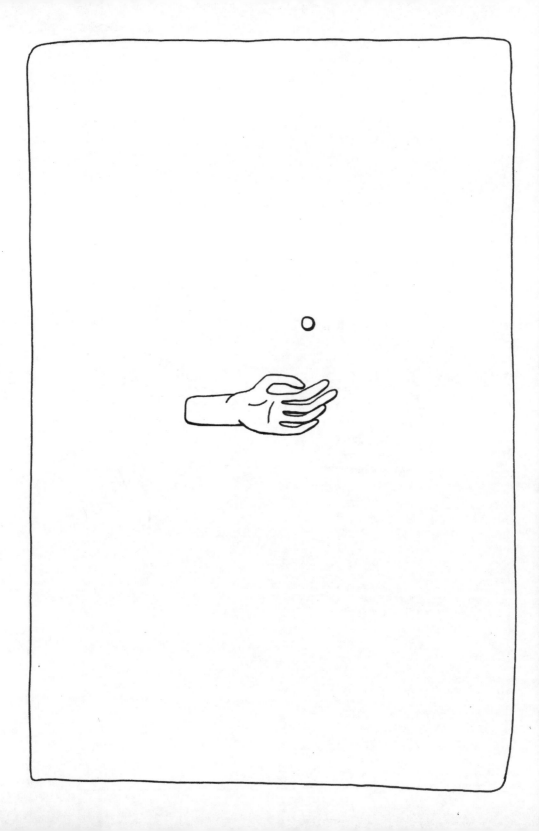

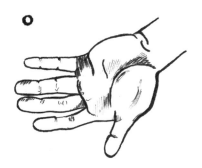

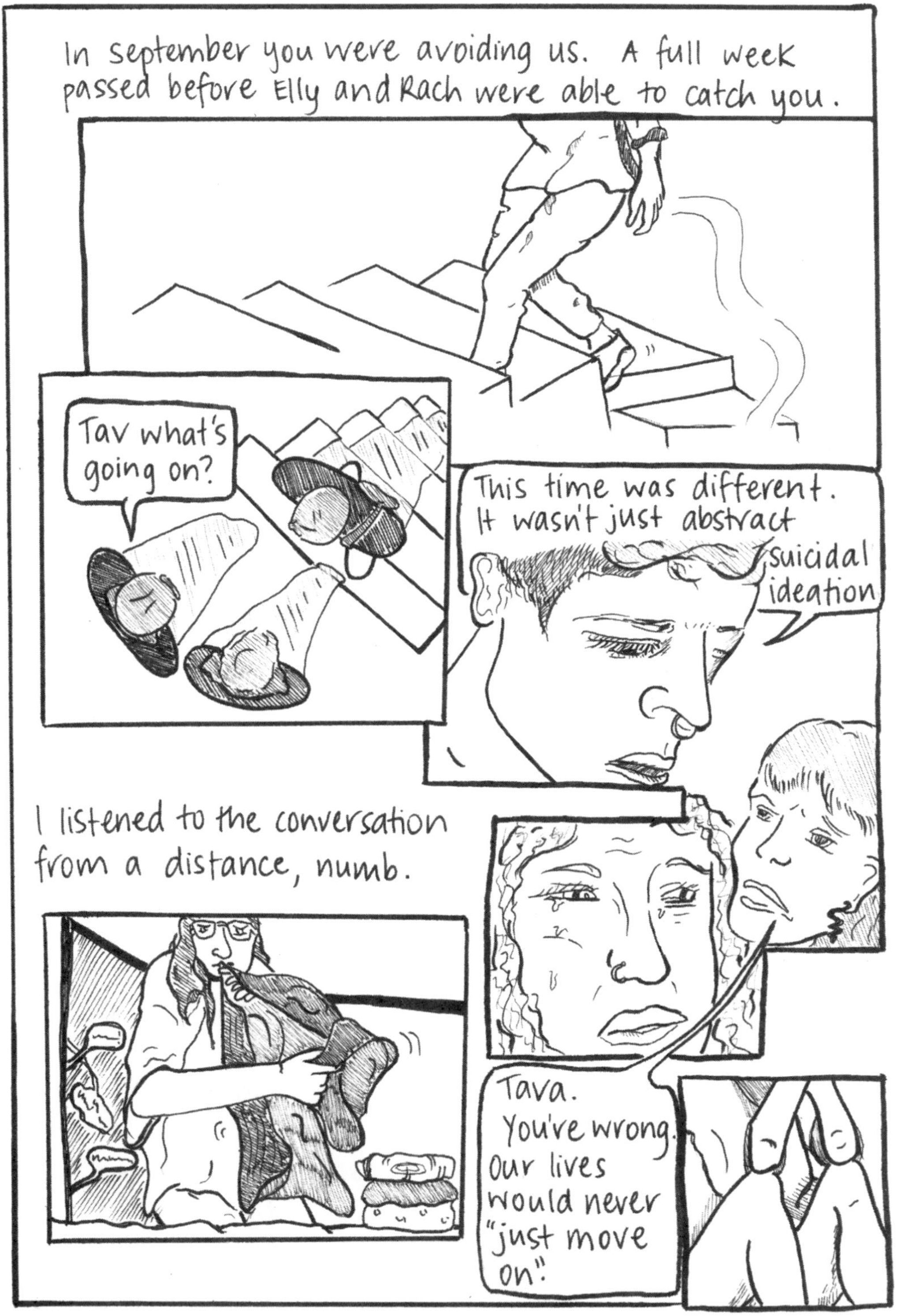

In september you were avoiding us. A full week passed before Elly and Rach were able to catch you.
Tav what's going on?
This time was different. It wasn't just abstract suicidal ideation
I listened to the conversation from a distance, numb.
Tava. You're wrong. Our lives would never "just move on."

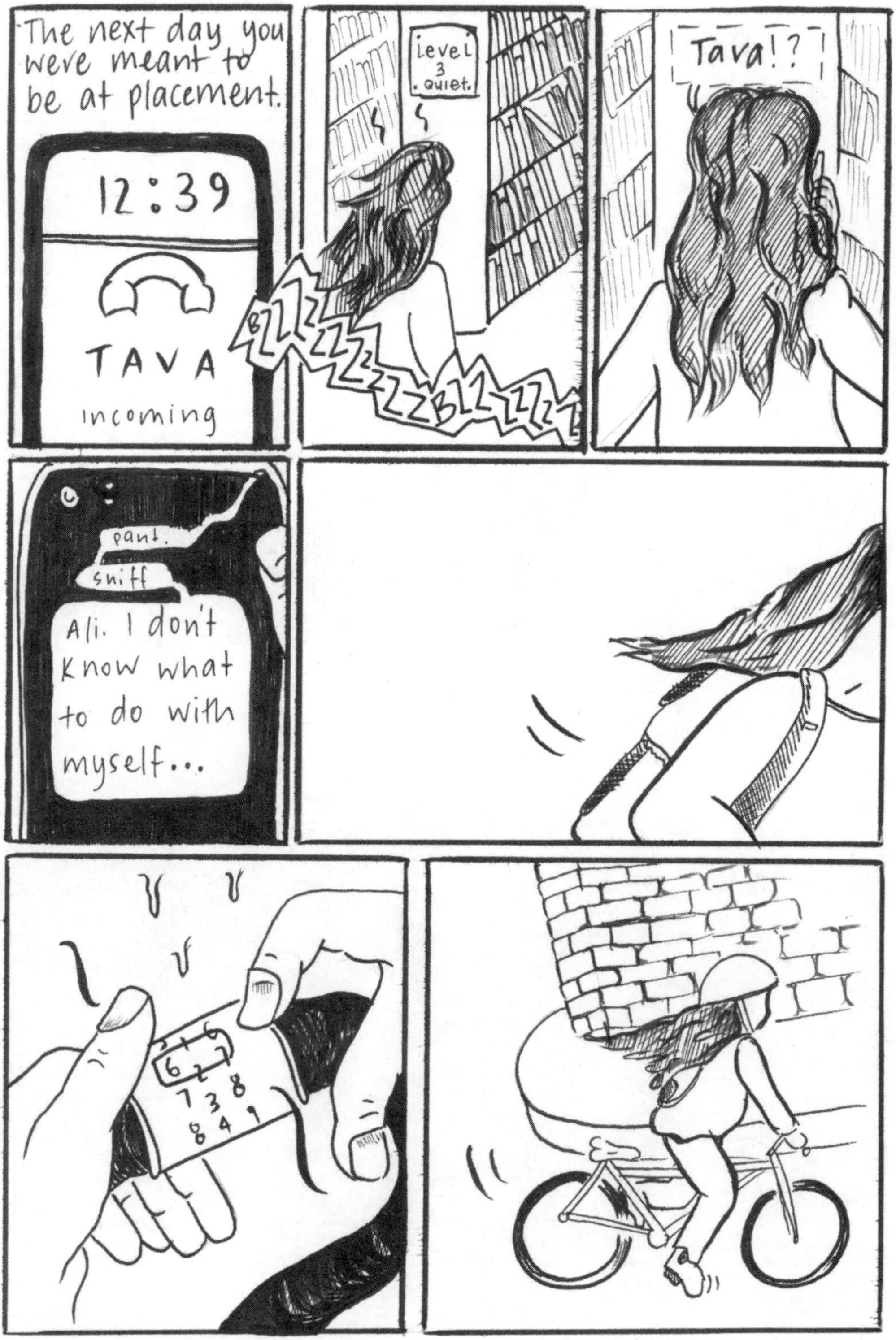
The next day you were meant to be at placement.
12:39
TAVA
incoming
level 3 quiet.
BZZZZZZZZZBZZZZZZZ
Tava!?
pant.
sniff
Ali. I don't know what to do with myself...

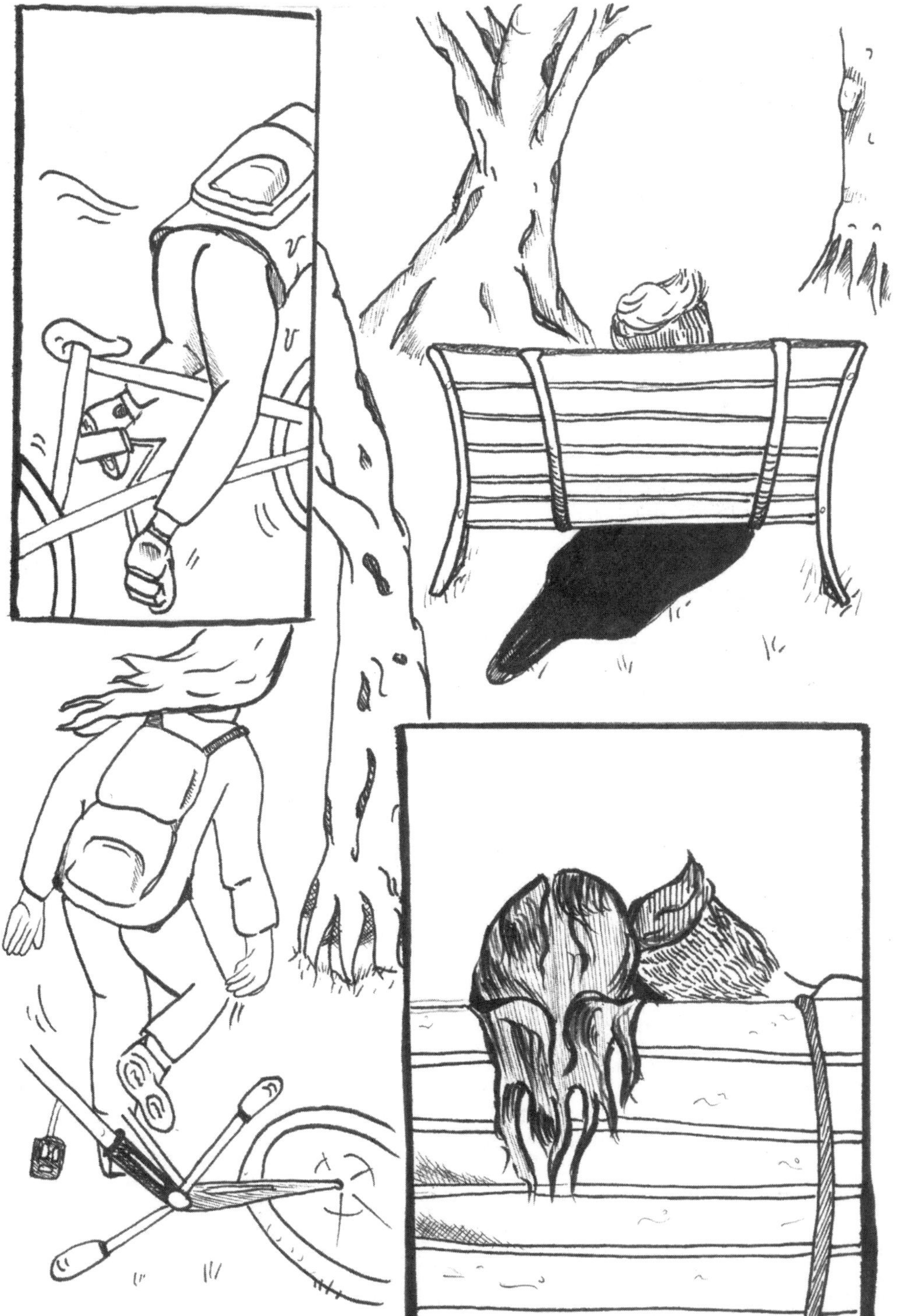

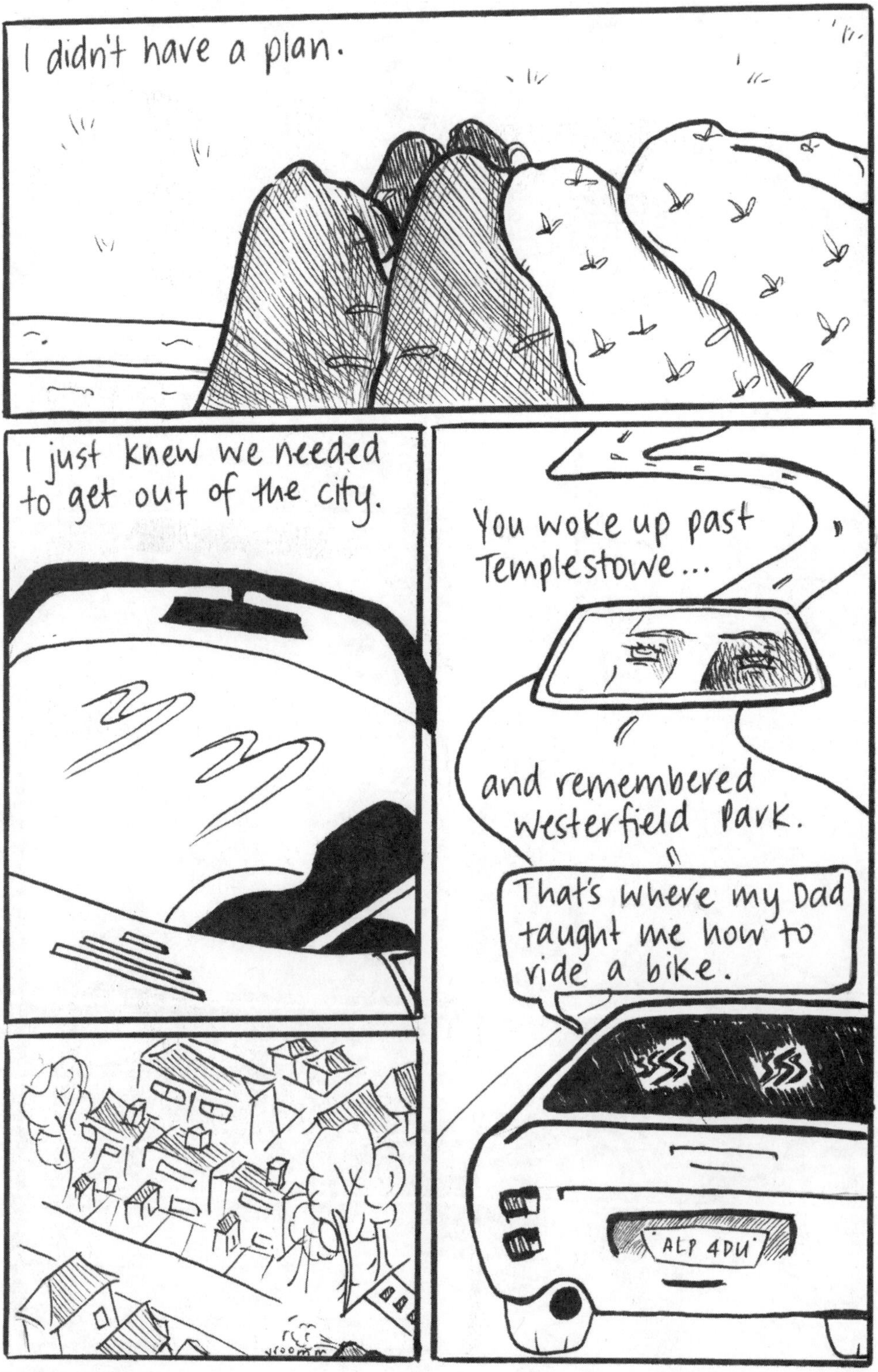
I didn't have a plan.
I just knew we needed to get out of the city.
You woke up past Templestowe...
and remembered Westerfield Park.
That's where my Dad taught me how to ride a bike.
ALP 4DU
vroomm

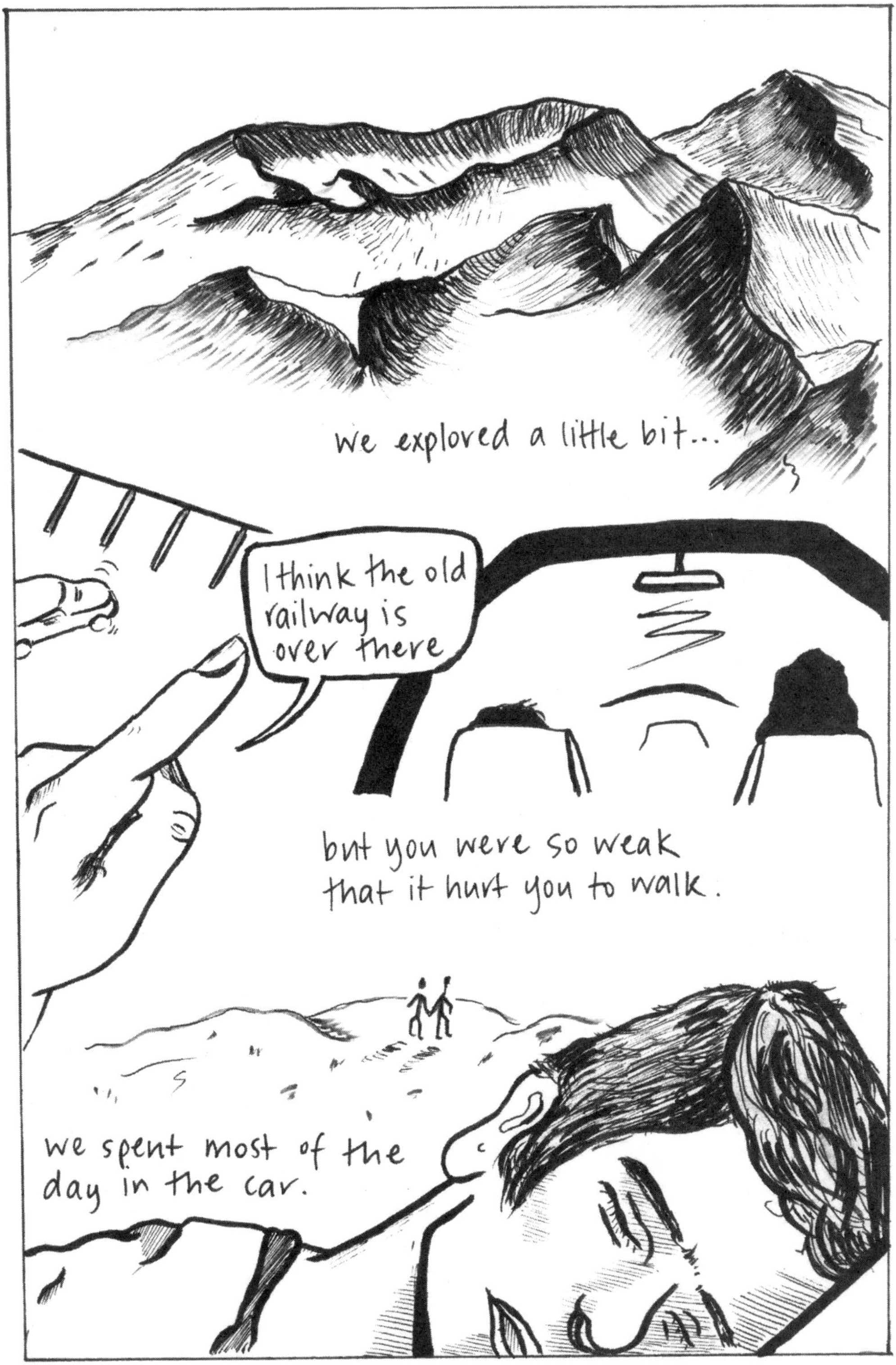
we explored a little bit...
I think the old railway is over there
but you were so weak that it hurt you to walk.
we spent most of the day in the car.

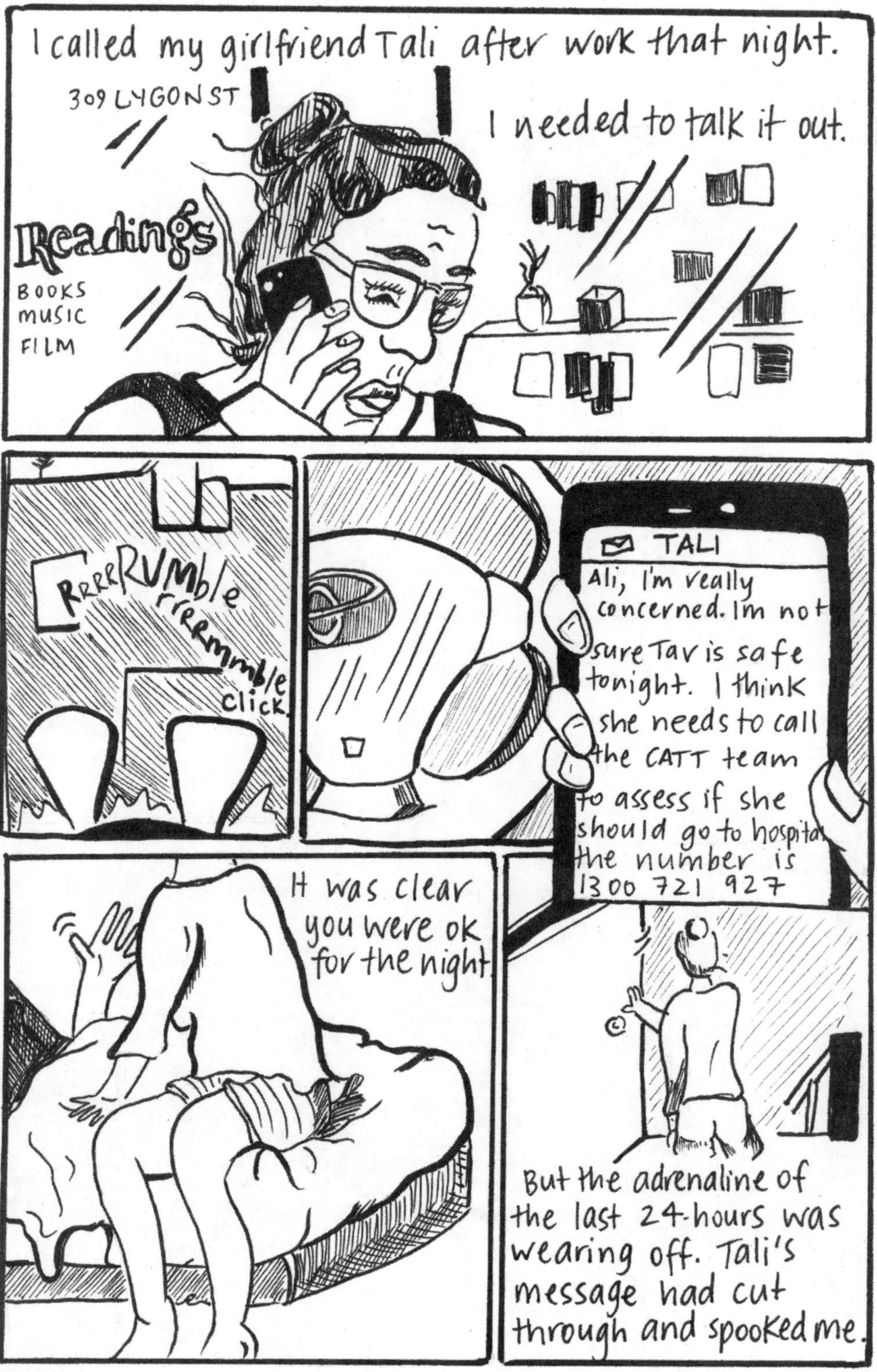
I called my girlfriend Tali after work that night.
309 LYGON ST
I needed to talk it out.
Readings
BOOKS
MUSIC
FILM
RRRRRUMble
rrrRmmble
click.
TALI
Ali, I'm really concerned. Im not sure Tav is safe tonight. I think she needs to call the CATT team to assess if she should go to hospital the number is 1300 721 927
It was clear you were ok for the night
But the adrenaline of the last 24-hours was wearing off. Tali's message had cut through and spooked me.

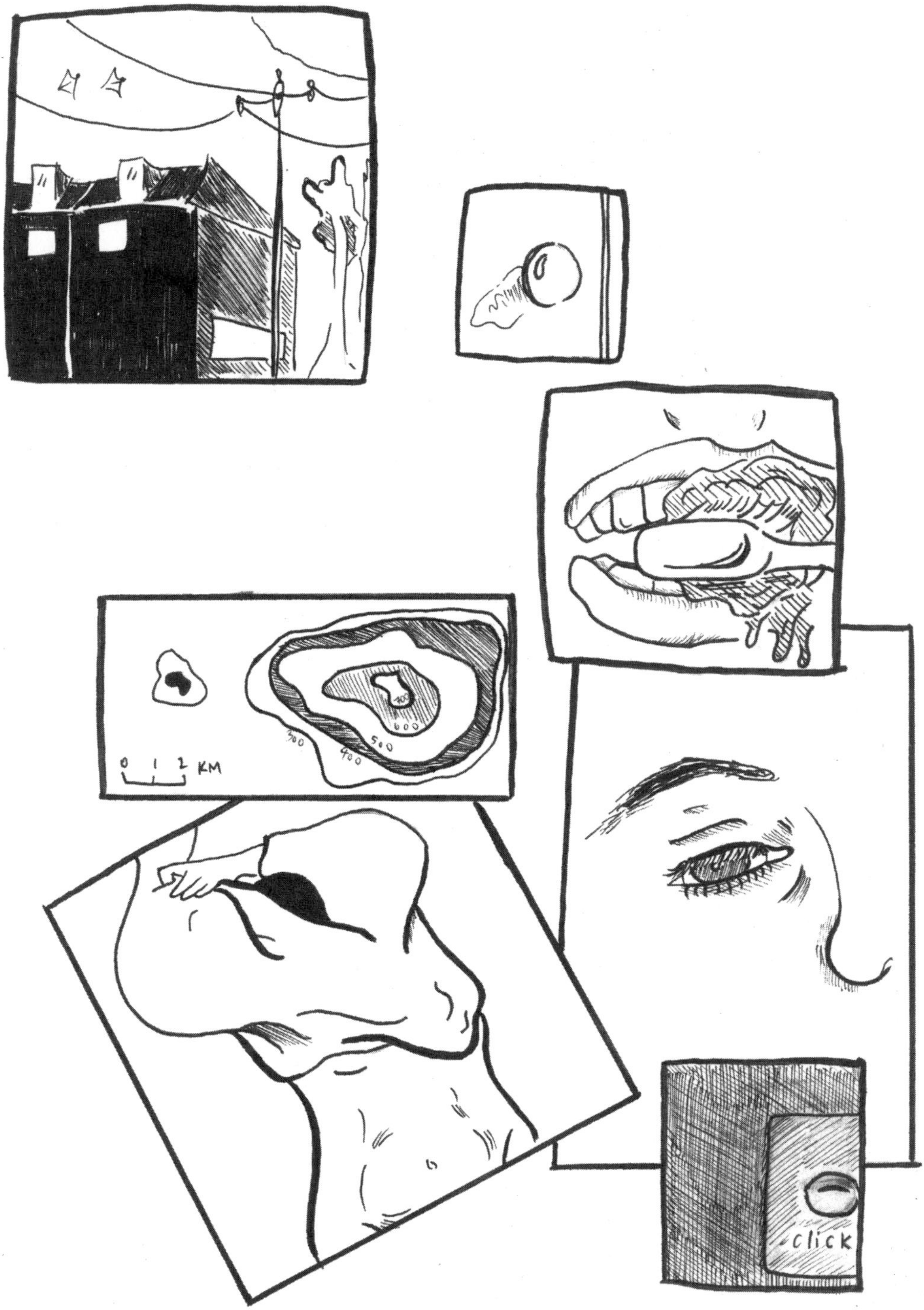
0 1 2 KM
300
400
500
600
700
click

I could finally feel it.

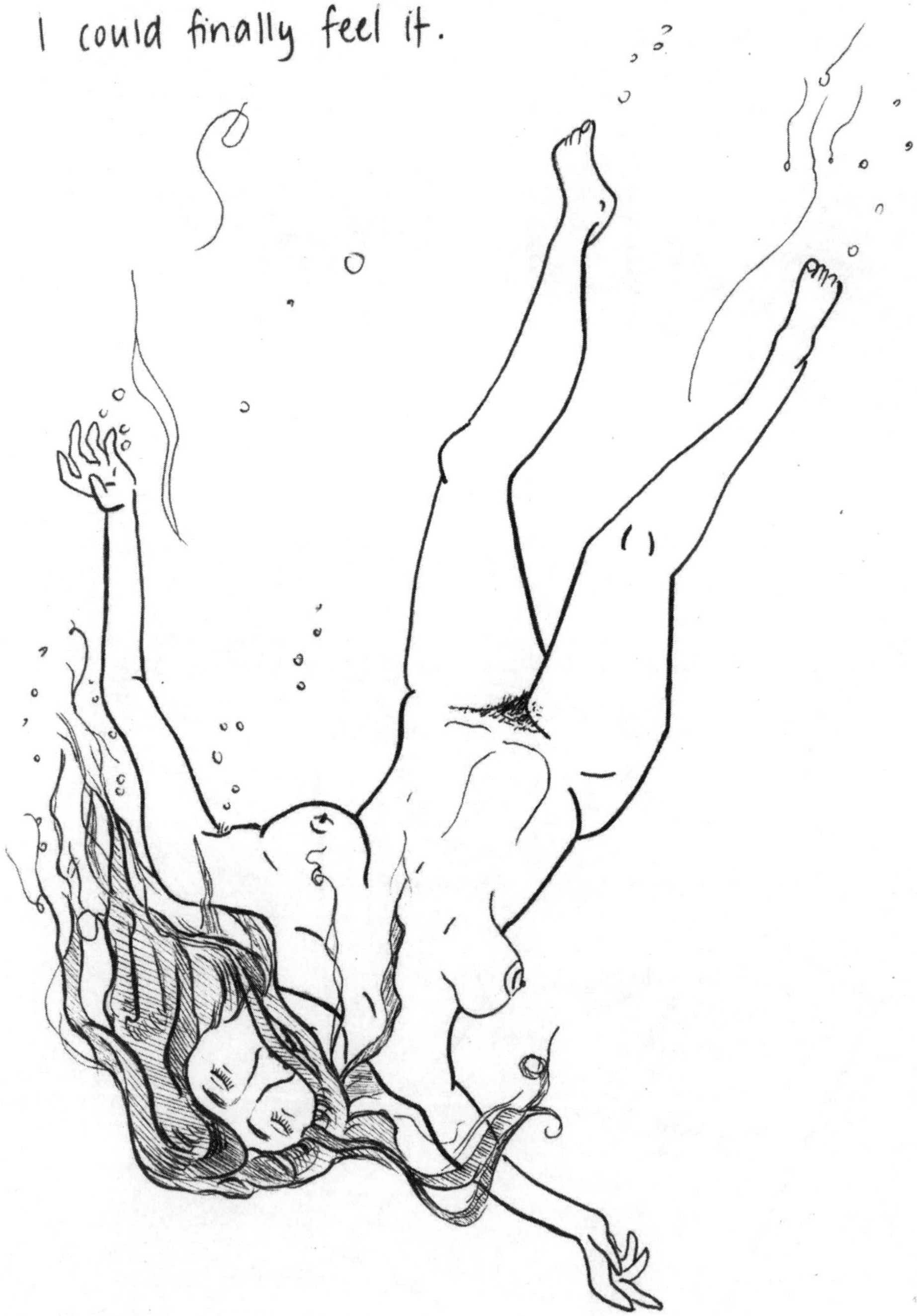

I was out of my depth.

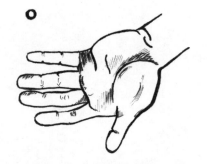

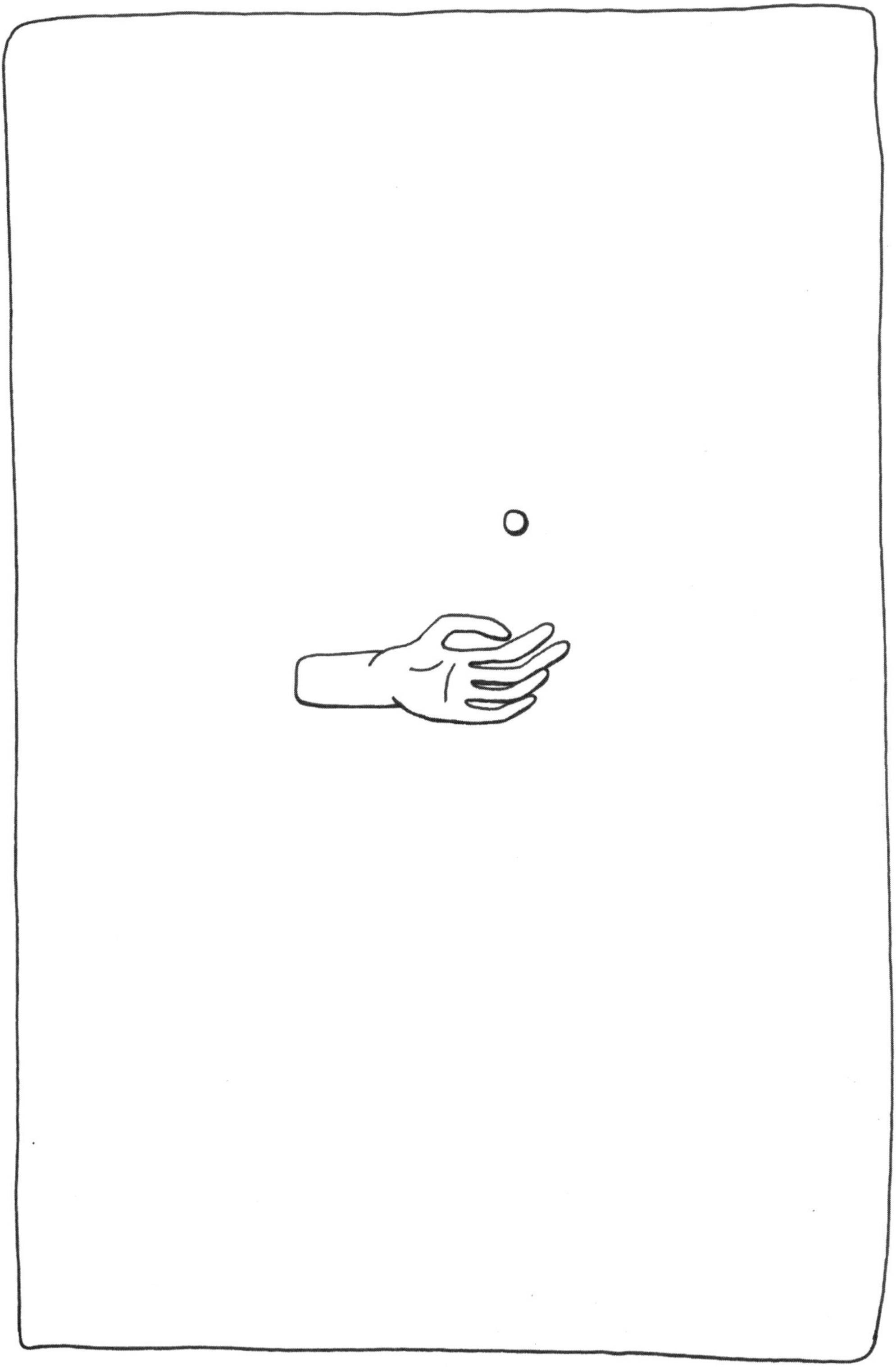

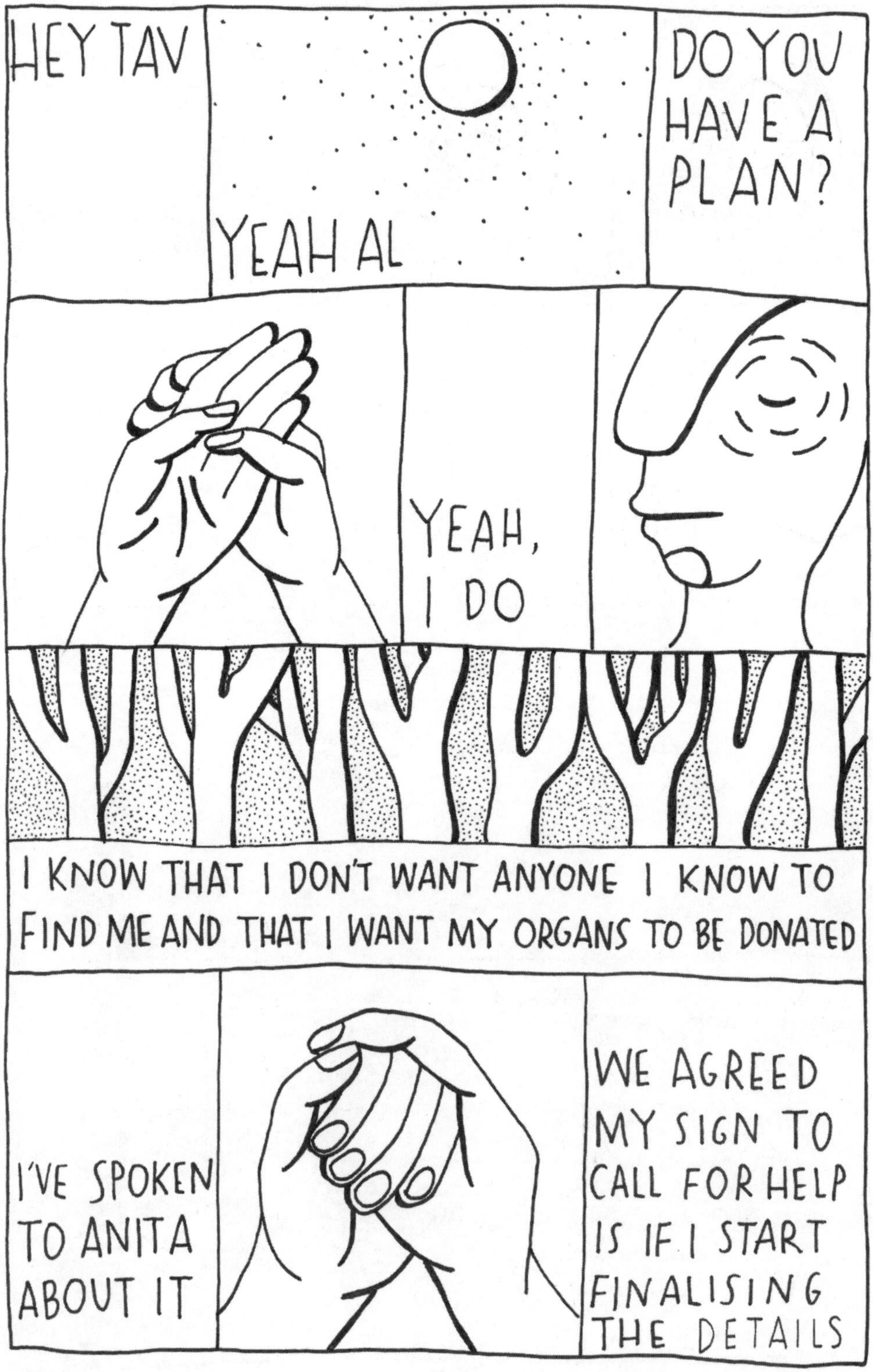
HEY TAV
YEAH AL
DO YOU HAVE A PLAN?
YEAH, I DO
I KNOW THAT I DON'T WANT ANYONE I KNOW TO FIND ME AND THAT I WANT MY ORGANS TO BE DONATED
I'VE SPOKEN TO ANITA ABOUT IT
WE AGREED MY SIGN TO CALL FOR HELP IS IF I START FINALISING THE DETAILS

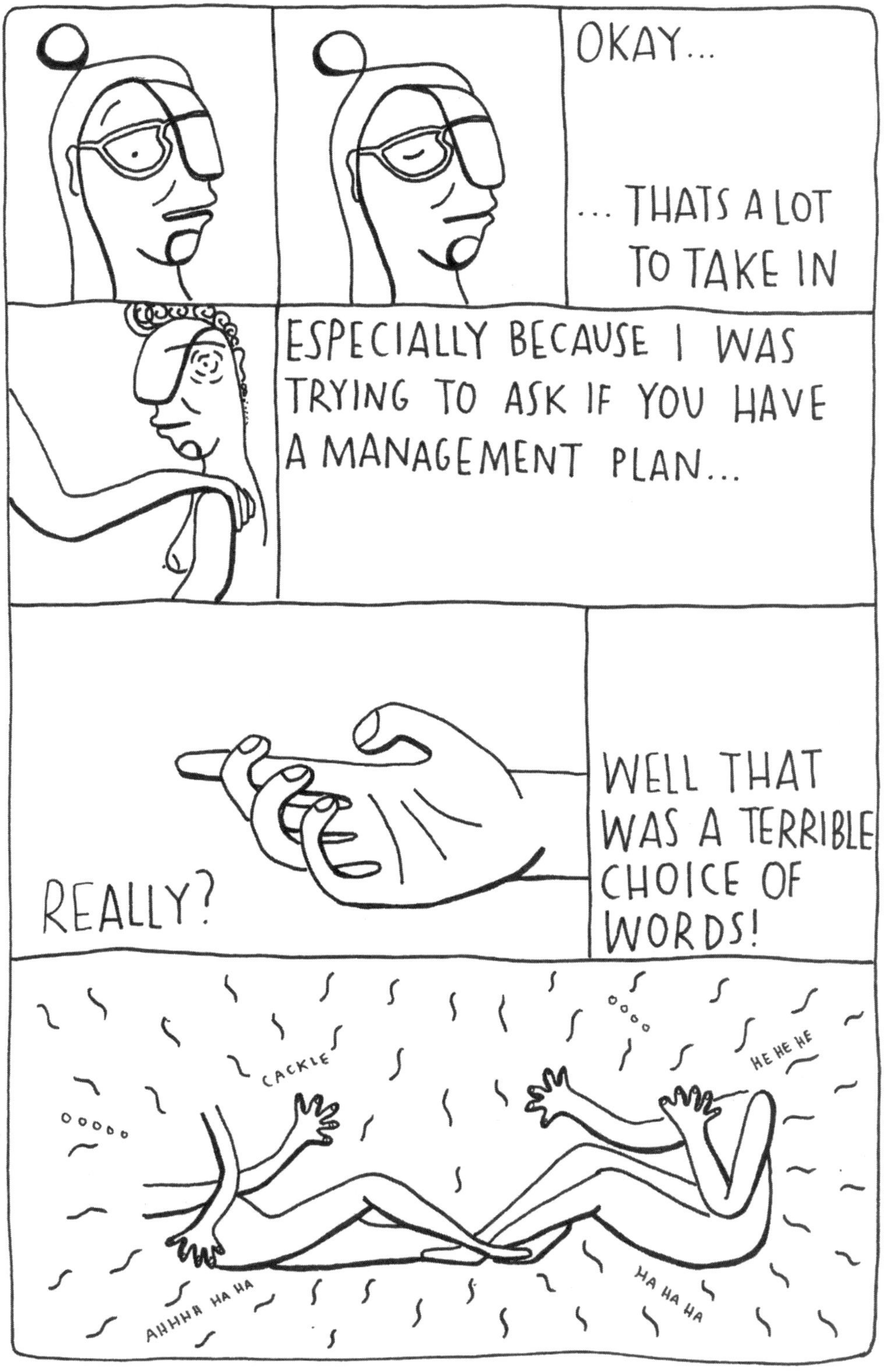
OKAY...
... THATS A LOT TO TAKE IN
ESPECIALLY BECAUSE I WAS TRYING TO ASK IF YOU HAVE A MANAGEMENT PLAN...
REALLY?
WELL THAT WAS A TERRIBLE CHOICE OF WORDS!
CACKLE
HE HE HE
AHHHA HA HA
HA HA HA

BUT SERIOUSLY TAV
DO YOU HAVE A STRATEGY FOR COPING WITH ALL THIS?
I DON'T KNOW ALI... IT'S HARD
IT DOESN'T FEEL LIKE THERE'S ALOT I CAN DO EXCEPT WAIT FOR THIS TO PASS
AND TRY TO DO AS LITTLE DAMAGE AS POSSIBLE...

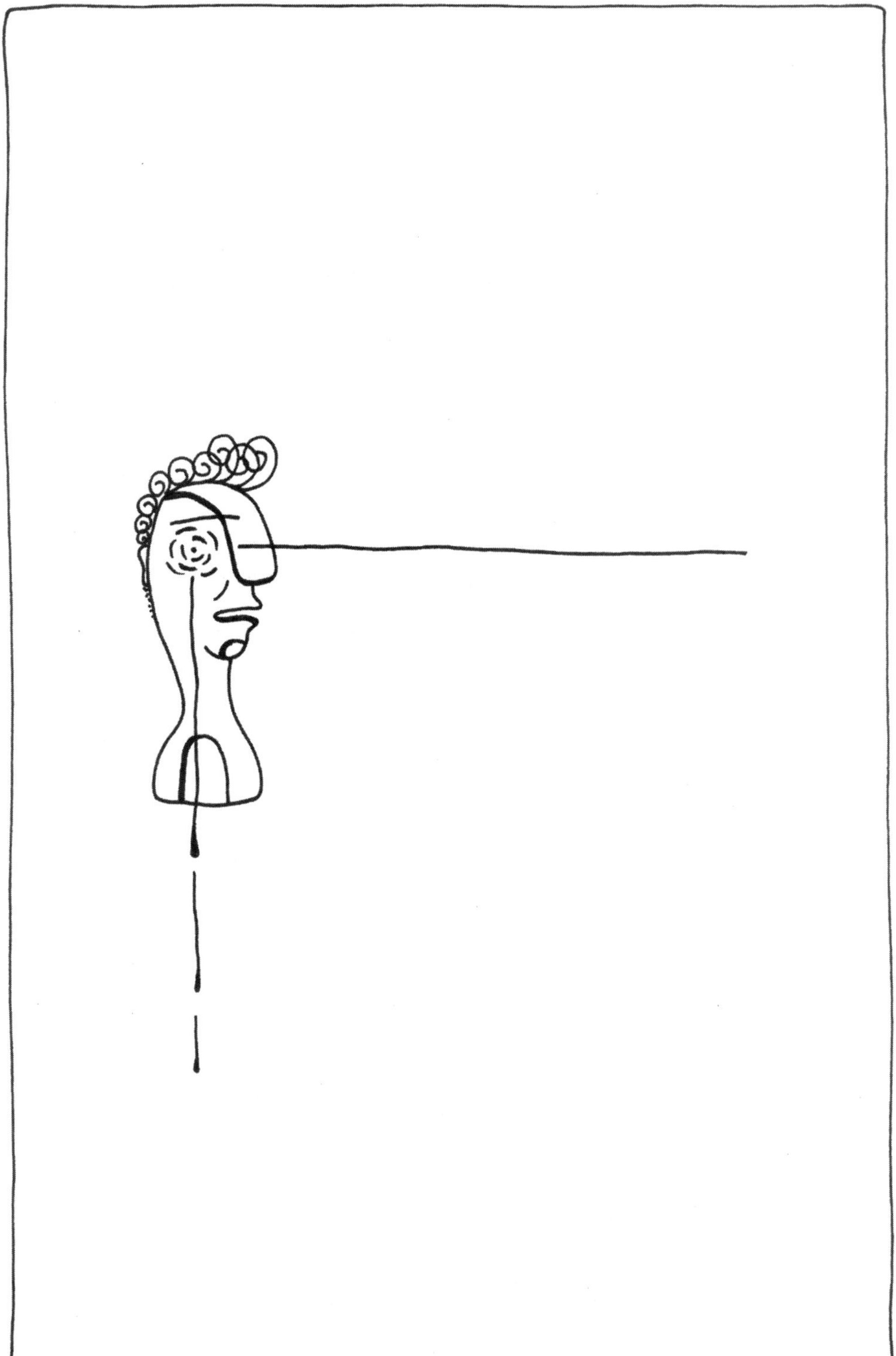

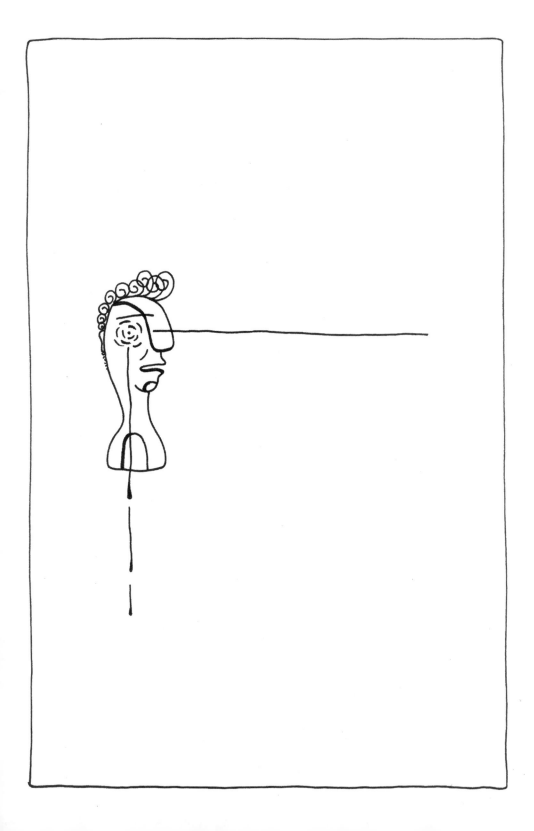

ANITA, I WANT OUT. I'M EXHAUSTED. I NEVER CHOSE TO BE BORN AND I FEEL LIKE I'VE GIVEN IT A GOOD SHOT, SO NOW I JUST WANT TO SAY 'THANKS FOR THE OPPORTUNITY BUT NO THANKS, THIS WHOLE LIFE THING ISN'T FOR ME.'

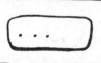

...

AND THE THING IS, EVERYONE WILL ADAPT, WE ALWAYS DO! IF I'M NOT HERE, SURE, IT'LL BE SAD AT FIRST BUT LIFE WILL CONTINUE AND IT WILL BE FINE...

THEY'LL ALL BE FINE IN THE LONG RUN...

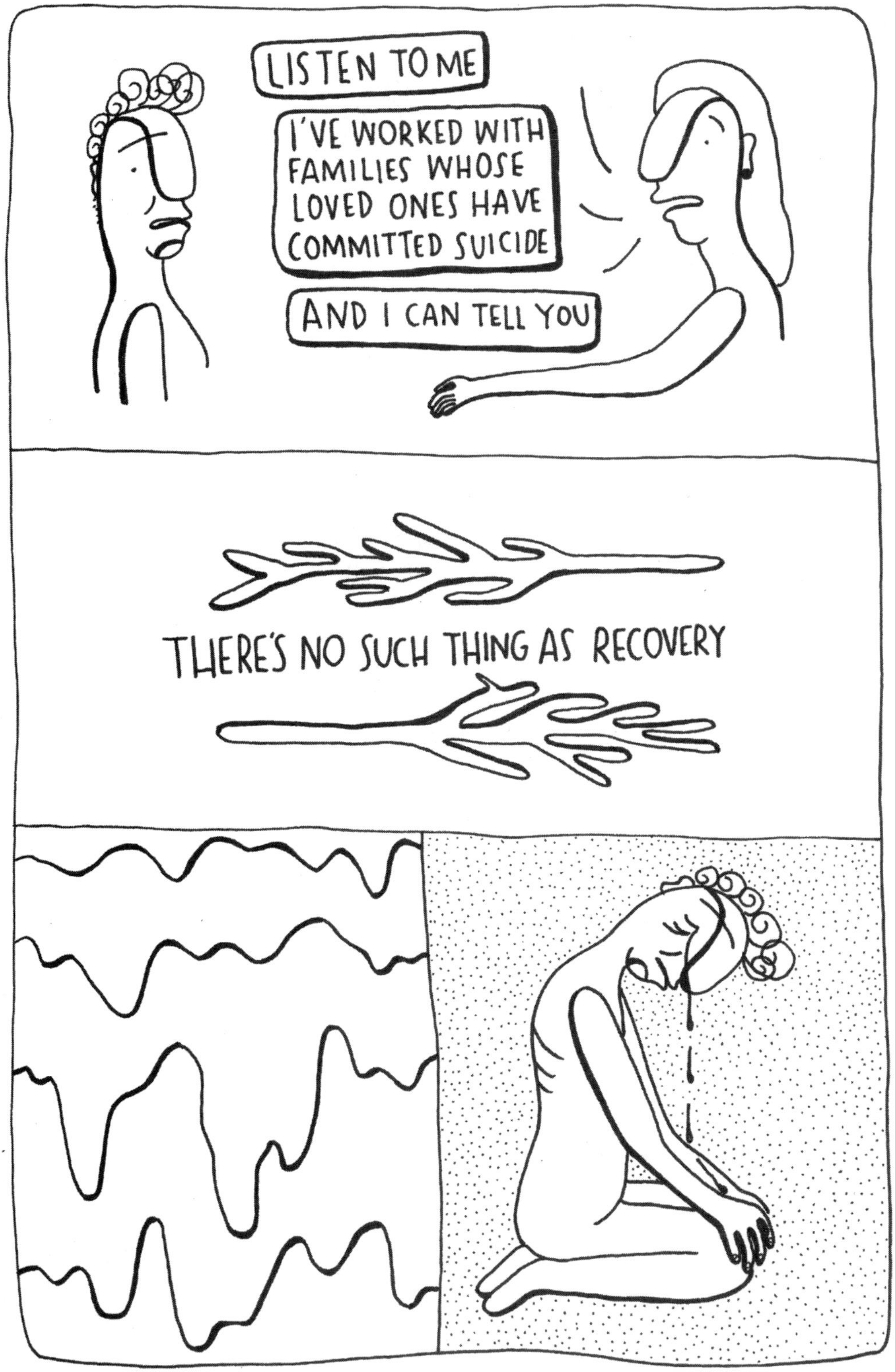
LISTEN TO ME
I'VE WORKED WITH FAMILIES WHOSE LOVED ONES HAVE COMMITTED SUICIDE
AND I CAN TELL YOU
THERE'S NO SUCH THING AS RECOVERY

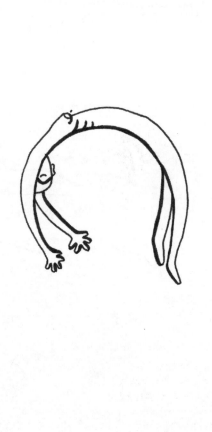

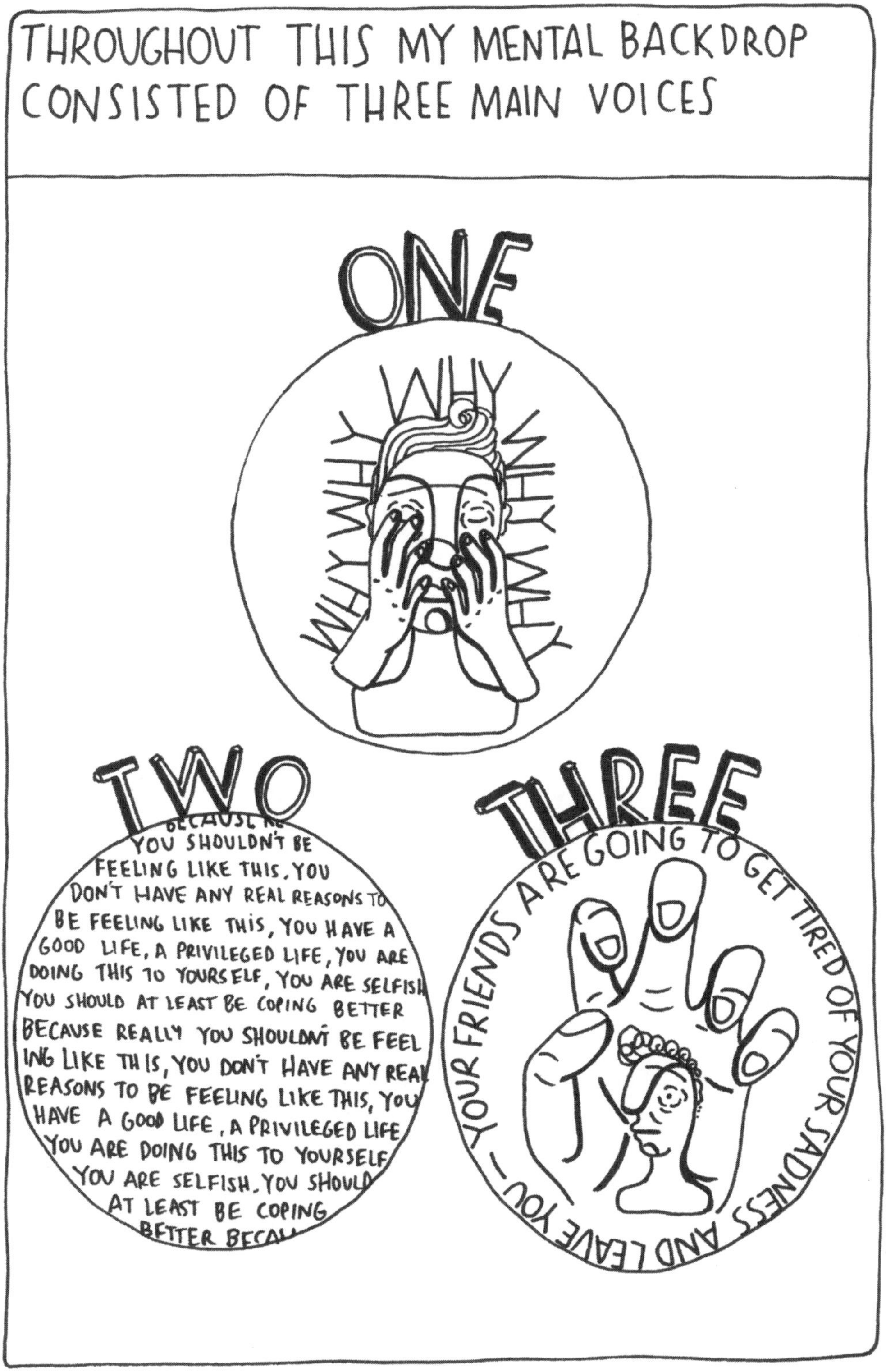

THROUGHOUT THIS MY MENTAL BACKDROP CONSISTED OF THREE MAIN VOICES

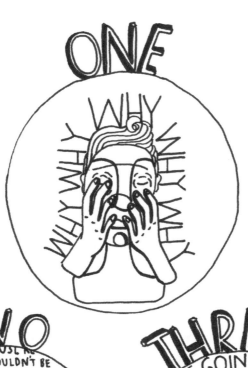

ONE

WHY WHY WHY...

TWO

BECAUSE RE YOU SHOULDN'T BE FEELING LIKE THIS, YOU DON'T HAVE ANY REAL REASONS TO BE FEELING LIKE THIS, YOU HAVE A GOOD LIFE, A PRIVILEGED LIFE, YOU ARE DOING THIS TO YOURSELF, YOU ARE SELFISH YOU SHOULD AT LEAST BE COPING BETTER BECAUSE REALLY YOU SHOULDN'T BE FEELING LIKE THIS, YOU DON'T HAVE ANY REAL REASONS TO BE FEELING LIKE THIS, YOU HAVE A GOOD LIFE, A PRIVILEGED LIFE YOU ARE DOING THIS TO YOURSELF YOU ARE SELFISH. YOU SHOULD AT LEAST BE COPING BETTER BECAU

THREE

YOUR FRIENDS ARE GOING TO GET TIRED OF YOUR SADNESS AND LEAVE YOU — YOUR FRIENDS ARE GOING TO GET TIRED OF YOUR SADNESS AND LEAVE YOU —

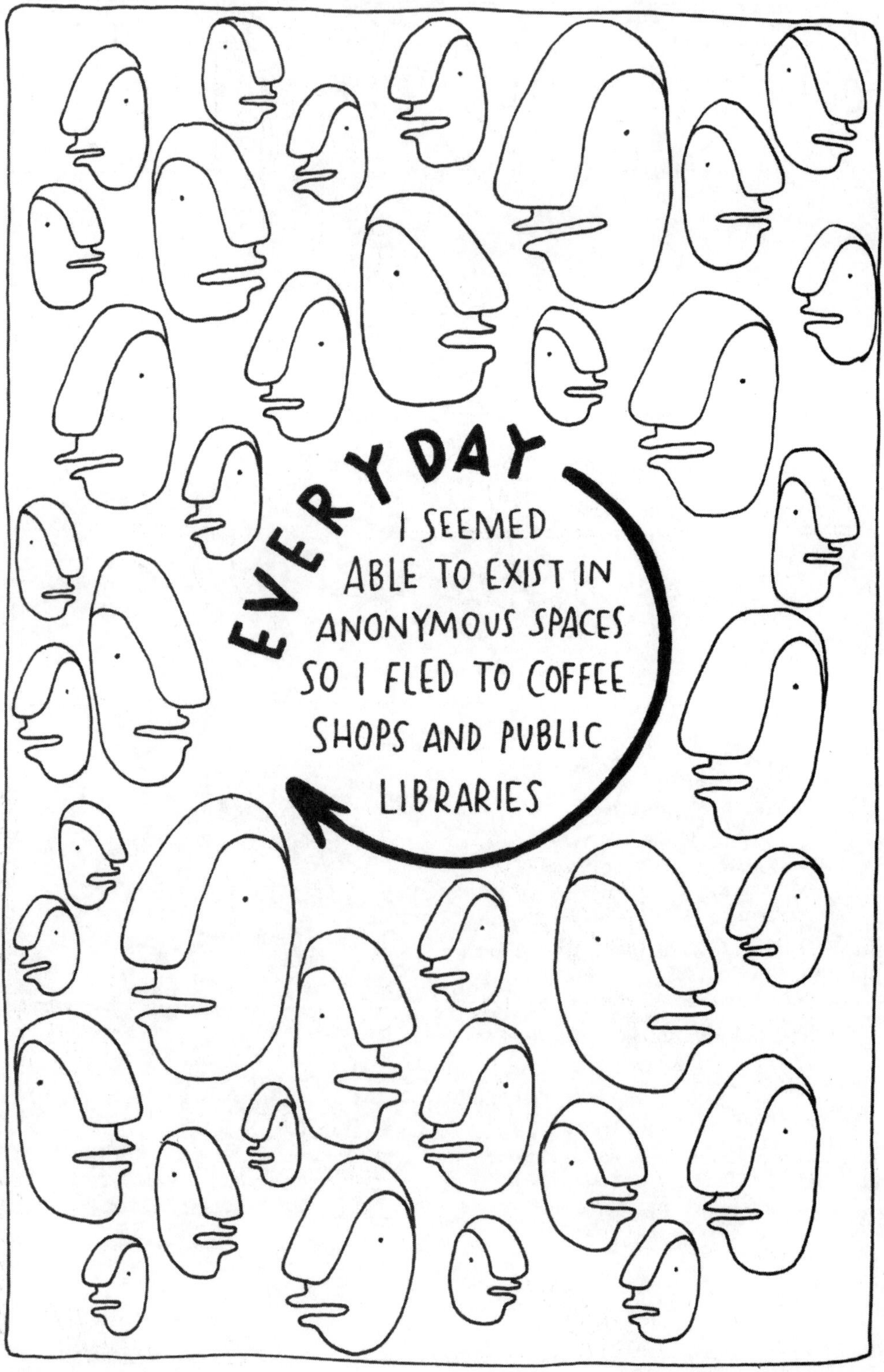
EVERYDAY
I SEEMED ABLE TO EXIST IN ANONYMOUS SPACES SO I FLED TO COFFEE SHOPS AND PUBLIC LIBRARIES

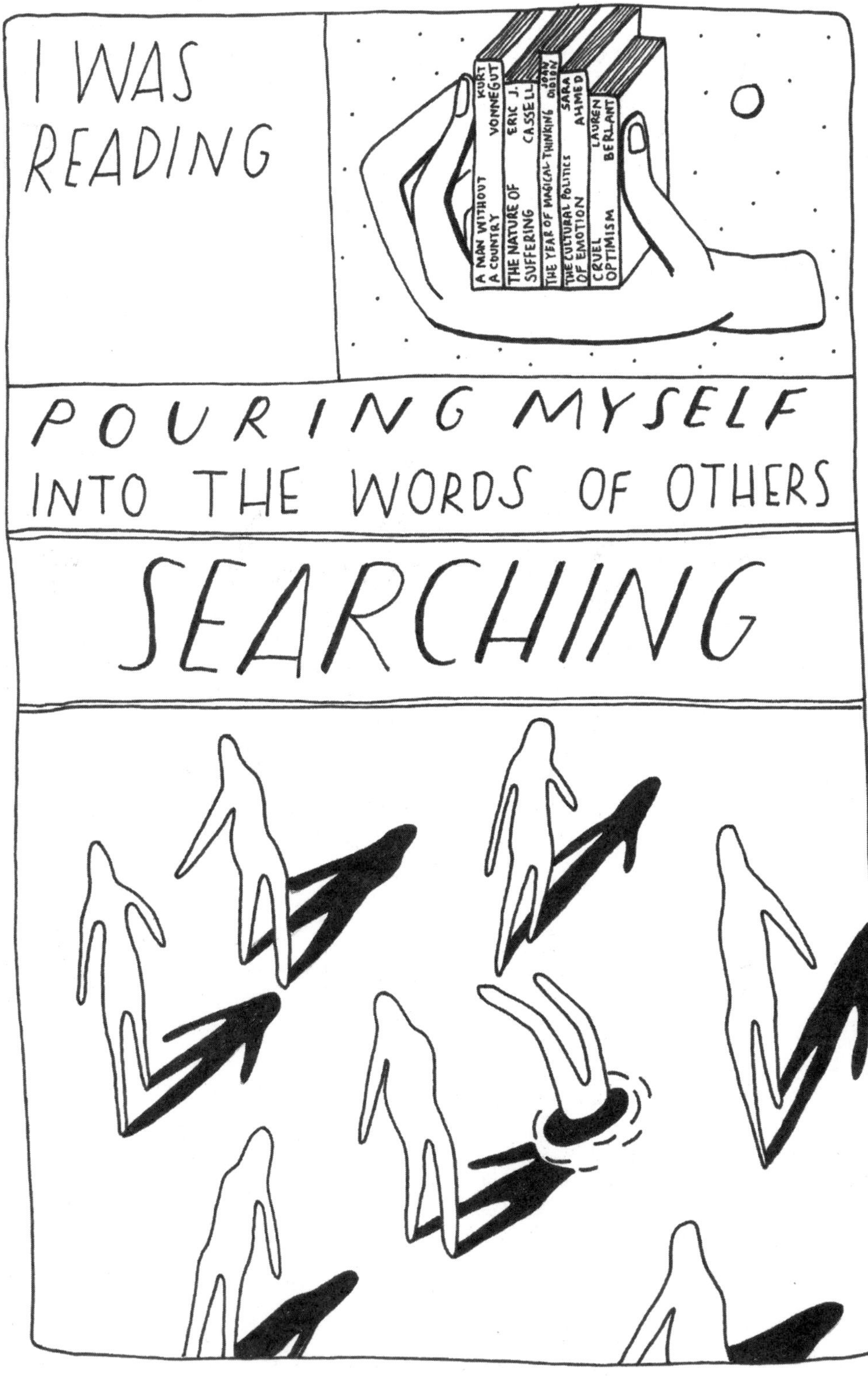
I WAS READING
KURT VONNEGUT
A MAN WITHOUT A COUNTRY
ERIC J. CASSELL
THE NATURE OF SUFFERING
JOAN DIDION
THE YEAR OF MAGICAL THINKING
SARA AHMED
THE CULTURAL POLITICS OF EMOTION
LAUREN BERLANT
CRUEL OPTIMISM
POURING MYSELF INTO THE WORDS OF OTHERS
SEARCHING

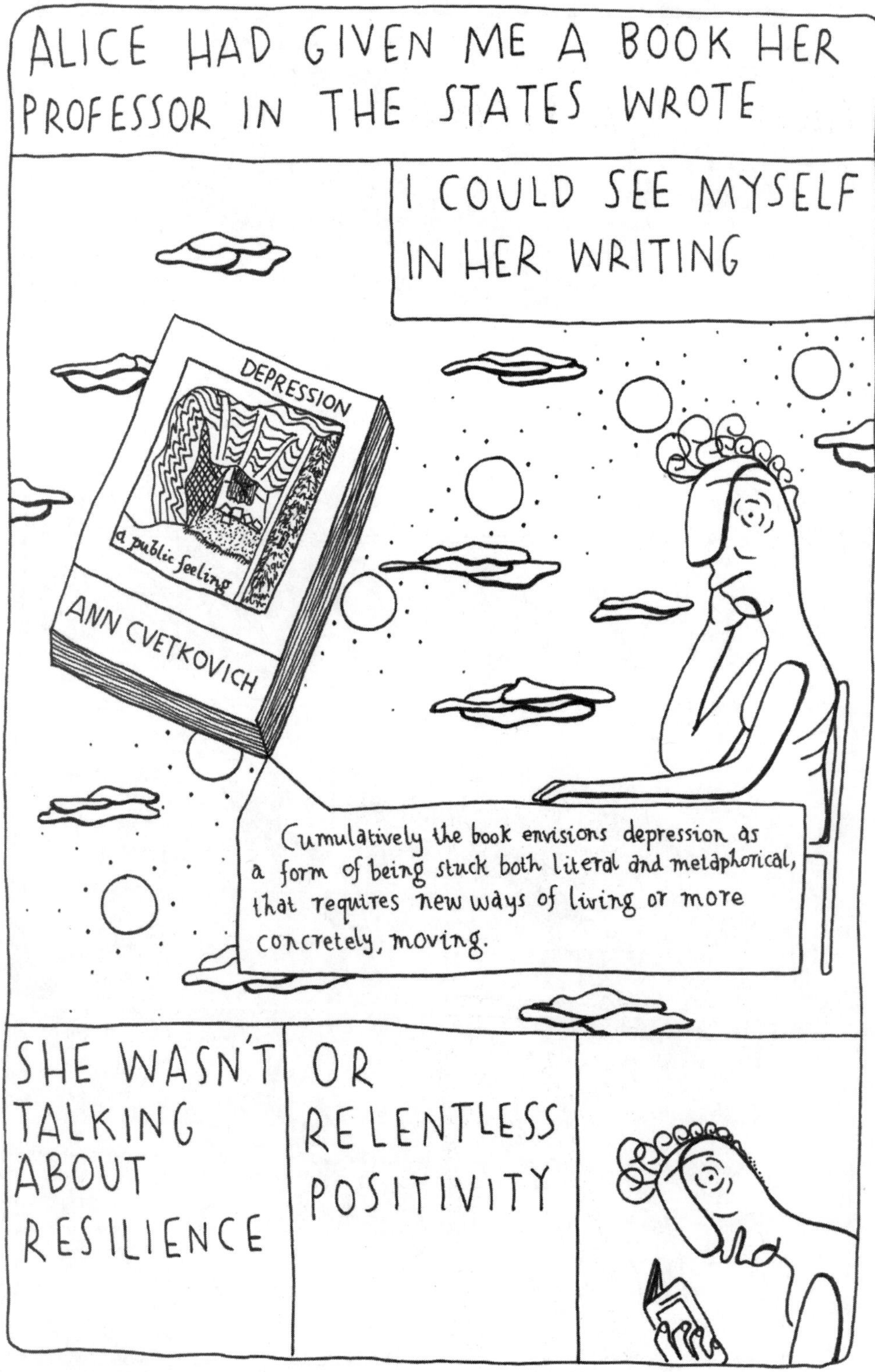

ALICE HAD GIVEN ME A BOOK HER PROFESSOR IN THE STATES WROTE
I COULD SEE MYSELF IN HER WRITING
DEPRESSION
a public feeling
ANN CVETKOVICH
Cumulatively the book envisions depression as a form of being stuck both literal and metaphorical, that requires new ways of living or more concretely, moving.
SHE WASN'T TALKING ABOUT RESILIENCE
OR RELENTLESS POSITIVITY

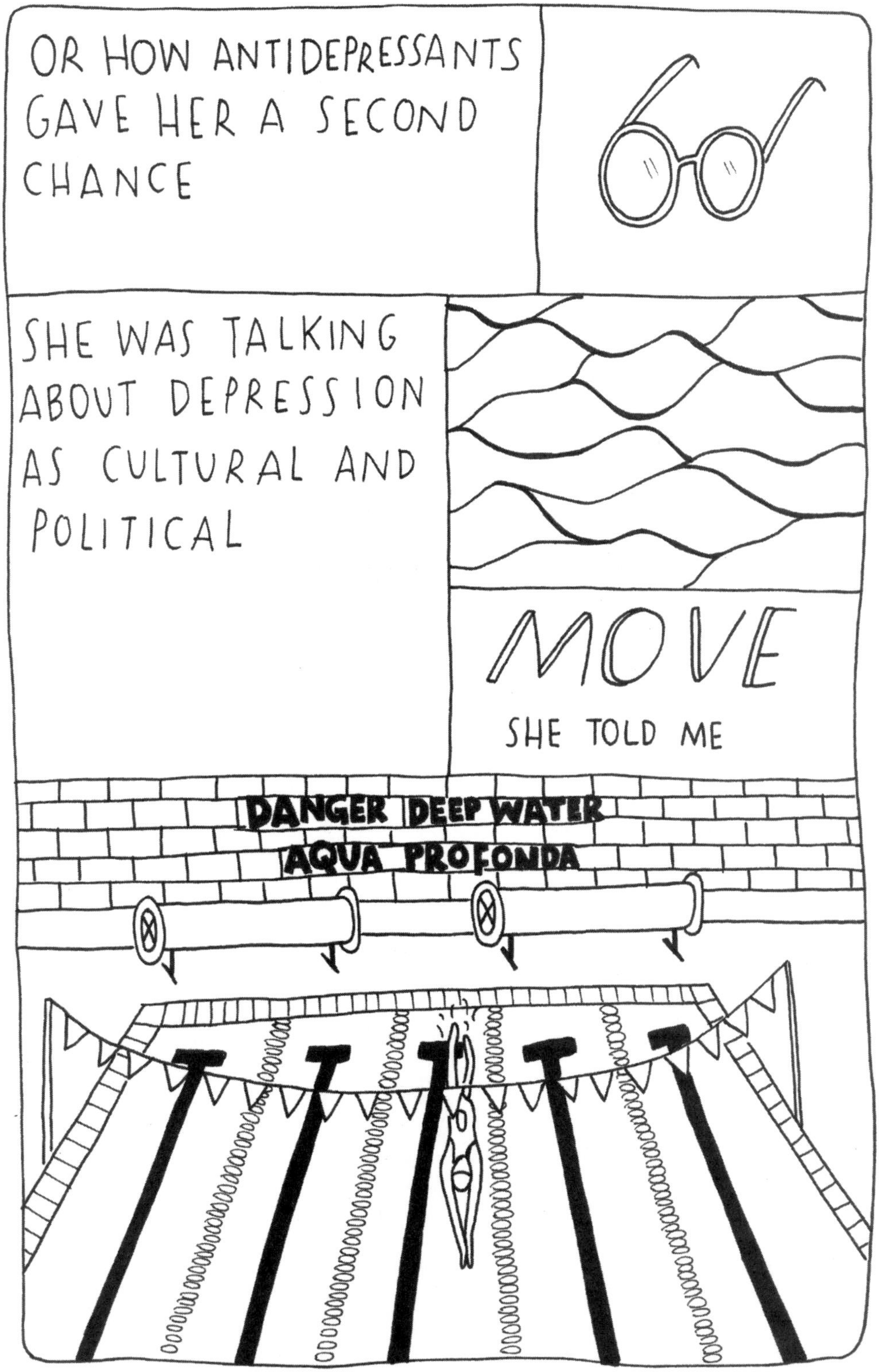
OR HOW ANTIDEPRESSANTS GAVE HER A SECOND CHANCE
SHE WAS TALKING ABOUT DEPRESSION AS CULTURAL AND POLITICAL
MOVE
SHE TOLD ME
DANGER DEEP WATER
AQUA PROFONDA

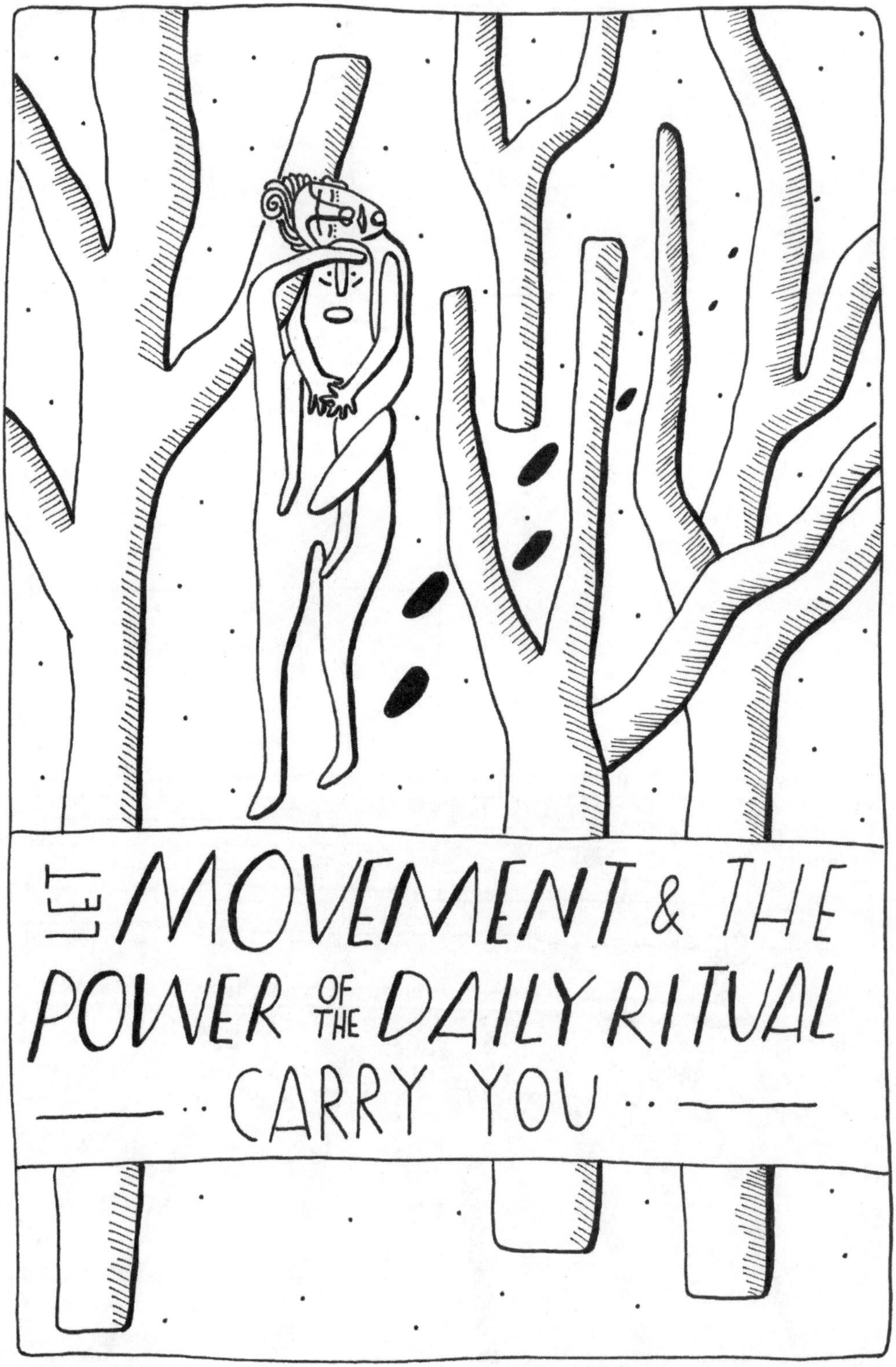
LET MOVEMENT & THE POWER OF THE DAILY RITUAL CARRY YOU

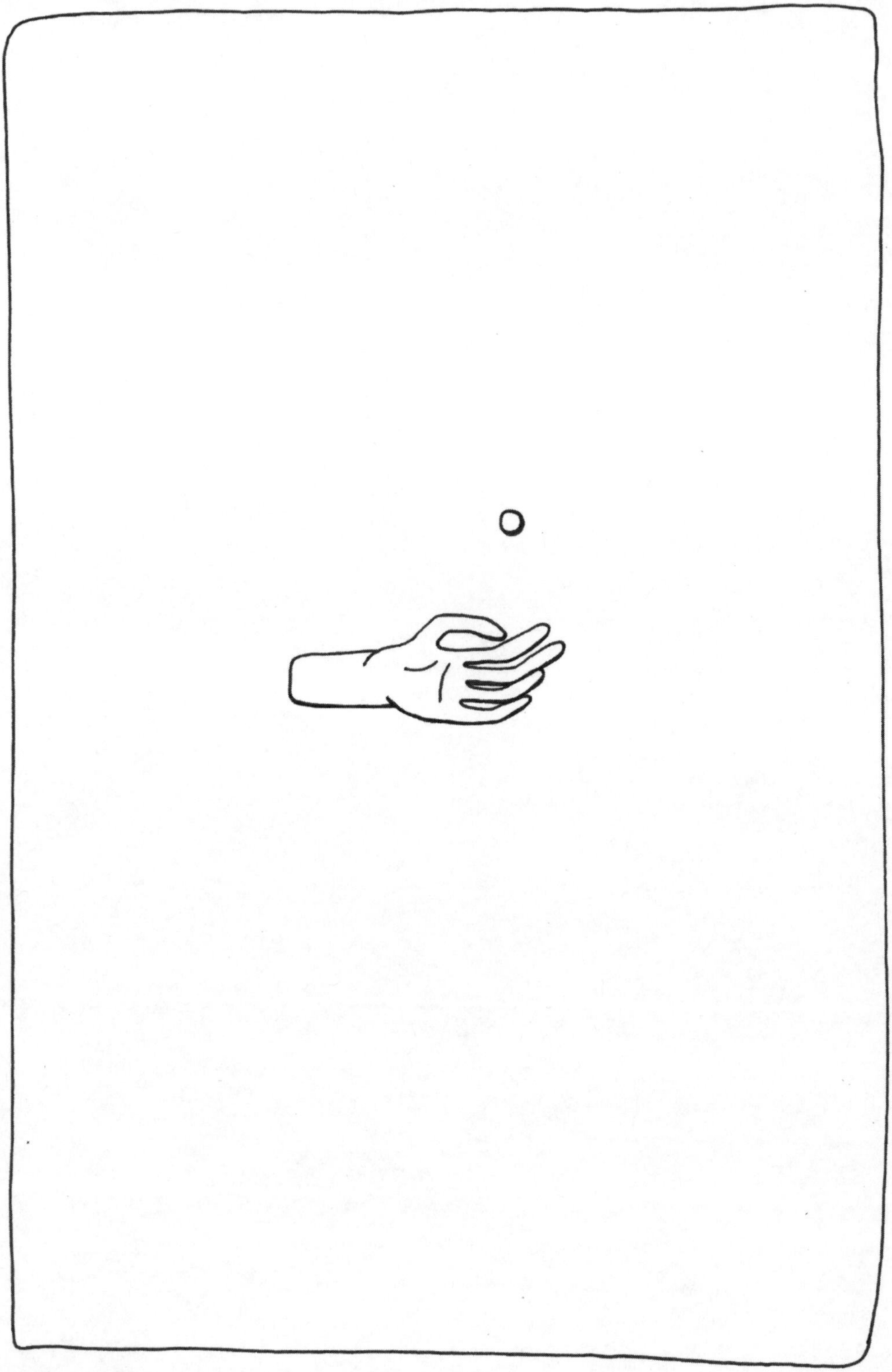

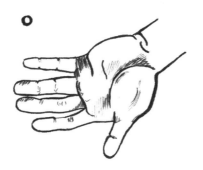

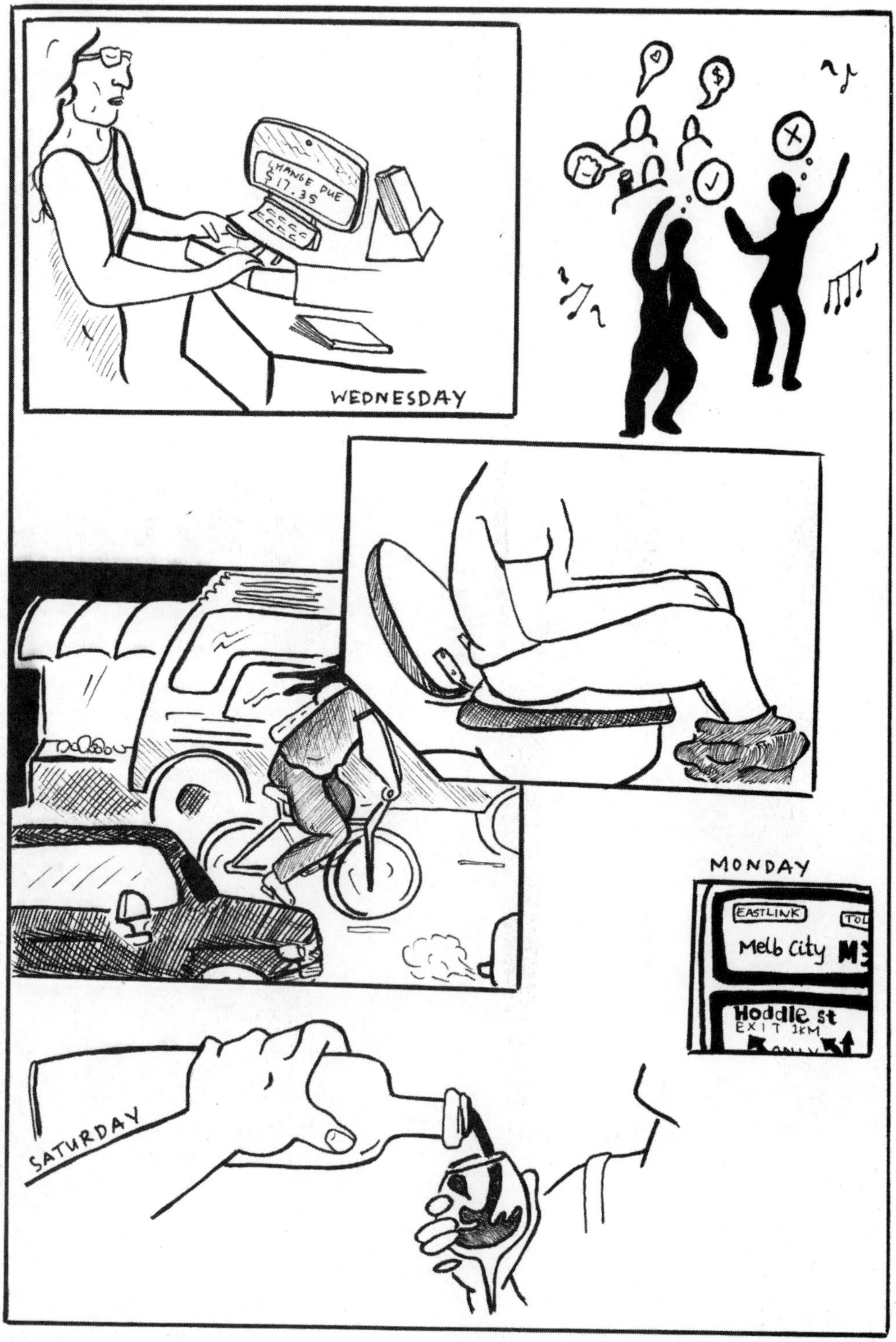
CHANGE DUE
$17.35
WEDNESDAY
MONDAY
EASTLINK
Melb City
Hoddle st
EXIT 1KM
SATURDAY

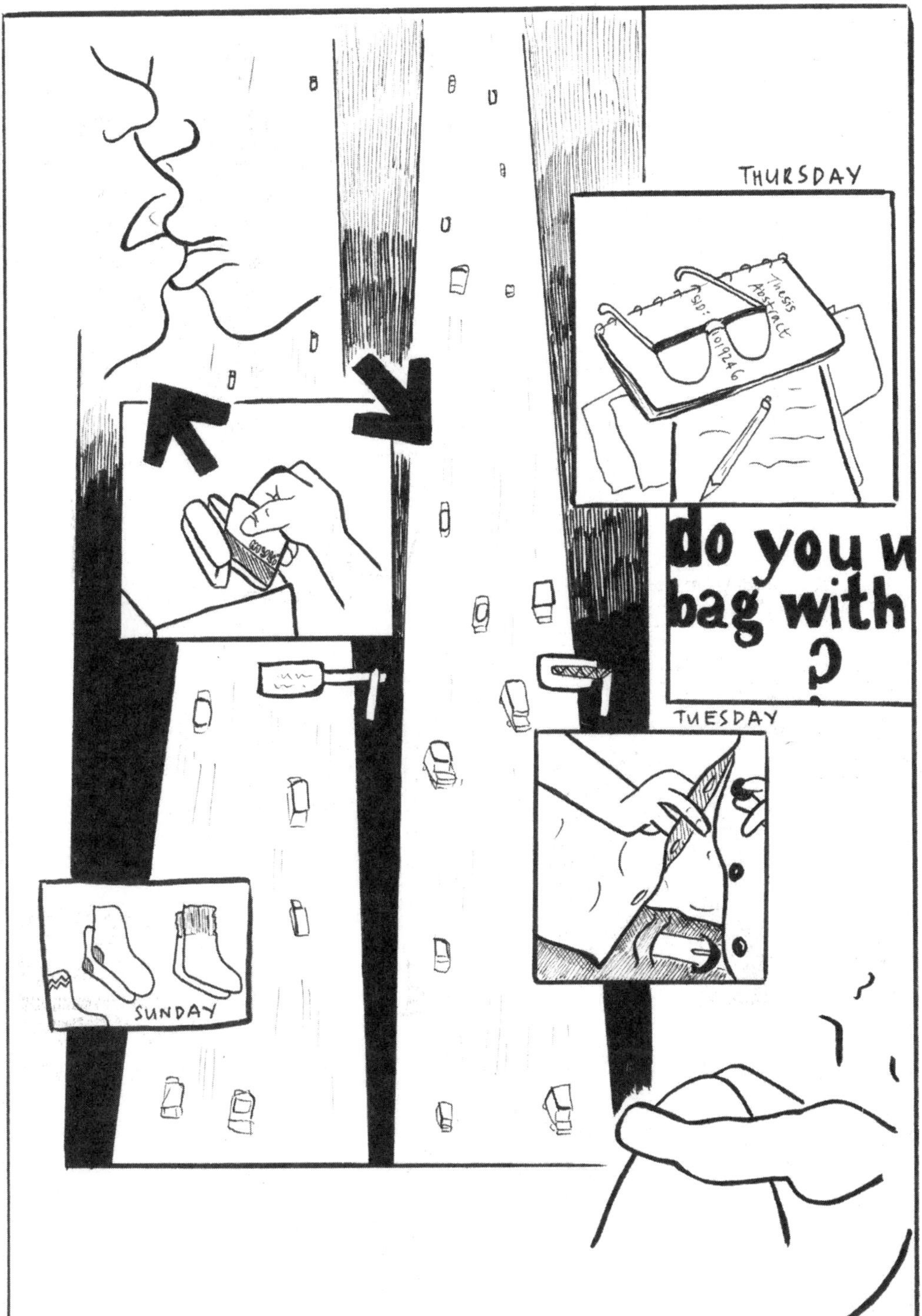
THURSDAY
Thesis Abstract
do you w
bag with
?
TUESDAY
SUNDAY

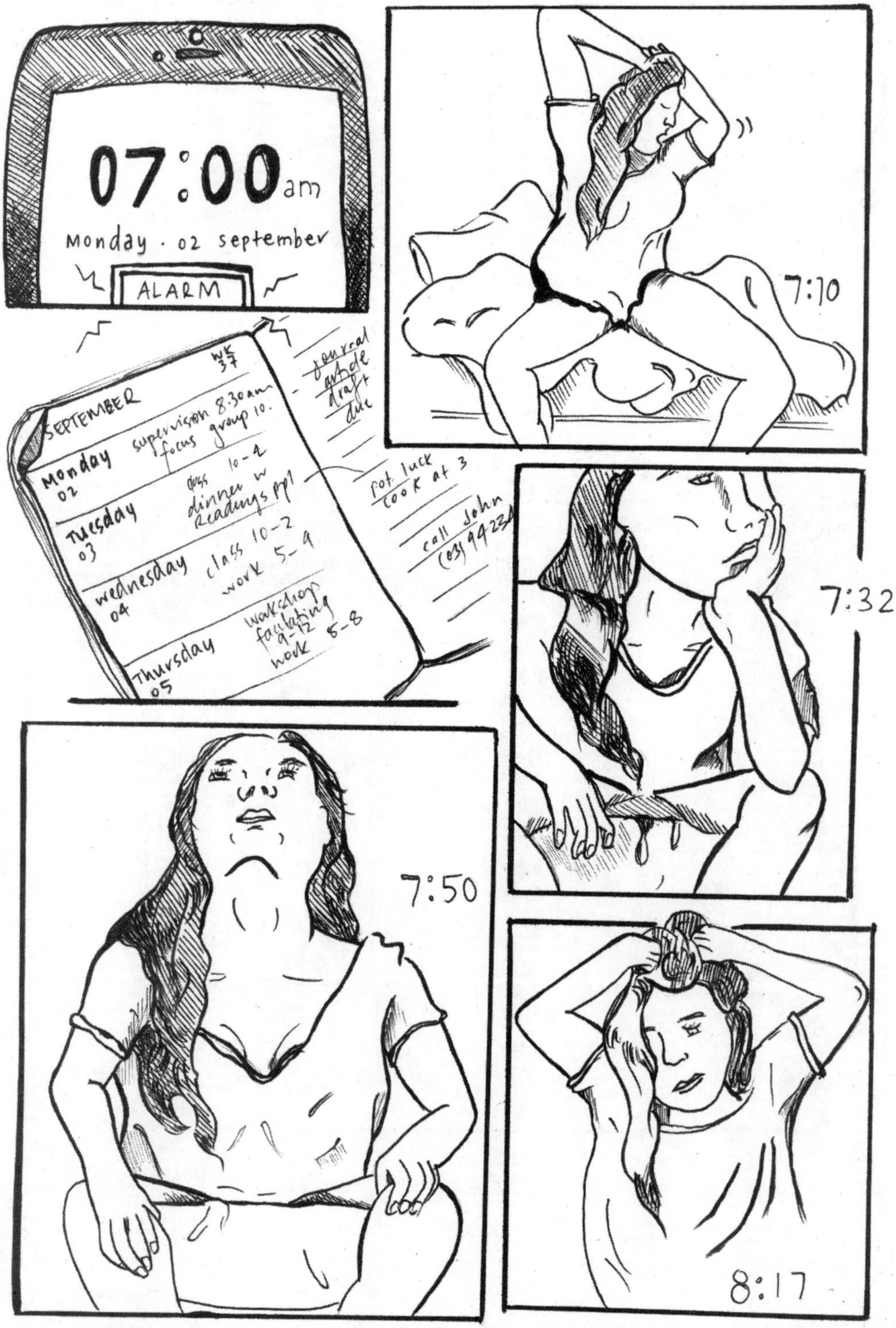
07:00am
Monday · 02 september
ALARM
SEPTEMBER
WK 37
Monday 02
supervision 8:30am
focus group 10.
Tuesday 03
class 10-4
dinner w Readings ppl
wednesday 04
class 10-2
work 5-9
Thursday 05
workshop facilitating 9-12
work 5-8
journal article draft due
pot luck cook at 3
call John
7:10
7:32
7:50
8:17

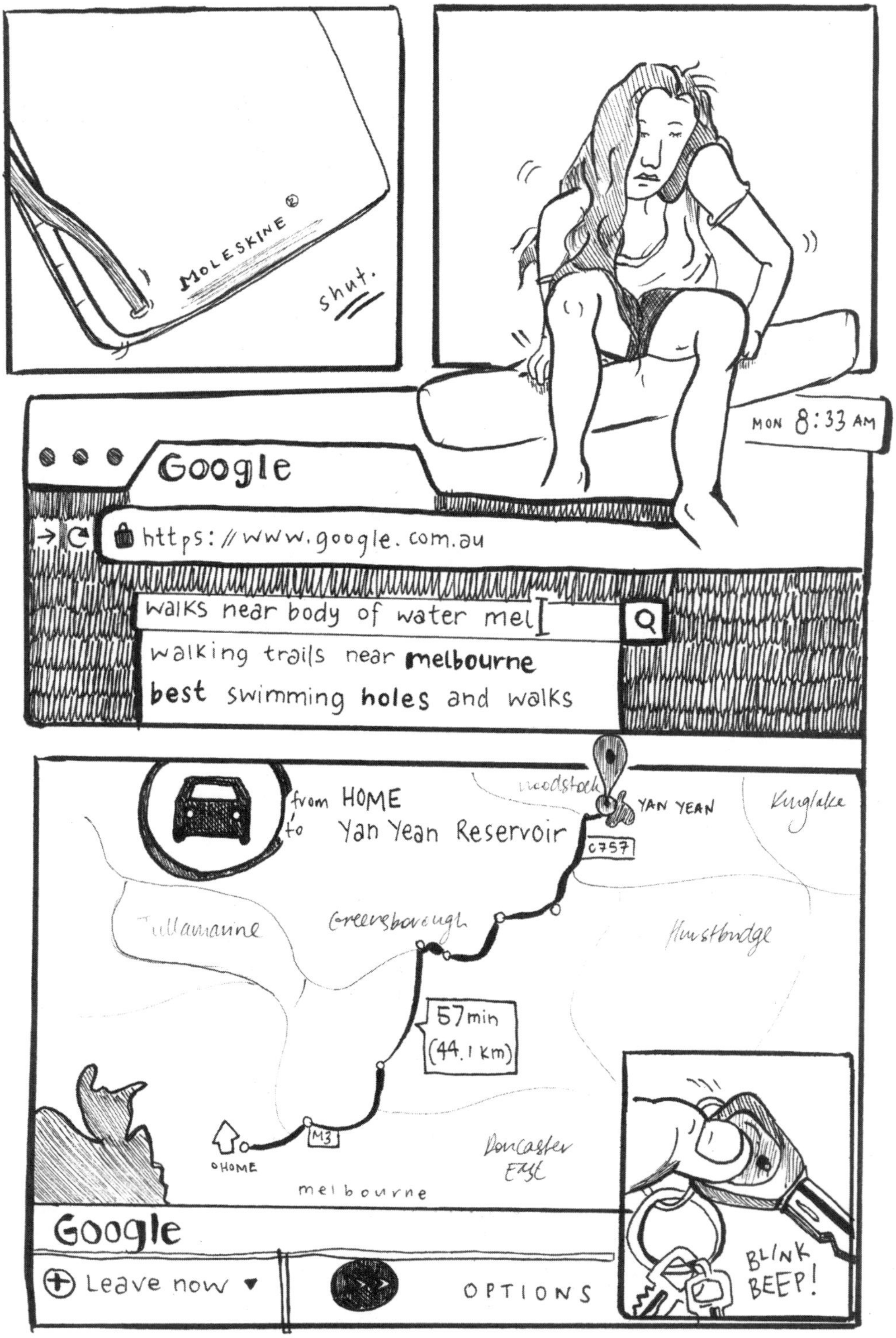

MOLESKINE®
shut.
MON 8:33 AM
Google
https://www.google.com.au
walks near body of water mel
walking trails near **melbourne**
best swimming **holes** and walks
from HOME
to Yan Yean Reservoir
YAN YEAN
C757
Greensborough
57min
(44.1 km)
M3
HOME
melbourne
Doncaster East
Google
Leave now
OPTIONS
BLINK
BEEP!

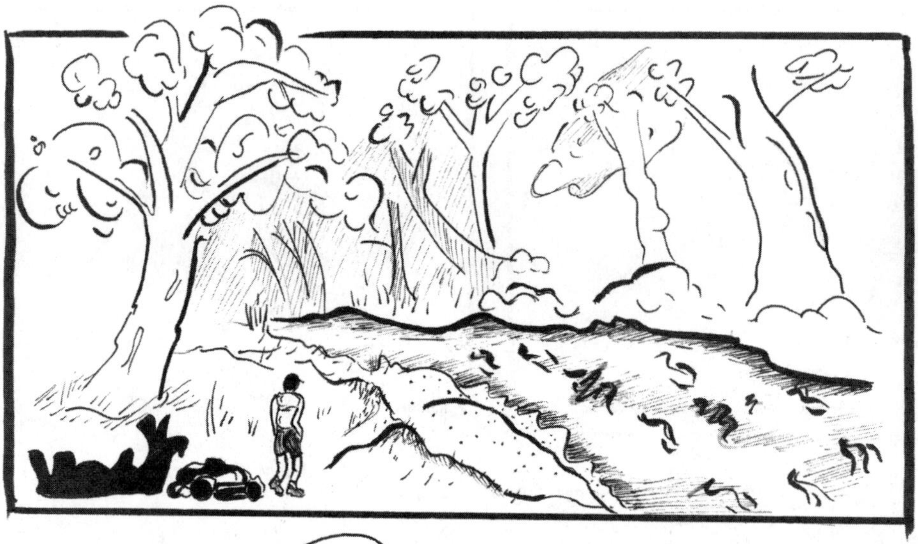

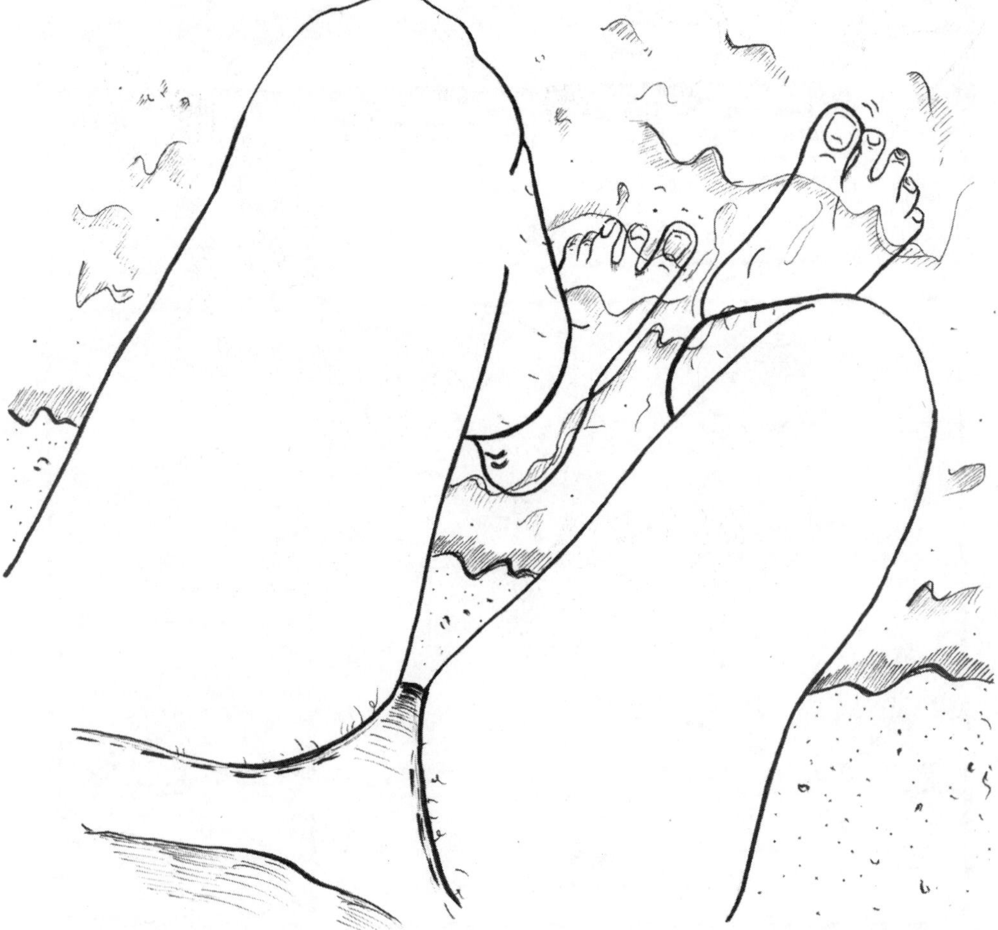

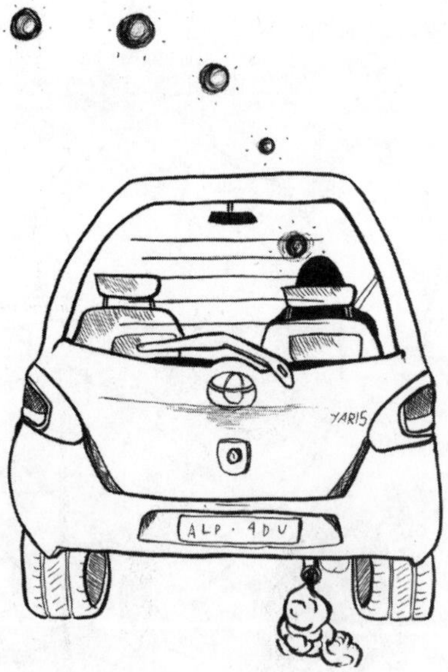
YARIS
ALP · 9DU

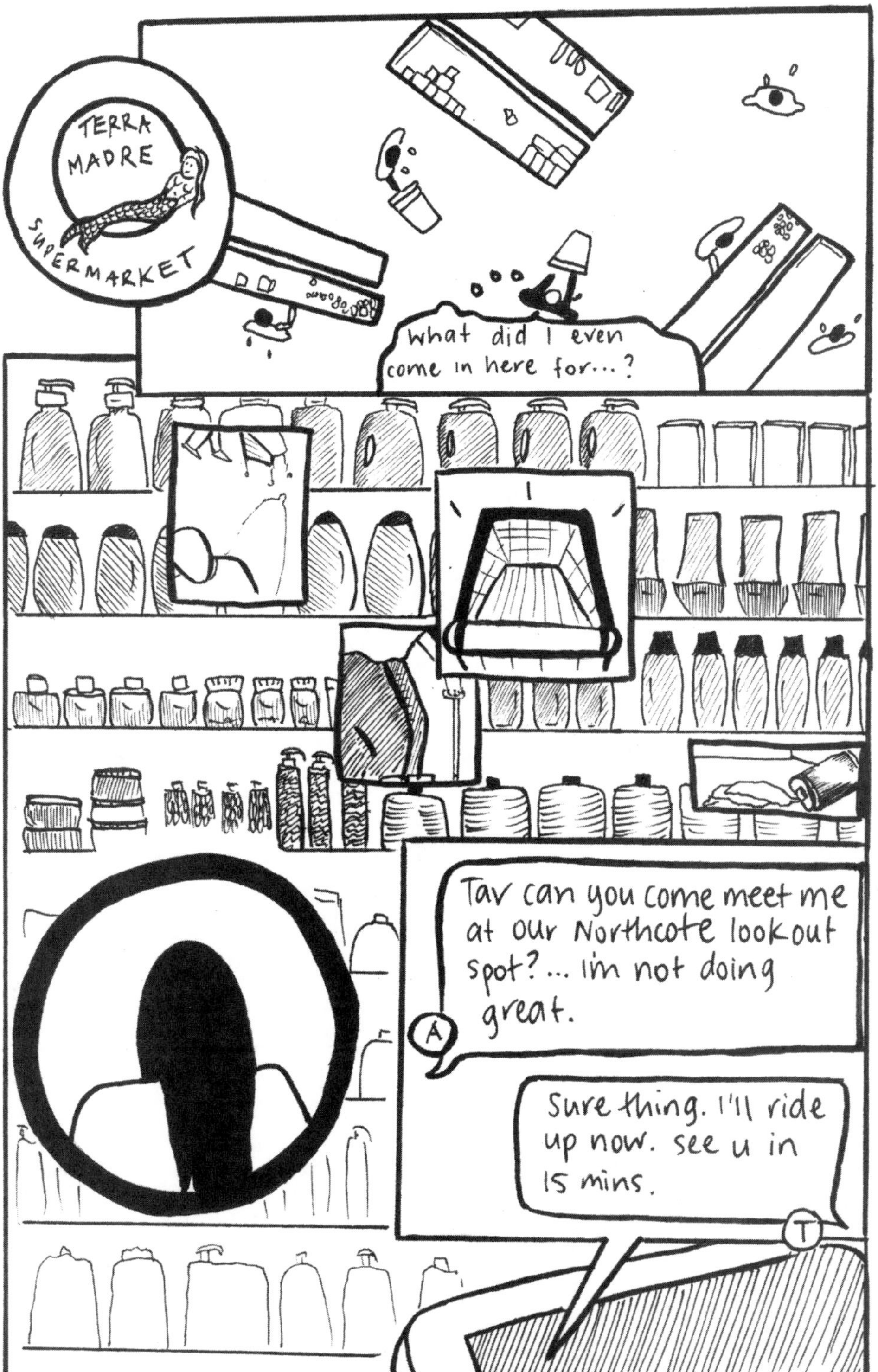
TERRA MADRE SUPERMARKET
what did I even come in here for...?
Tav can you come meet me at our Northcote lookout spot?... im not doing great.
A
Sure thing. I'll ride up now. see u in 15 mins.
T

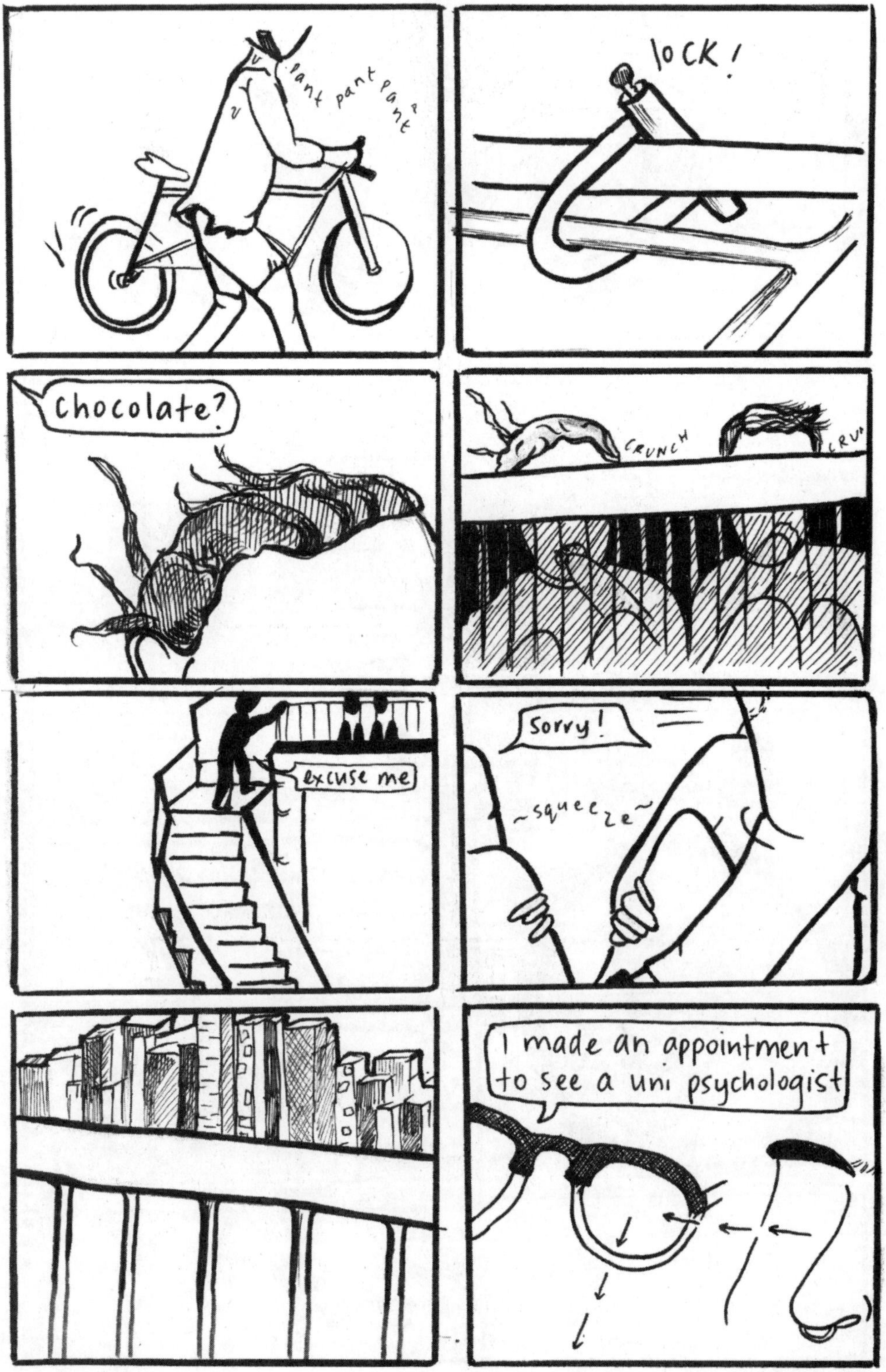
pant pant pant
lock!
Chocolate?
CRUNCH
excuse me
Sorry!
~squeeze~
I made an appointment to see a uni psychologist

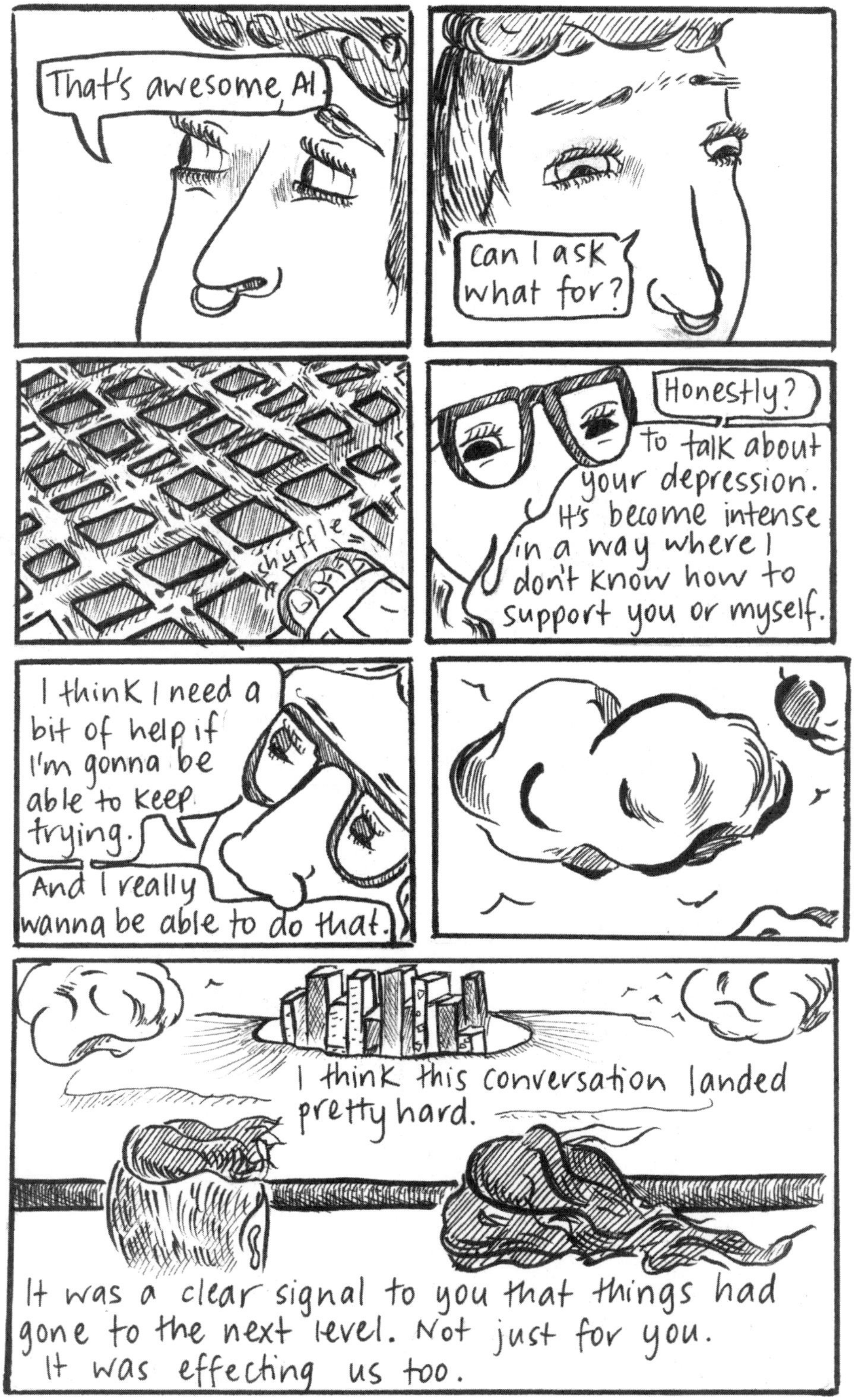
That's awesome, Al.
Can I ask what for?
shuffle
Honestly?
to talk about your depression. It's become intense in a way where I don't know how to support you or myself.
I think I need a bit of help if I'm gonna be able to keep trying.
And I really wanna be able to do that.
I think this conversation landed pretty hard.
It was a clear signal to you that things had gone to the next level. Not just for you. It was effecting us too.

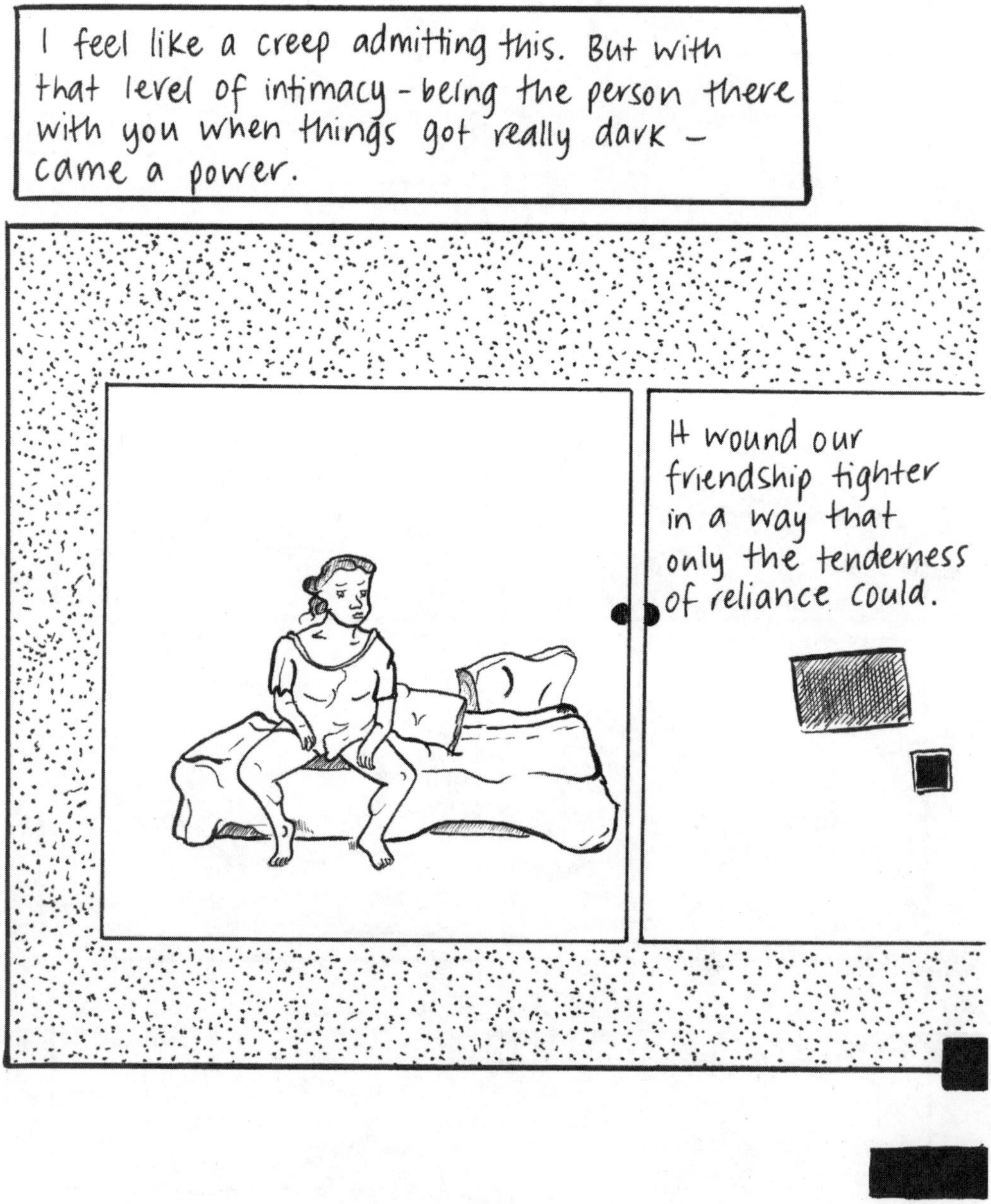
I feel like a creep admitting this. But with that level of intimacy - being the person there with you when things got really dark - came a power.
It wound our friendship tighter in a way that only the tenderness of reliance could.

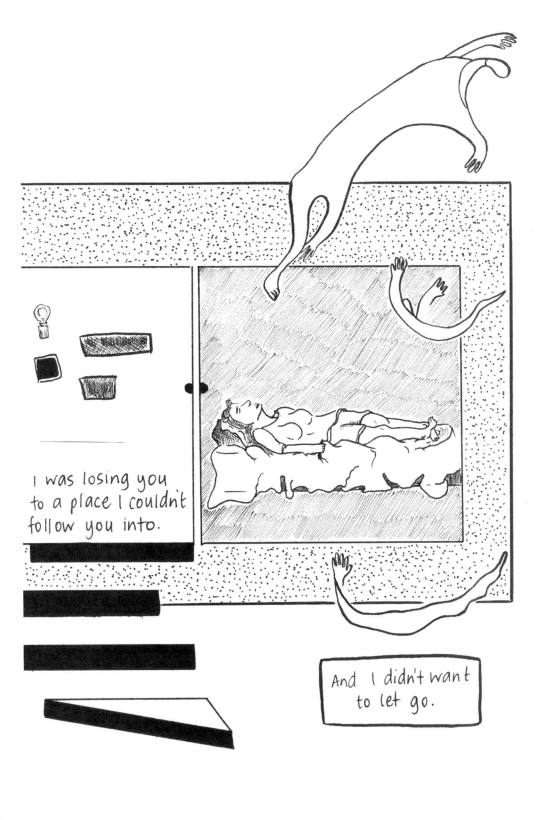

I was losing you to a place I couldn't follow you into.

And I didn't want to let go.

TREADINGS

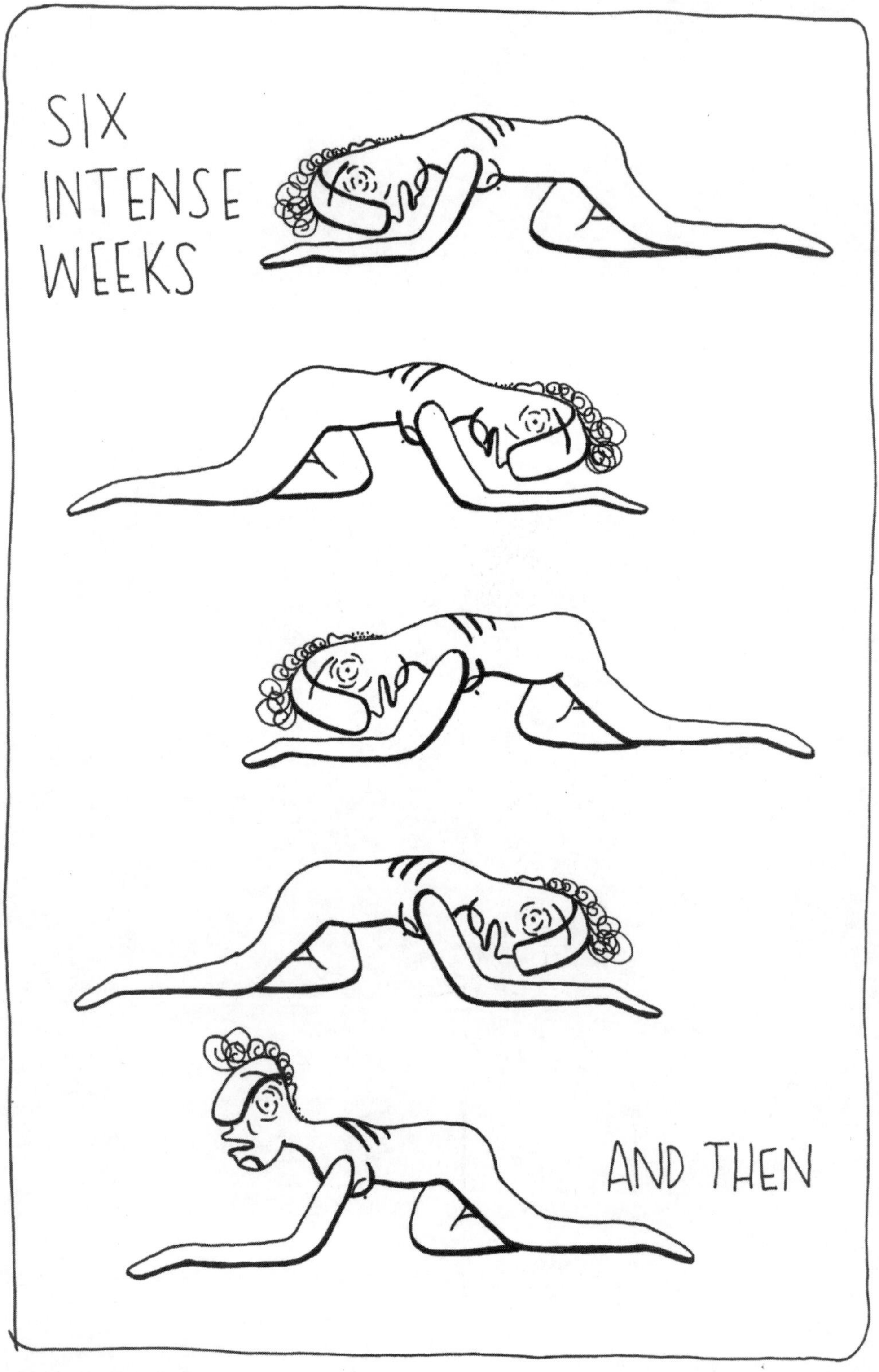
SIX INTENSE WEEKS
AND THEN

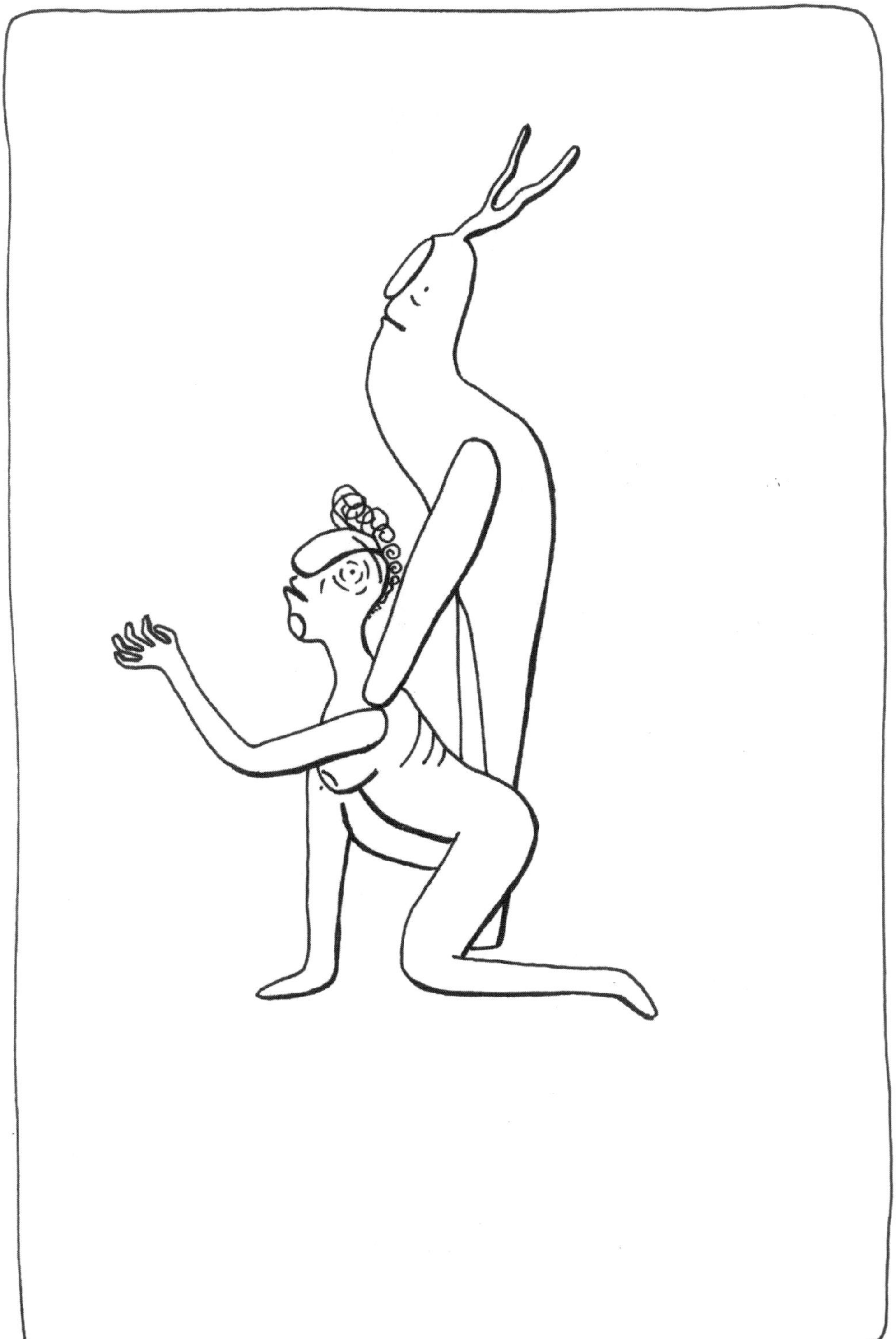

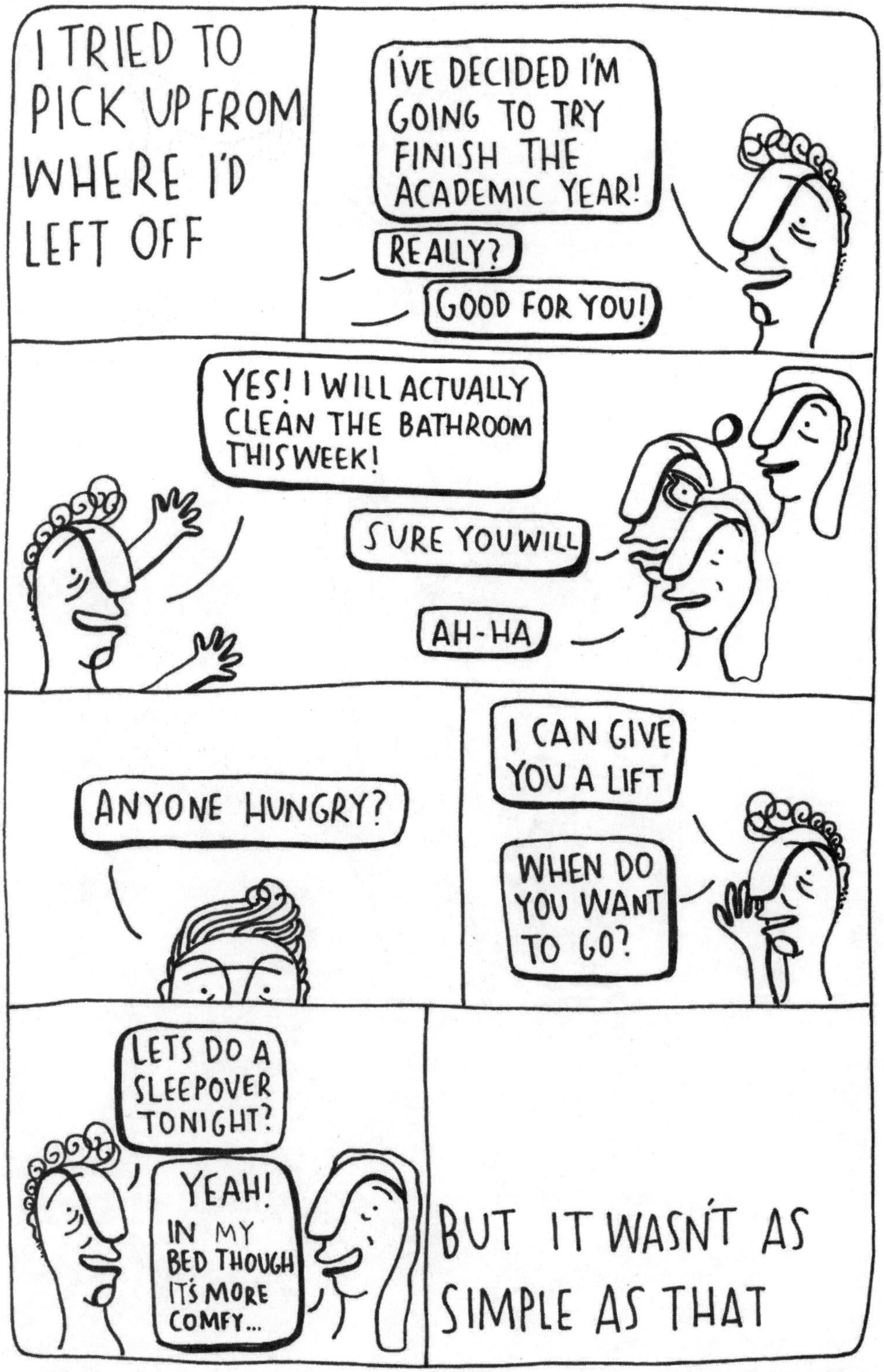
I TRIED TO PICK UP FROM WHERE I'D LEFT OFF
I'VE DECIDED I'M GOING TO TRY FINISH THE ACADEMIC YEAR!
REALLY?
GOOD FOR YOU!
YES! I WILL ACTUALLY CLEAN THE BATHROOM THIS WEEK!
SURE YOU WILL
AH-HA
ANYONE HUNGRY?
I CAN GIVE YOU A LIFT
WHEN DO YOU WANT TO GO?
LETS DO A SLEEPOVER TONIGHT?
YEAH! IN MY BED THOUGH IT'S MORE COMFY...
BUT IT WASN'T AS SIMPLE AS THAT

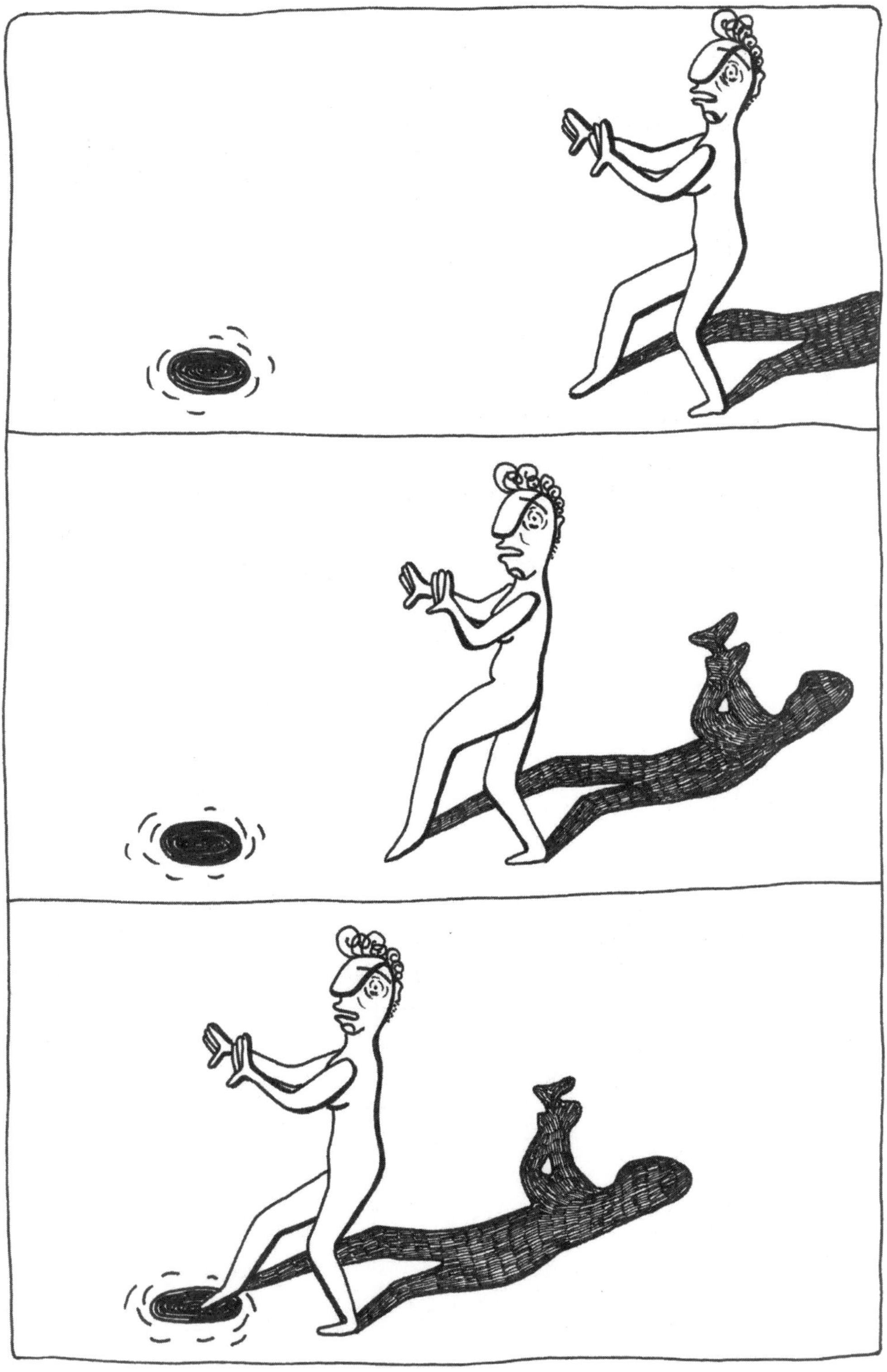

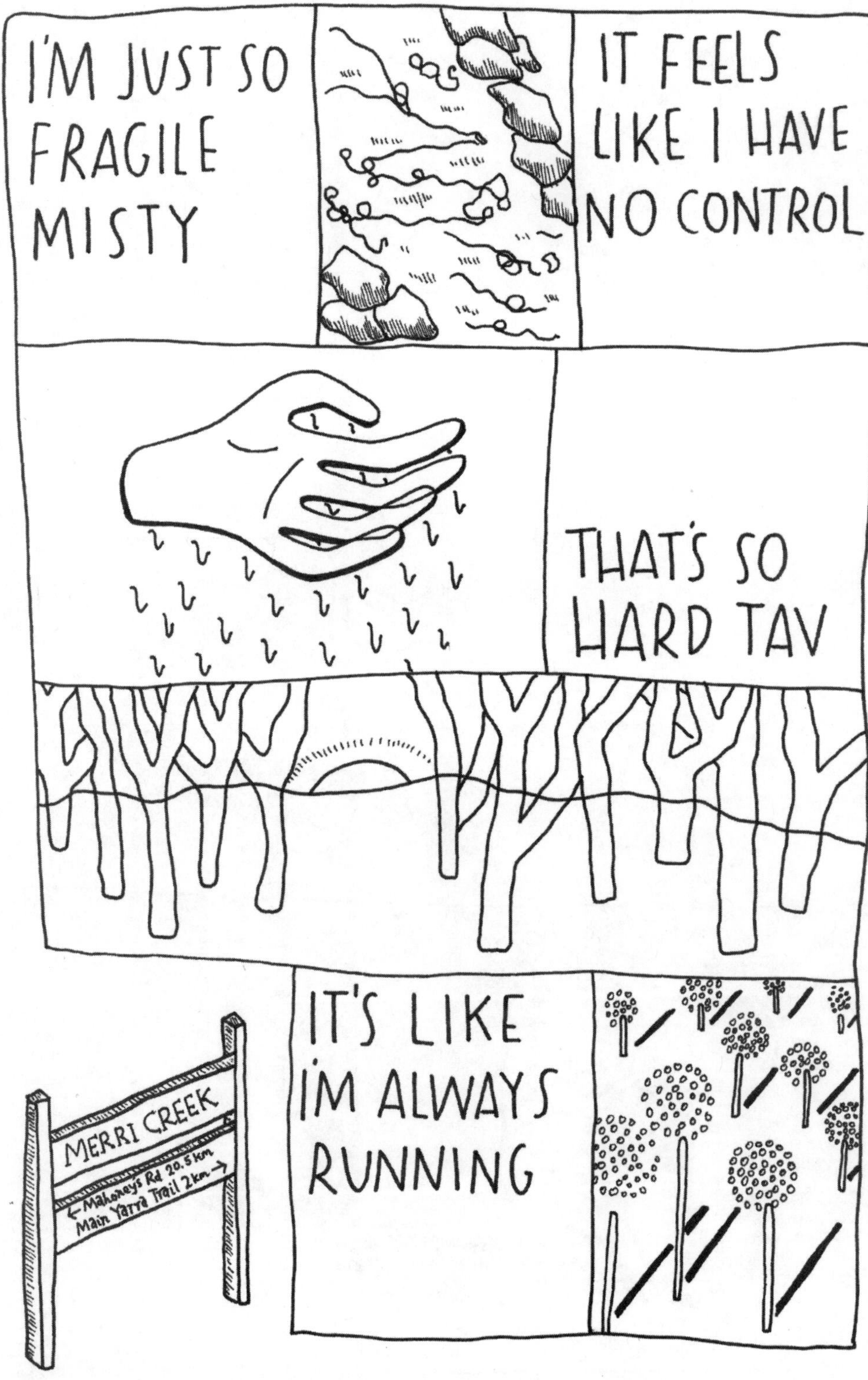
I'M JUST SO FRAGILE MISTY
IT FEELS LIKE I HAVE NO CONTROL
THAT'S SO HARD TAV
MERRI CREEK
← Mahoneys Rd 20.5 km
Main Yarra Trail 2 km →
IT'S LIKE I'M ALWAYS RUNNING

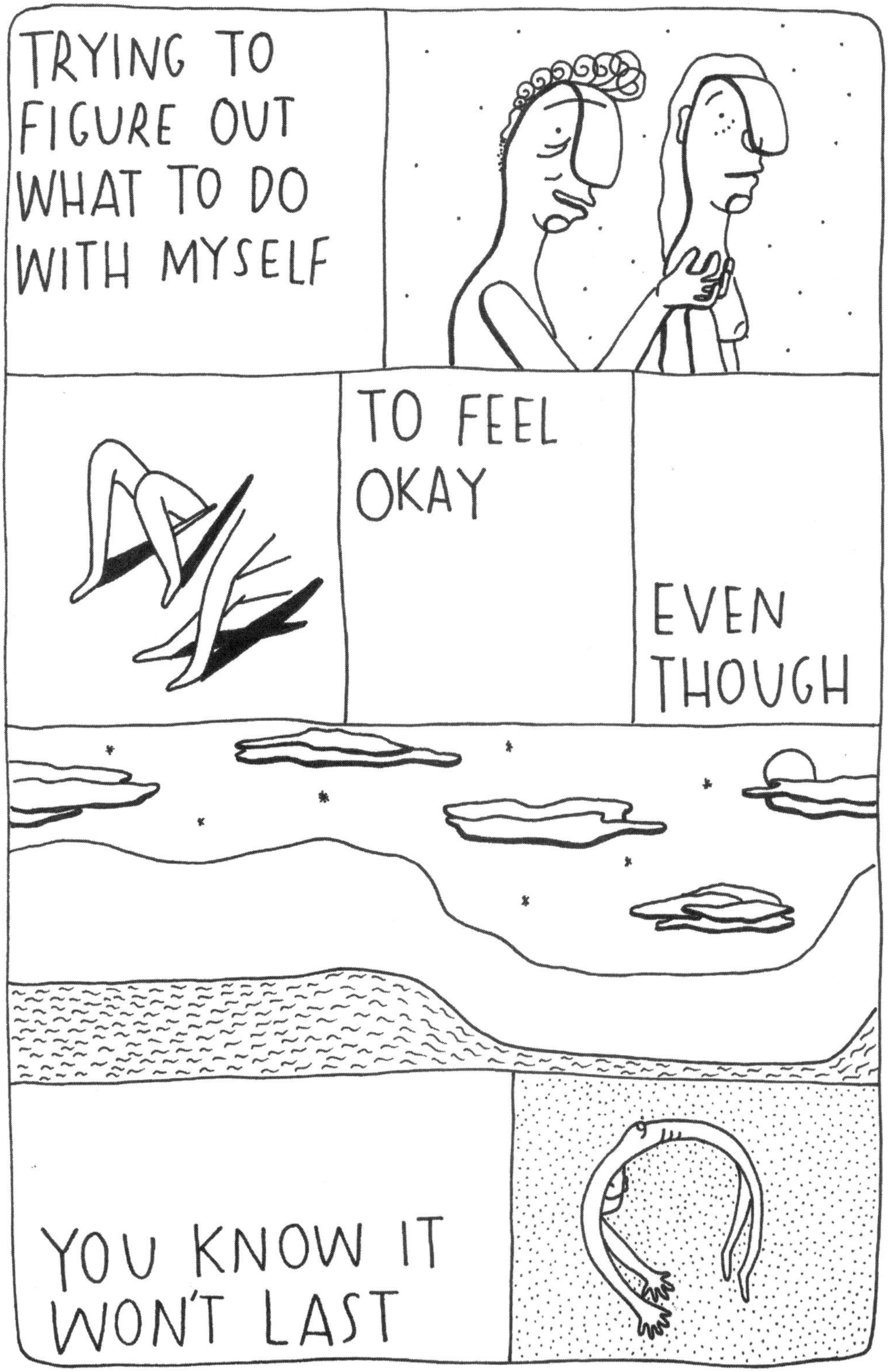
TRYING TO FIGURE OUT WHAT TO DO WITH MYSELF
TO FEEL OKAY
EVEN THOUGH
YOU KNOW IT WON'T LAST

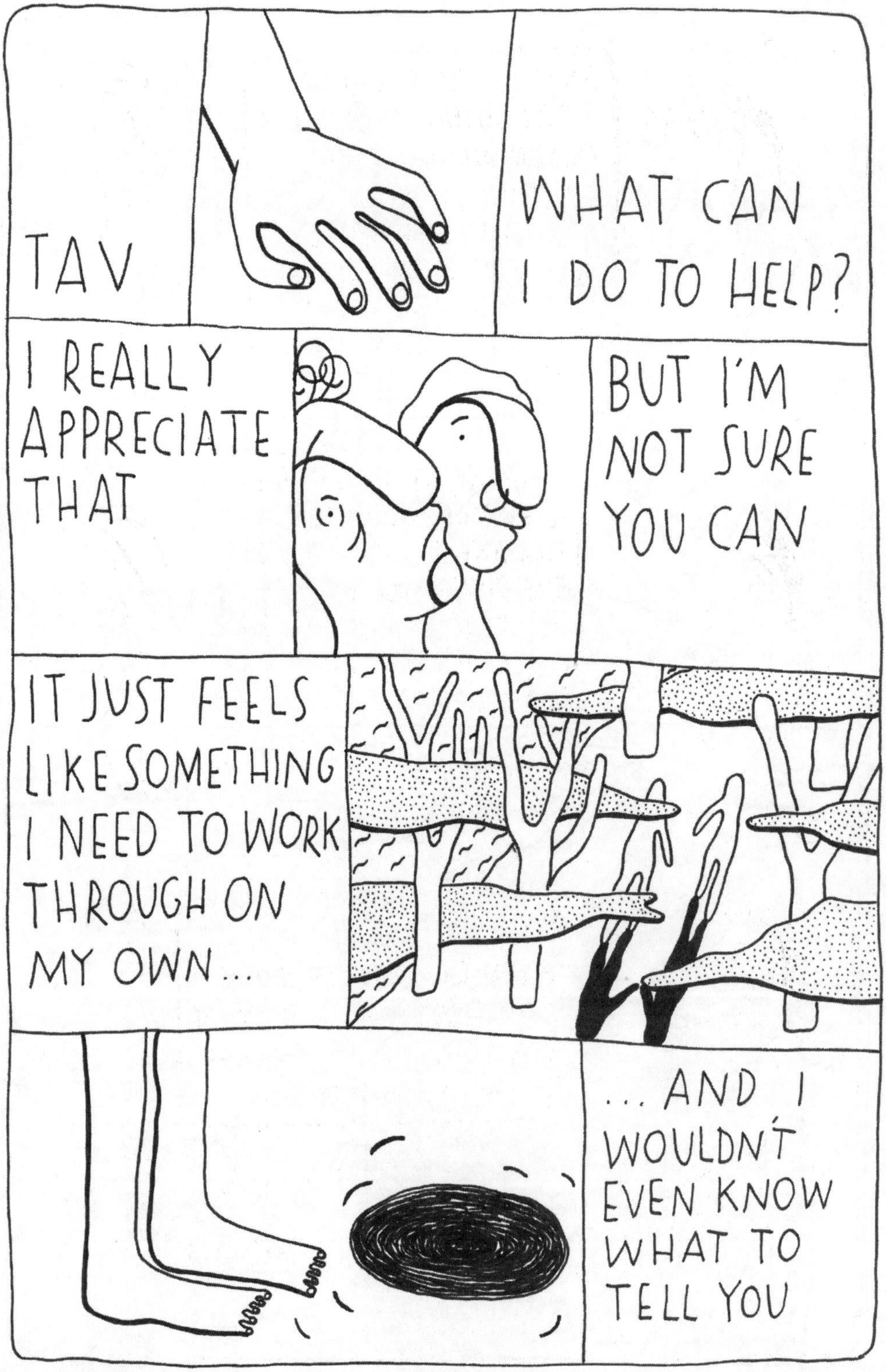
TAV
WHAT CAN I DO TO HELP?
I REALLY APPRECIATE THAT
BUT I'M NOT SURE YOU CAN
IT JUST FEELS LIKE SOMETHING I NEED TO WORK THROUGH ON MY OWN...
...AND I WOULDN'T EVEN KNOW WHAT TO TELL YOU

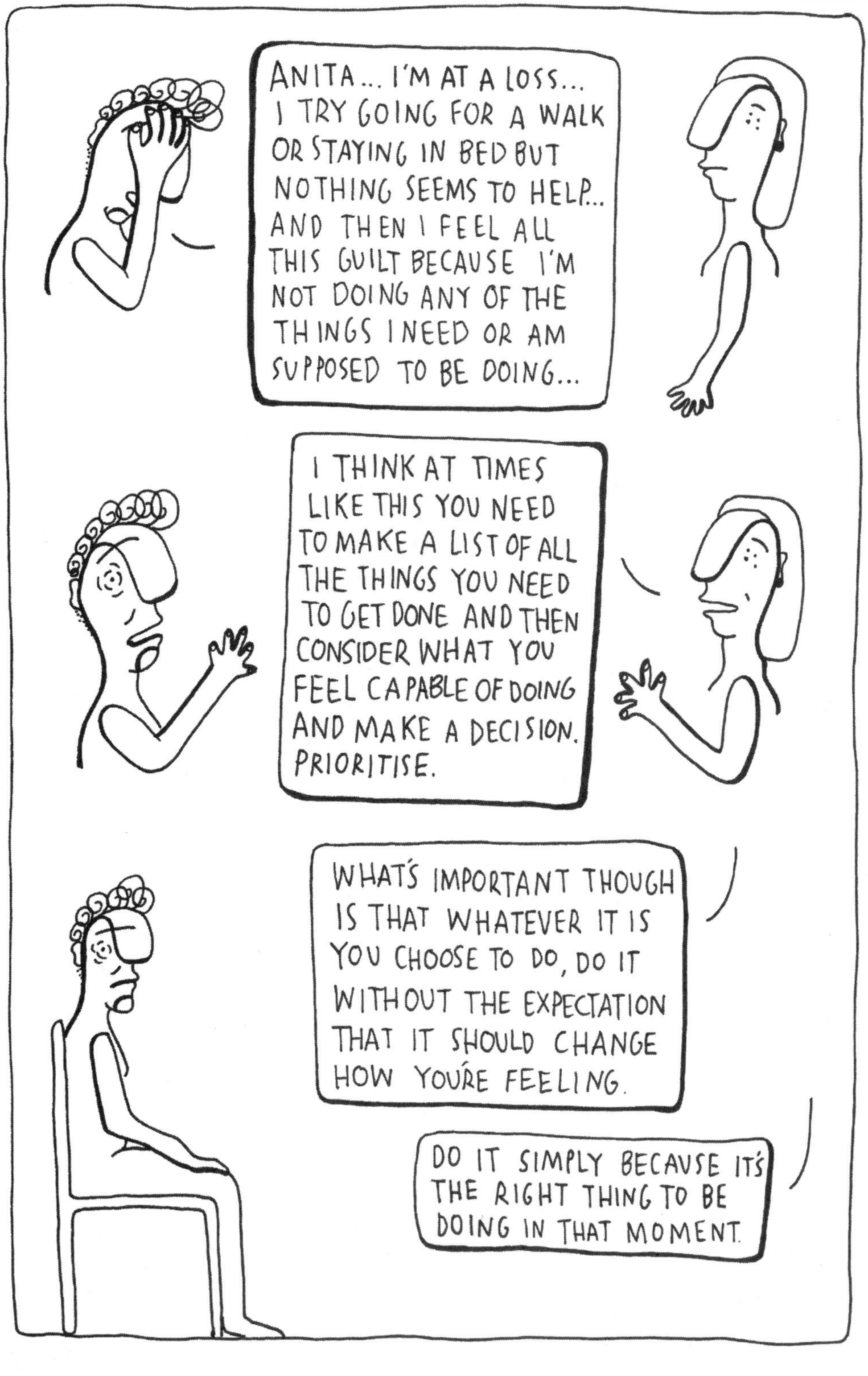
ANITA... I'M AT A LOSS... I TRY GOING FOR A WALK OR STAYING IN BED BUT NOTHING SEEMS TO HELP... AND THEN I FEEL ALL THIS GUILT BECAUSE I'M NOT DOING ANY OF THE THINGS I NEED OR AM SUPPOSED TO BE DOING...
I THINK AT TIMES LIKE THIS YOU NEED TO MAKE A LIST OF ALL THE THINGS YOU NEED TO GET DONE AND THEN CONSIDER WHAT YOU FEEL CAPABLE OF DOING AND MAKE A DECISION. PRIORITISE.
WHAT'S IMPORTANT THOUGH IS THAT WHATEVER IT IS YOU CHOOSE TO DO, DO IT WITHOUT THE EXPECTATION THAT IT SHOULD CHANGE HOW YOU'RE FEELING.
DO IT SIMPLY BECAUSE IT'S THE RIGHT THING TO BE DOING IN THAT MOMENT.

A SINGLE MOTTO EMERGED
DO WHATEVER YOU NEED TO STAY ALIVE
ONE DAY AT A TIME

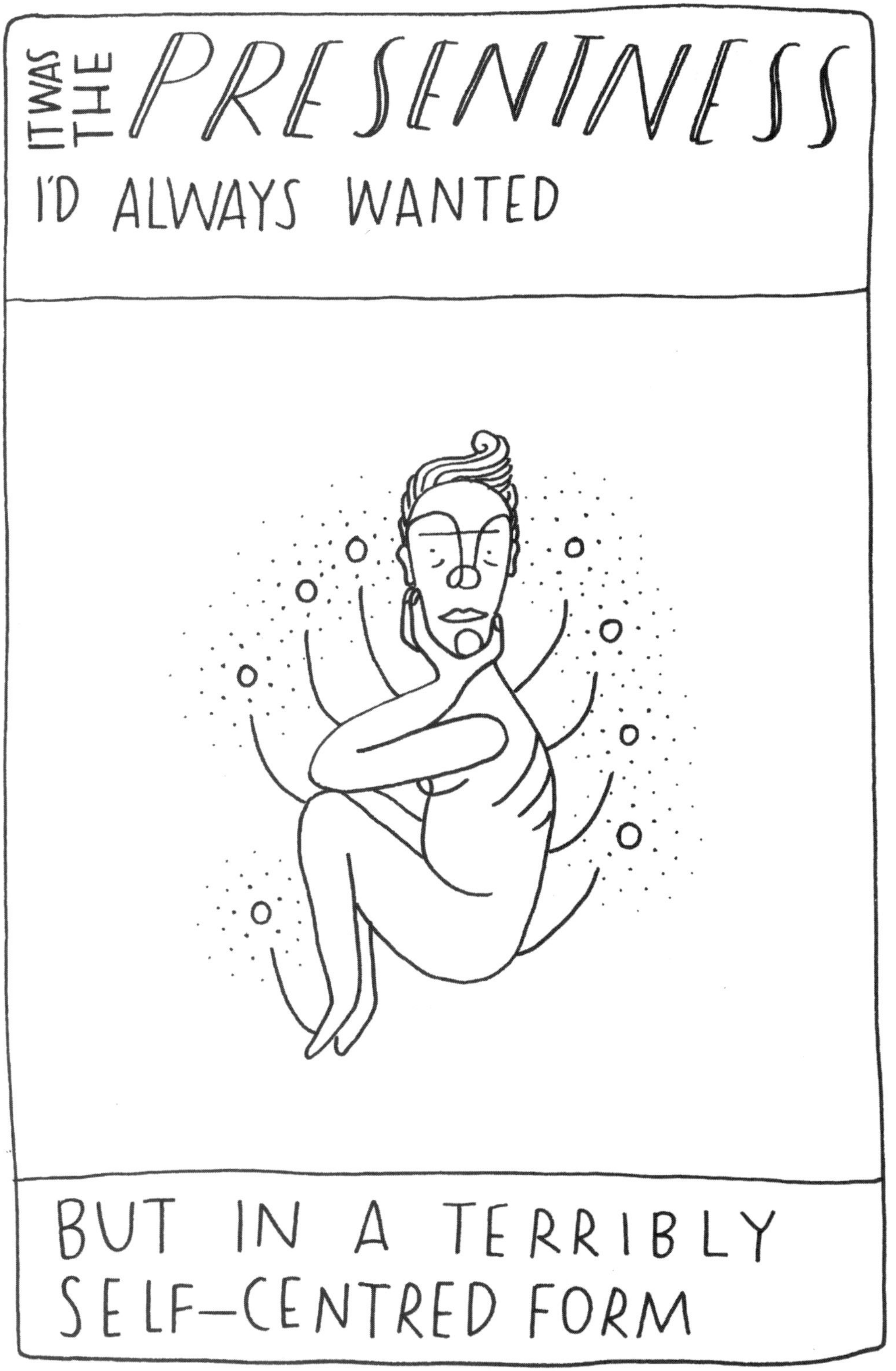
IT WAS THE PRESENTNESS
I'D ALWAYS WANTED
BUT IN A TERRIBLY SELF-CENTRED FORM

SOME BEAUTIFUL
RELATIONSHIPS
DEVELOPED

WAYS TO BE HELD

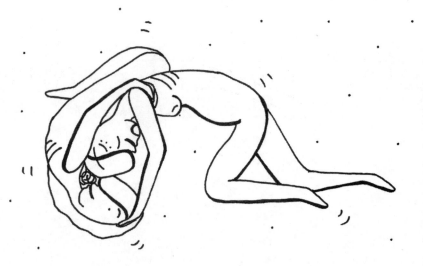

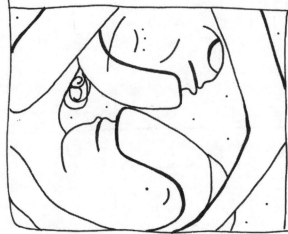

TO BE
SAFE
IF ONLY FOR A...

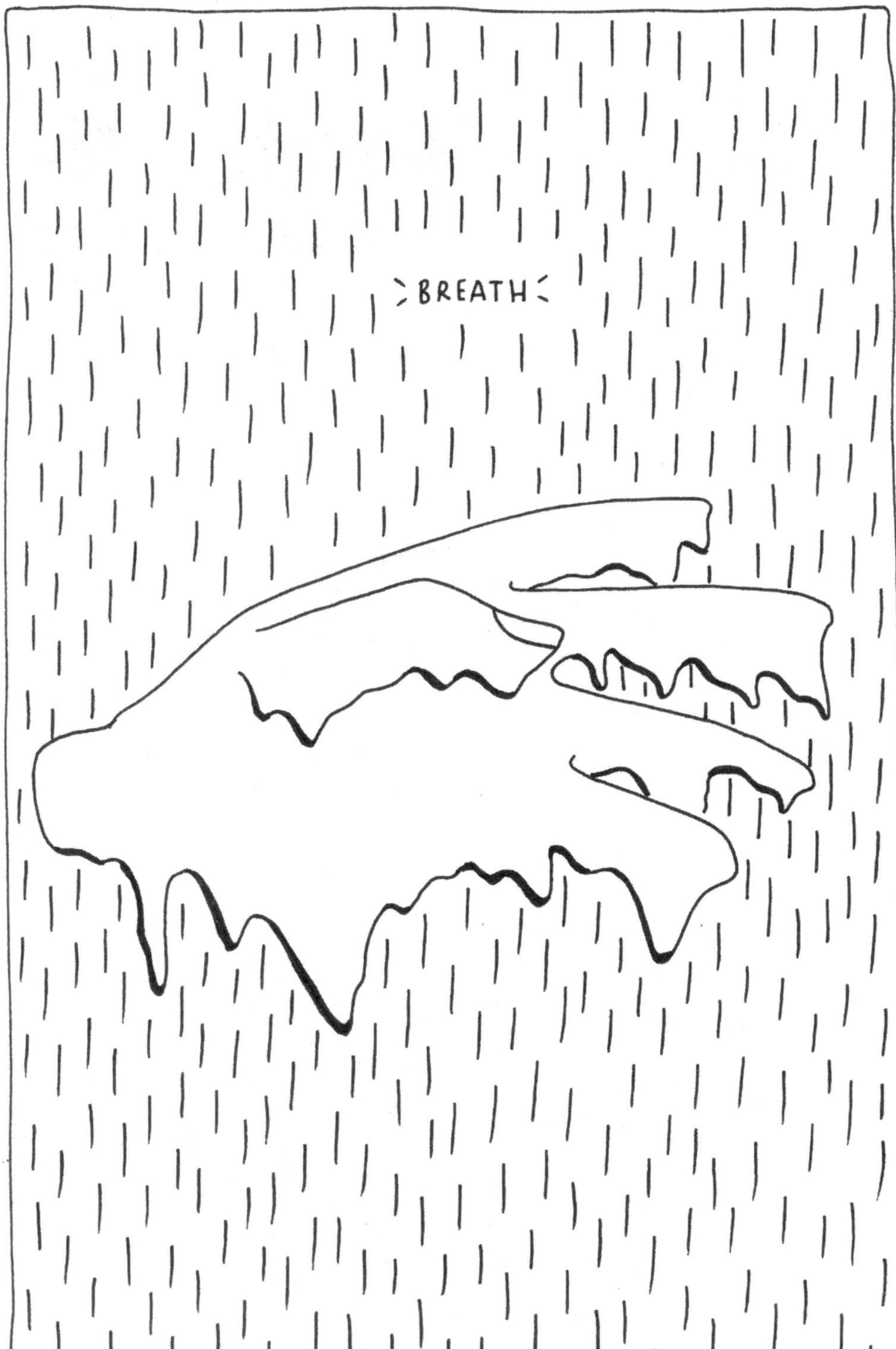
BREATH

BUT THIS SELF CENTREDNESS ALSO DID ALOT OF DAMAGE TO EXISTING FRIENDSHIPS AND RELATIONSHIPS

DAMAGE THAT I'M STILL TRYING TO REPAIR

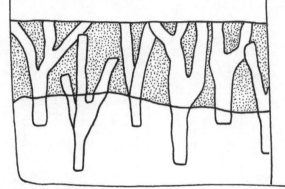

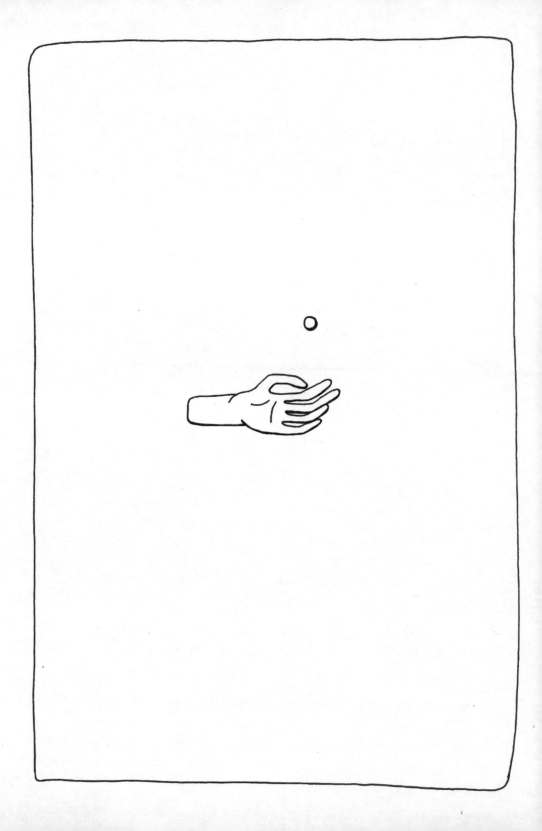

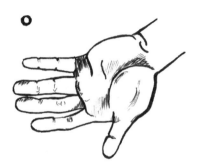

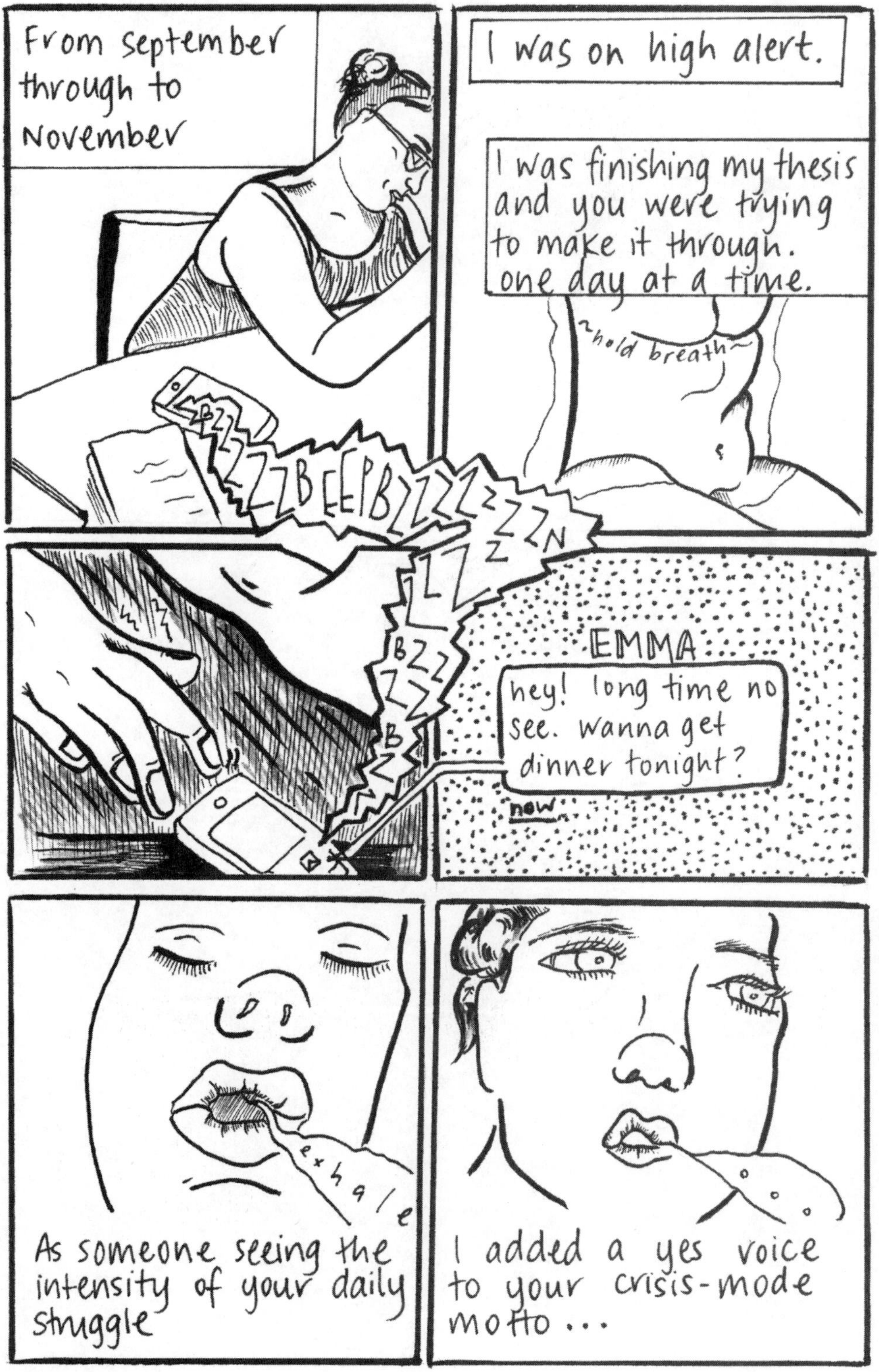
From september through to November
I was on high alert.
I was finishing my thesis and you were trying to make it through. one day at a time.
~hold breath~
BZZZZZZBEEPBZZZZZZZZN
ZZBZZZZBZ
EMMA
hey! long time no see. wanna get dinner tonight?
now
exhale
As someone seeing the intensity of your daily struggle
I added a yes voice to your crisis-mode motto...

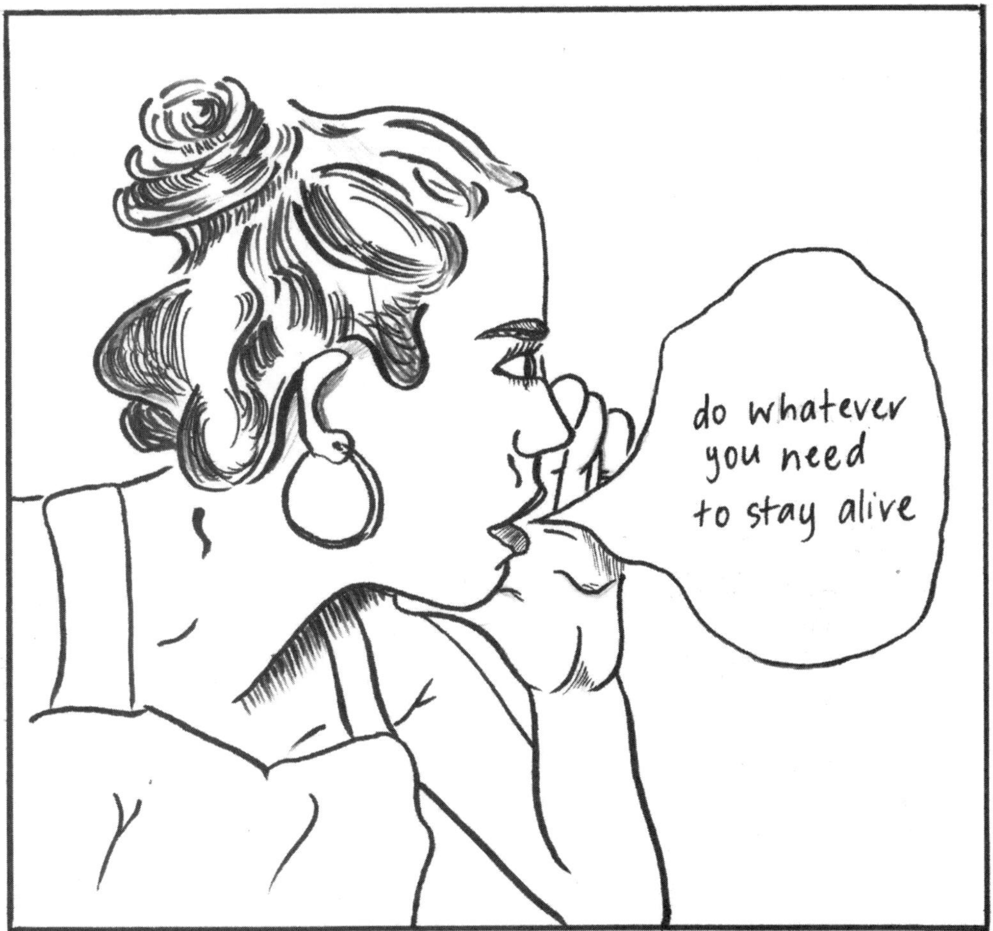
do whatever you need to stay alive

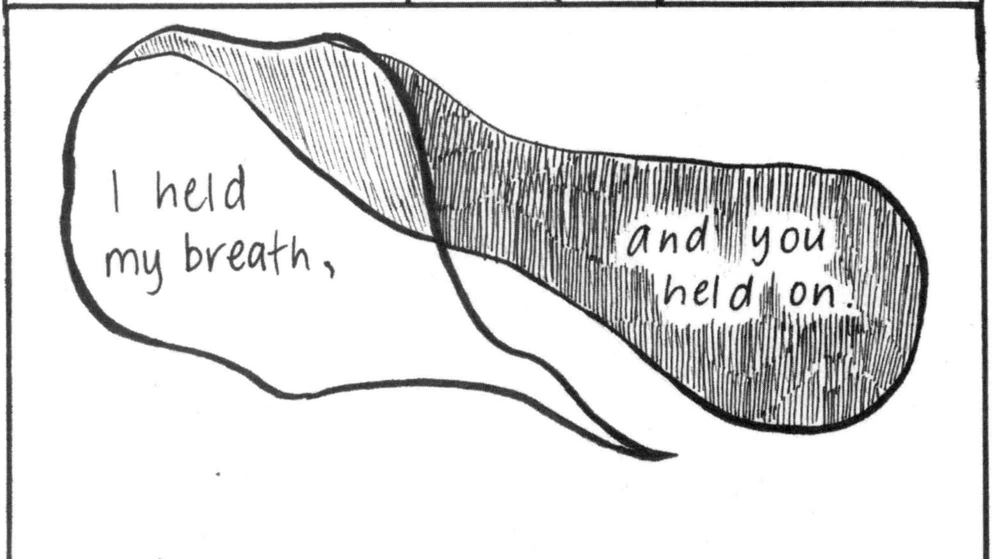
I held my breath,
and you held on.

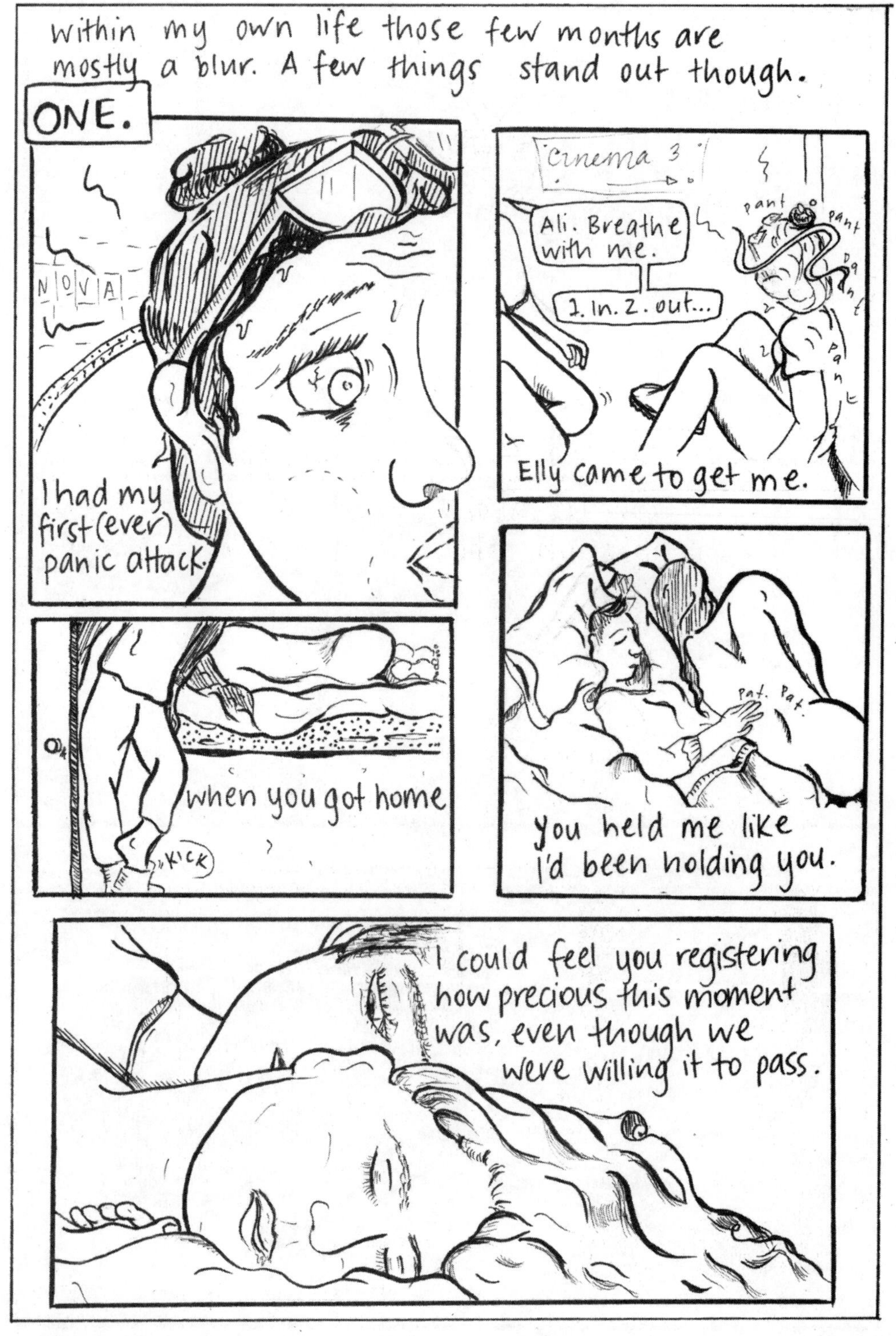
within my own life those few months are mostly a blur. A few things stand out though.
ONE.
NOVA
I had my first (ever) panic attack.
Cinema 3
Ali. Breathe with me.
1. In. 2. out...
pant pant pant pant
Elly came to get me.
when you got home
KICK
Pat. Pat.
You held me like I'd been holding you.
I could feel you registering how precious this moment was, even though we were willing it to pass.

TWO.

my birthday.

You snuck out early...

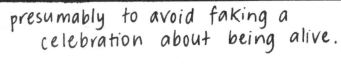

presumably to avoid faking a celebration about being alive.

16:38

FRIDAY, SEPT 11

TAVA

swipeeee

I love you.

I knew what you meant.

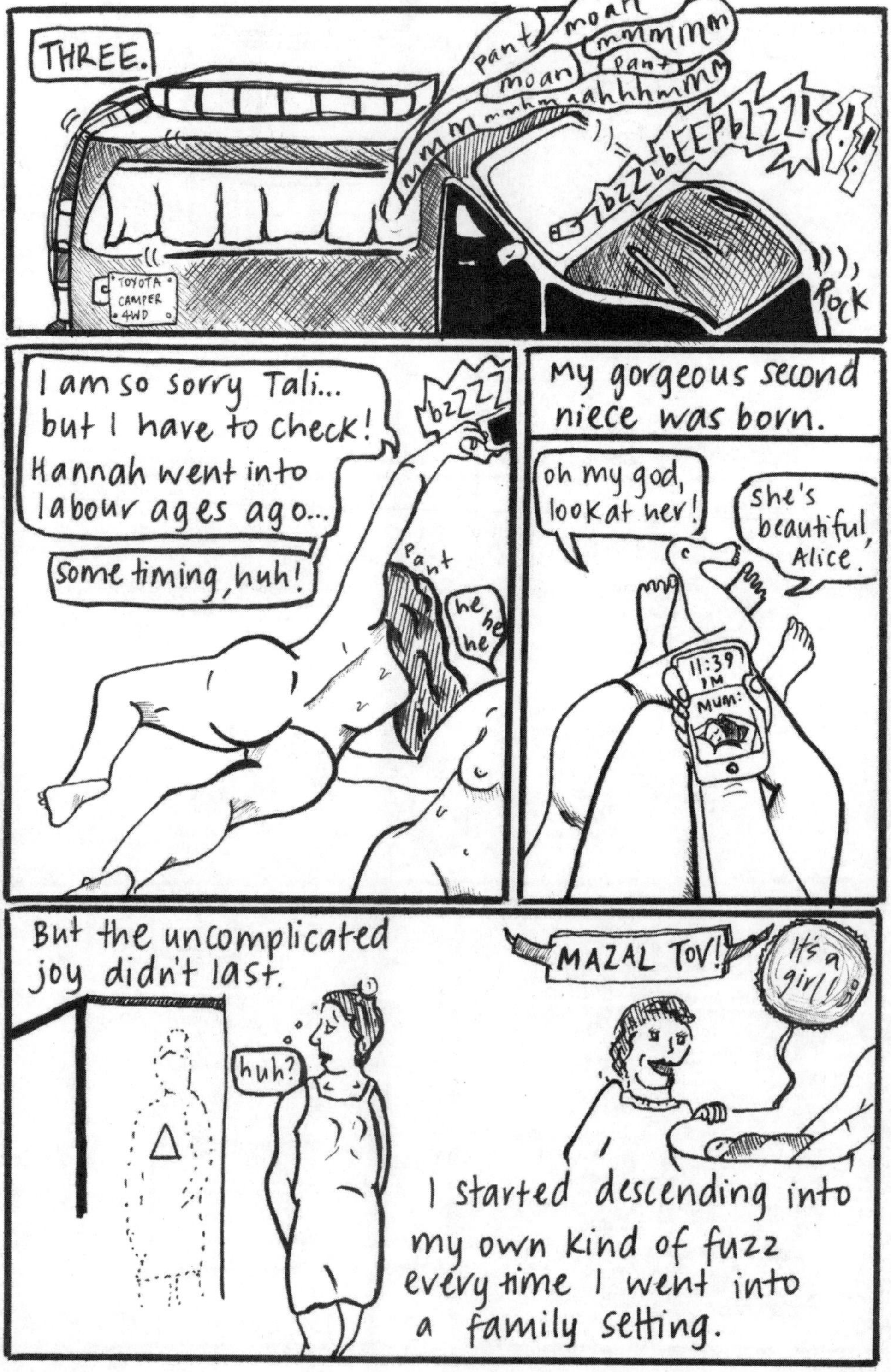
THREE.
pant
moan
mmmmm
moan
pant
mmmmmmmmm aahhhmmm
bzzbbEEPbZZZ!
!!?!
TOYOTA CAMPER 4WD
ROCK
I am so sorry Tali... but I have to check! Hannah went into labour ages ago...
some timing, huh!
bzzzz
pant
he he he
My gorgeous second niece was born.
oh my god, look at her!
She's beautiful, Alice.
11:39 PM
MUM:
But the uncomplicated joy didn't last.
MAZAL TOV!
It's a girl!
huh?
I started descending into my own kind of fuzz every time I went into a family setting.

It was the usual gender stuff

I think my grandson may have just found his first girlfriend!

ha ha

he he

oh, cute!

But this time, with everything going on with you, I wasn't strong enough to handle it.

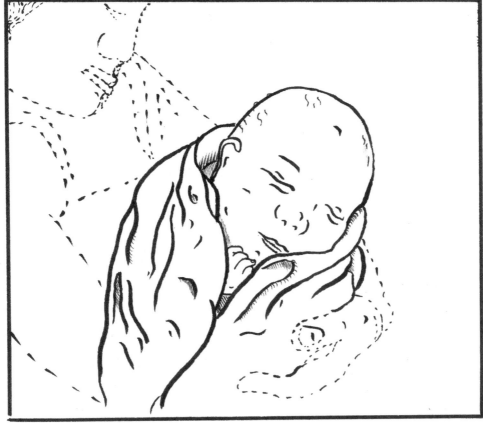

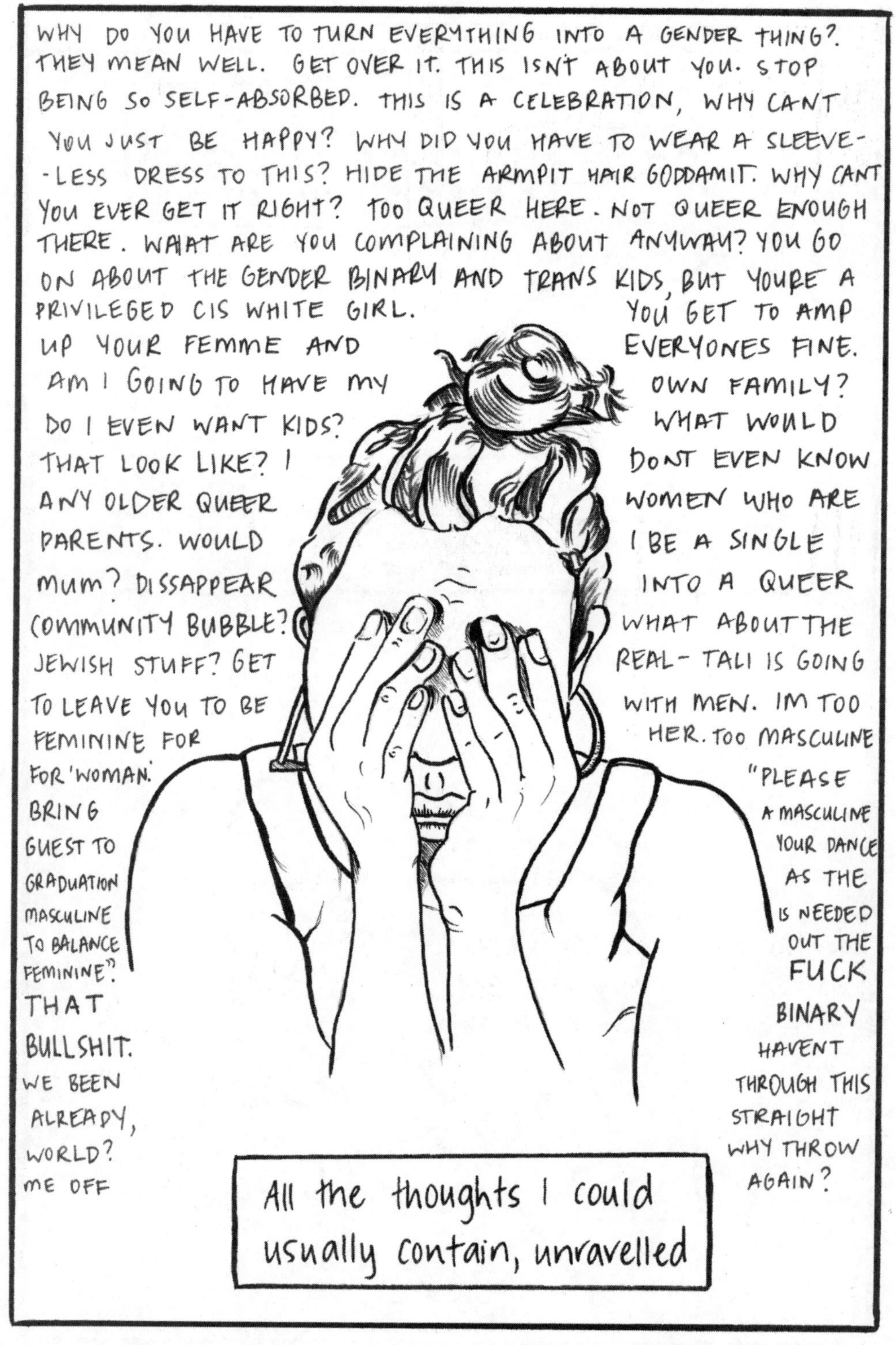
WHY DO YOU HAVE TO TURN EVERYTHING INTO A GENDER THING? THEY MEAN WELL. GET OVER IT. THIS ISN'T ABOUT YOU. STOP BEING SO SELF-ABSORBED. THIS IS A CELEBRATION, WHY CANT YOU JUST BE HAPPY? WHY DID YOU HAVE TO WEAR A SLEEVE--LESS DRESS TO THIS? HIDE THE ARMPIT HAIR GODDAMIT. WHY CANT YOU EVER GET IT RIGHT? TOO QUEER HERE. NOT QUEER ENOUGH THERE. WHAT ARE YOU COMPLAINING ABOUT ANYWAY? YOU GO ON ABOUT THE GENDER BINARY AND TRANS KIDS, BUT YOURE A PRIVILEGED CIS WHITE GIRL.
YOU GET TO AMP
UP YOUR FEMME AND
EVERYONES FINE.
AM I GOING TO HAVE MY
OWN FAMILY?
DO I EVEN WANT KIDS?
WHAT WOULD
THAT LOOK LIKE? I
DONT EVEN KNOW
ANY OLDER QUEER
WOMEN WHO ARE
PARENTS. WOULD
I BE A SINGLE
MUM? DISSAPPEAR
INTO A QUEER
COMMUNITY BUBBLE?
WHAT ABOUT THE
JEWISH STUFF? GET
REAL - TALI IS GOING
TO LEAVE YOU TO BE
WITH MEN. IM TOO
FEMININE FOR
HER. TOO MASCULINE
FOR 'WOMAN.'
"PLEASE
BRING
A MASCULINE
GUEST TO
YOUR DANCE
GRADUATION
AS THE
MASCULINE
IS NEEDED
TO BALANCE
OUT THE
FEMININE".
FUCK
THAT
BINARY
BULLSHIT.
HAVENT
WE BEEN
THROUGH THIS
ALREADY,
STRAIGHT
WORLD?
WHY THROW
ME OFF
AGAIN?
All the thoughts I could usually contain, unravelled

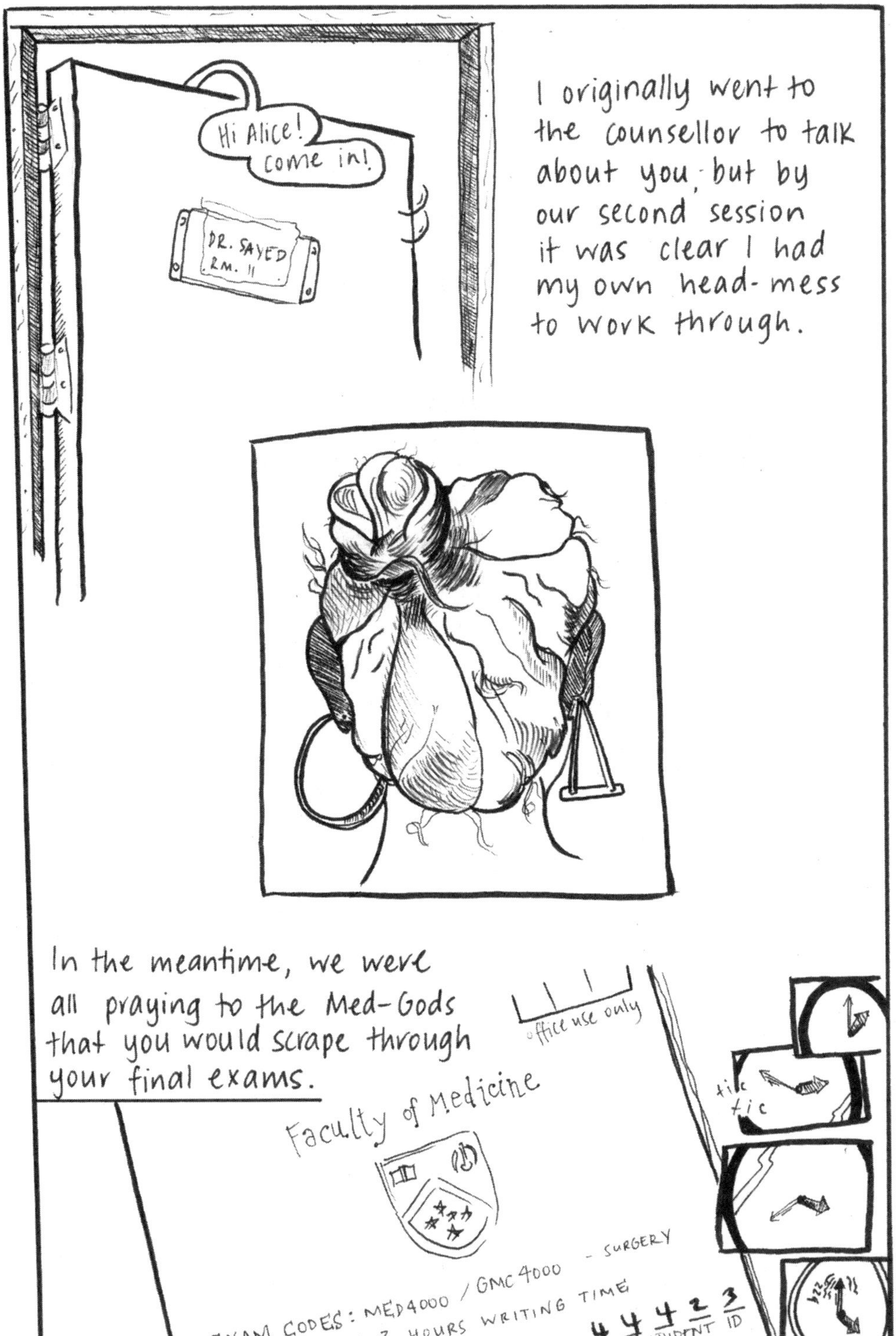
Hi Alice! come in!
DR. SAYED RM. 11
I originally went to the counsellor to talk about you, but by our second session it was clear I had my own head-mess to work through.
In the meantime, we were all praying to the Med-Gods that you would scrape through your final exams.
office use only
Faculty of Medicine
tic tic
EXAM CODES: MED4000 / GMC4000 - SURGERY
3 HOURS WRITING TIME
4 4 4 2 3
STUDENT ID

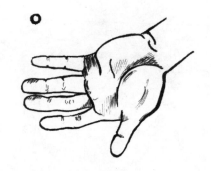

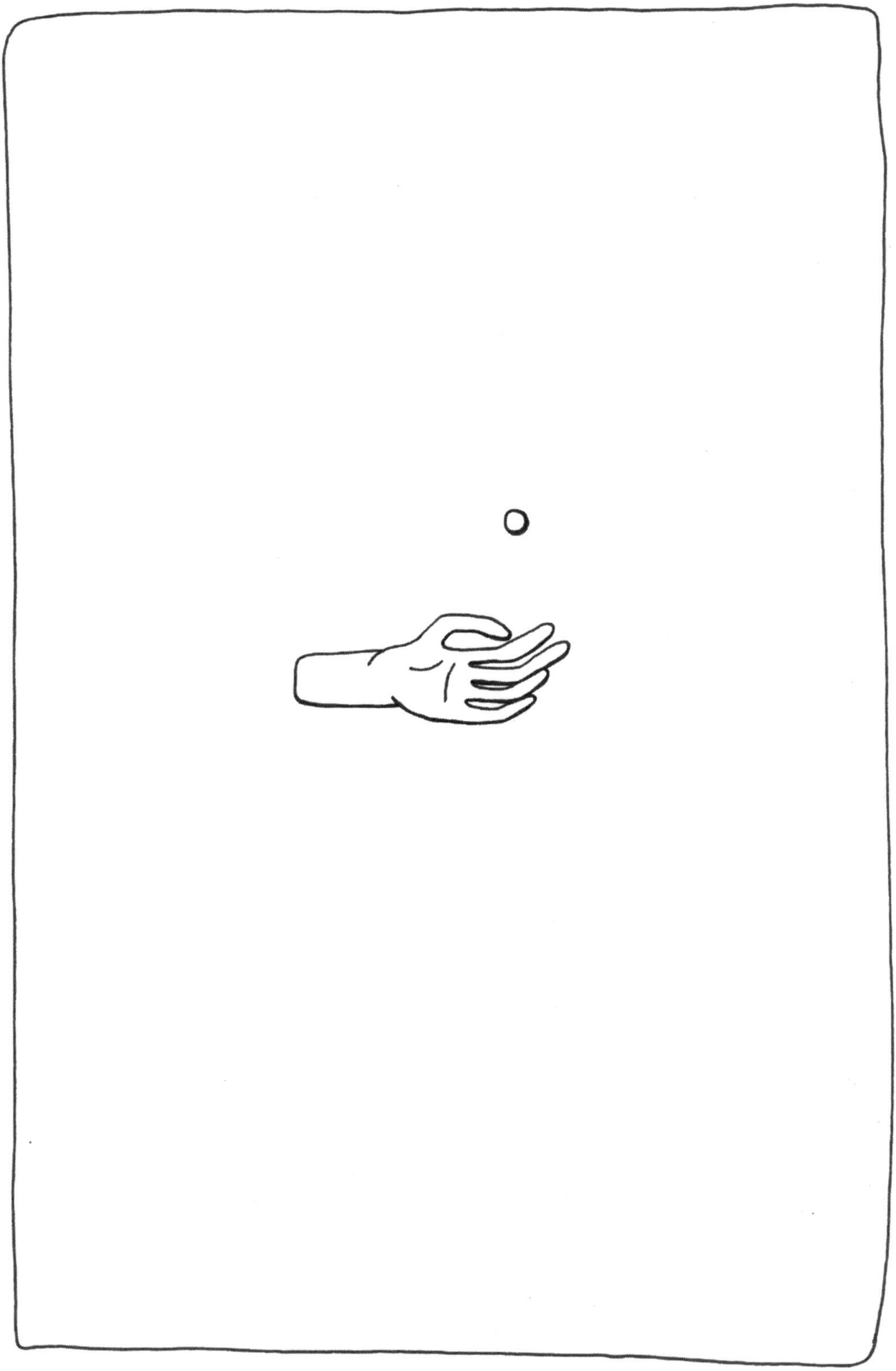

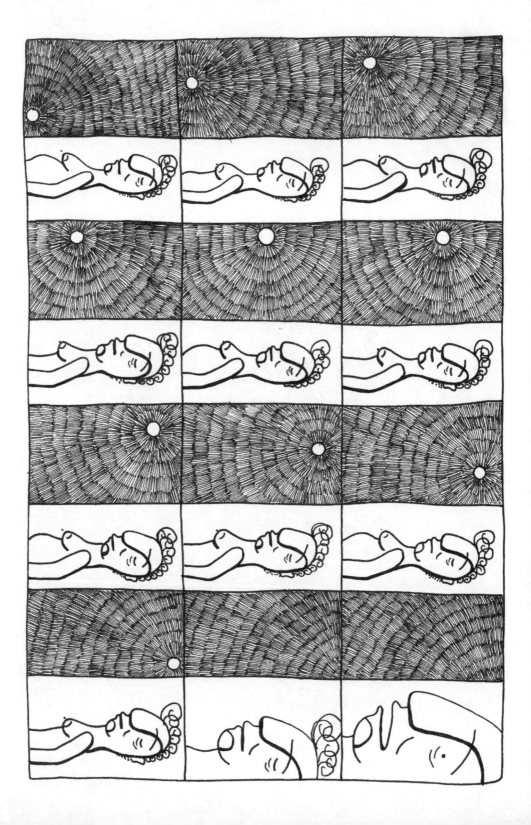

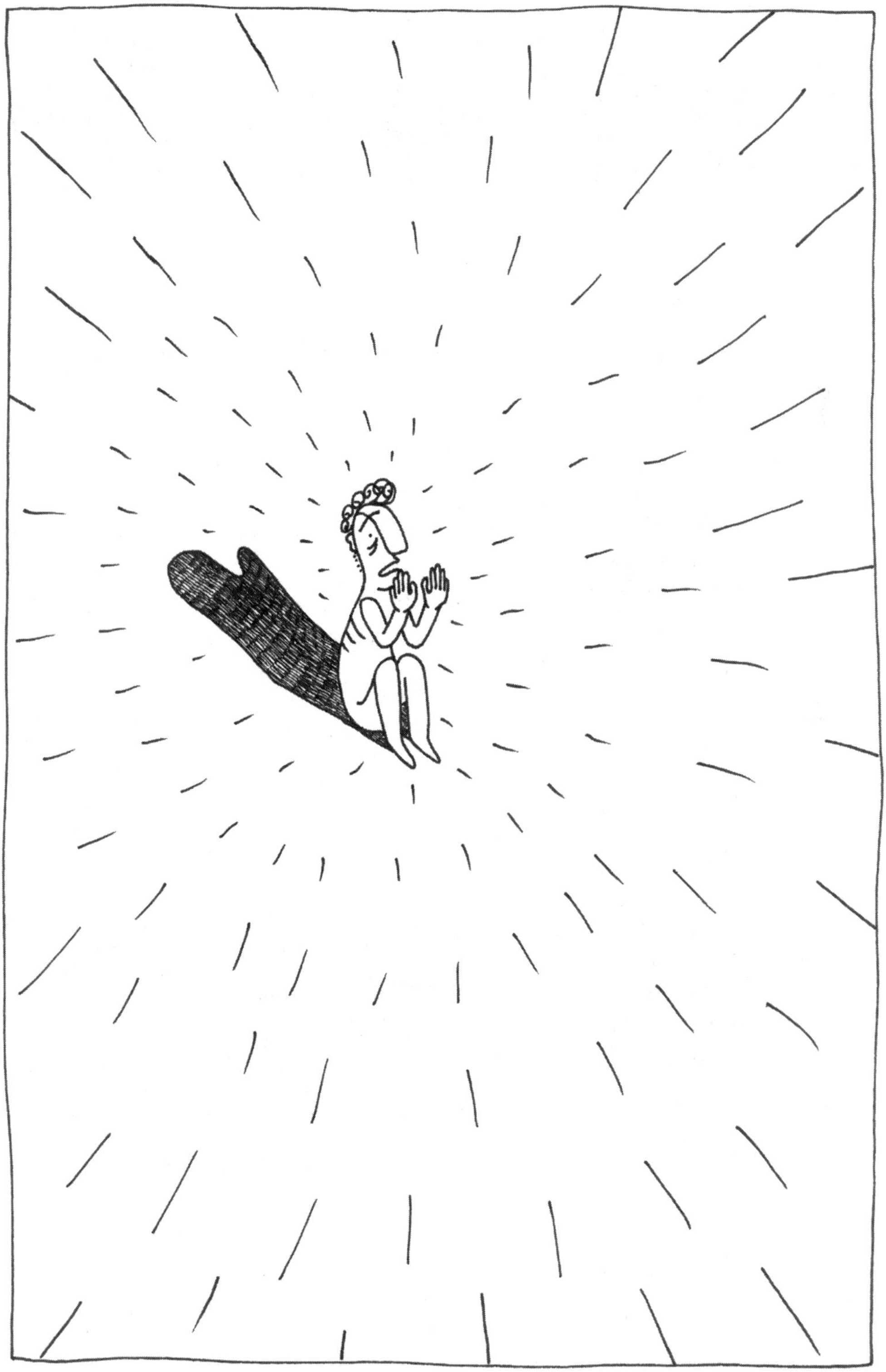

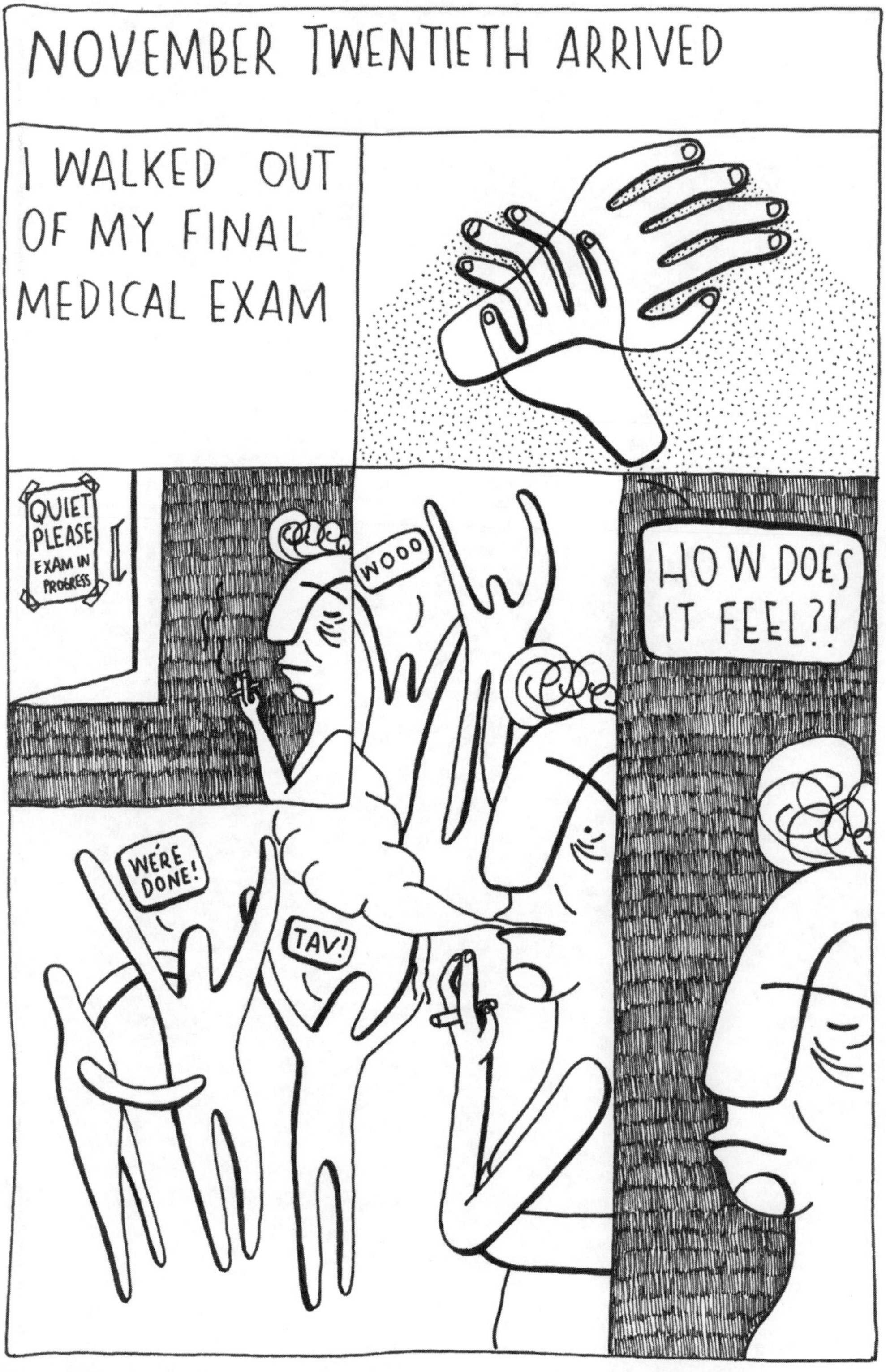
NOVEMBER TWENTIETH ARRIVED
I WALKED OUT OF MY FINAL MEDICAL EXAM
QUIET PLEASE EXAM IN PROGRESS
WOOO
HOW DOES IT FEEL?!
WE'RE DONE!
TAV!

THIS PAGE IS INTENTIONALLY LEFT BLANK

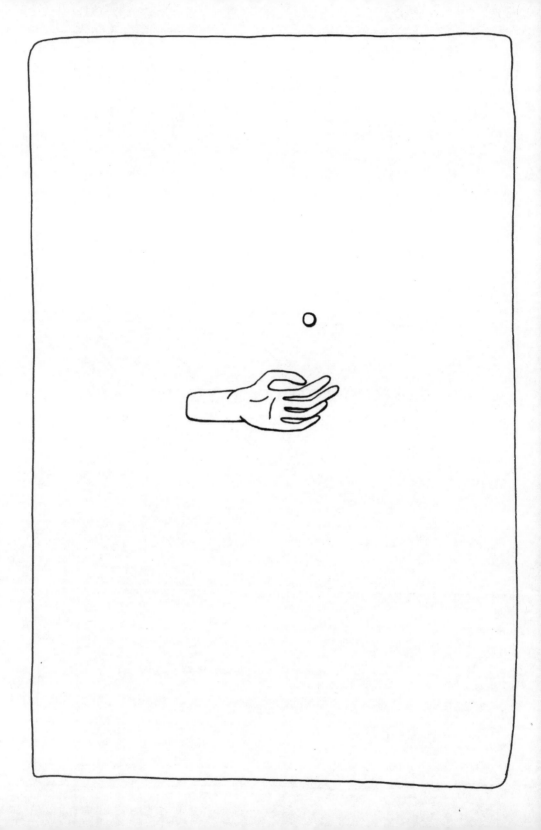

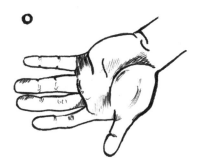

I think I was even more relieved than you when we eventually found out you had passed.

T1
QANTAS DOMESTIC

T2
INTERNATIONAL DEPARTURES →

T2 LANES 1 + 2

Give them both big hugs from me, yeah?

For sure, Al.

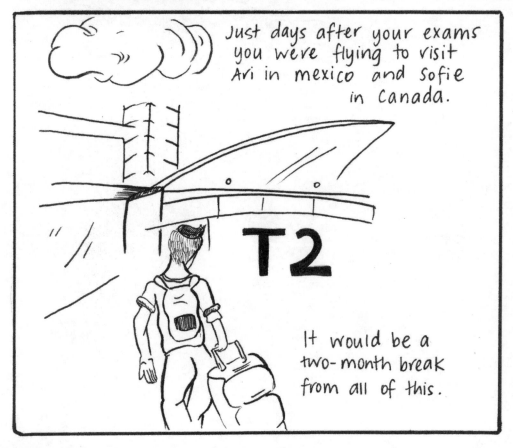

Just days after your exams you were flying to visit Ari in mexico and Sofie in Canada.

T2

It would be a two-month break from all of this.

And that was it.
After eight scary and
intense months, you were just
gone.

SIFTINGS

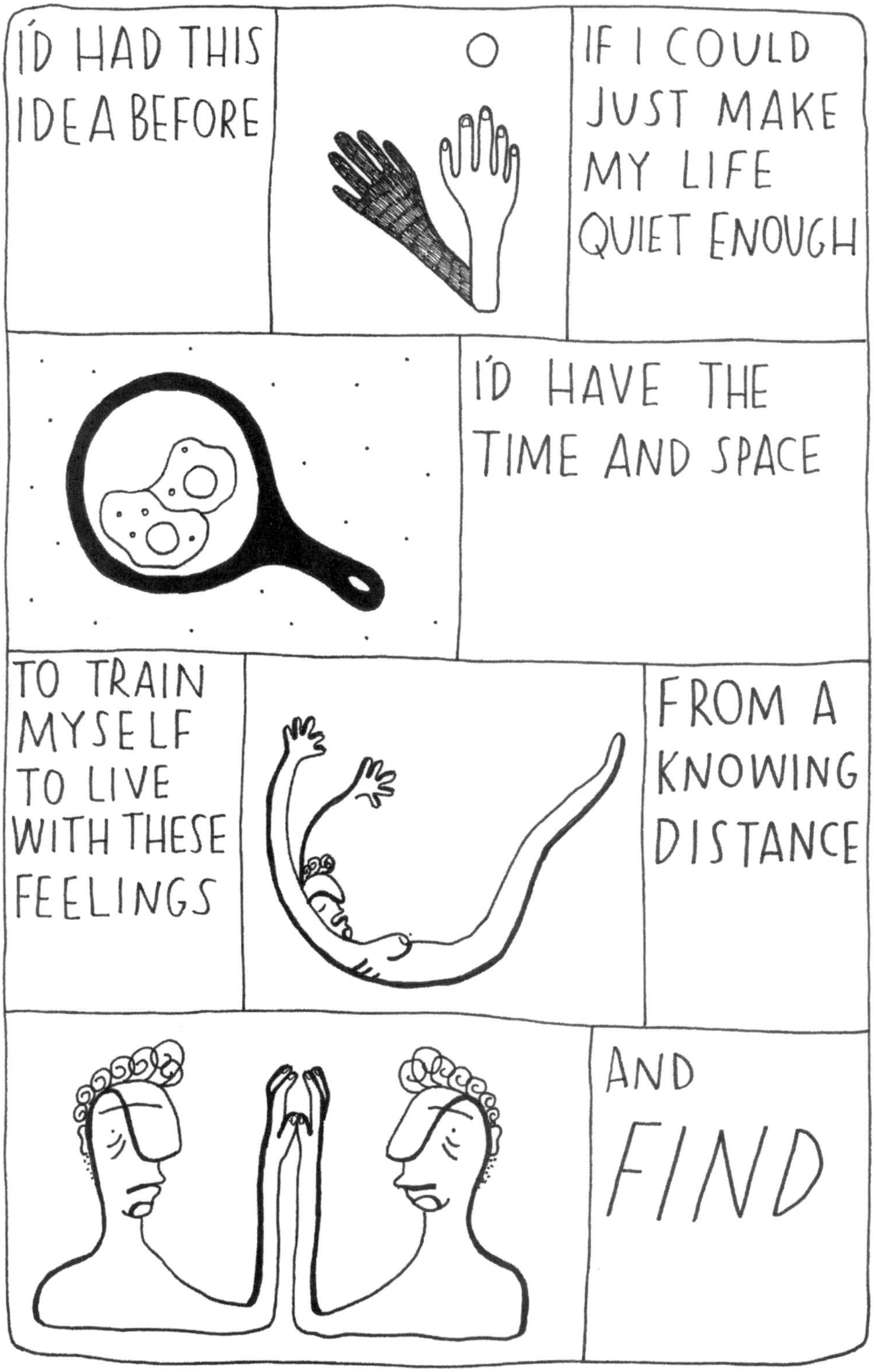

I'D HAD THIS IDEA BEFORE

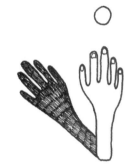

IF I COULD JUST MAKE MY LIFE QUIET ENOUGH

I'D HAVE THE TIME AND SPACE

TO TRAIN MYSELF TO LIVE WITH THESE FEELINGS

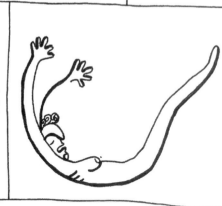

FROM A KNOWING DISTANCE

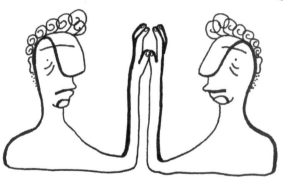

AND *FIND*

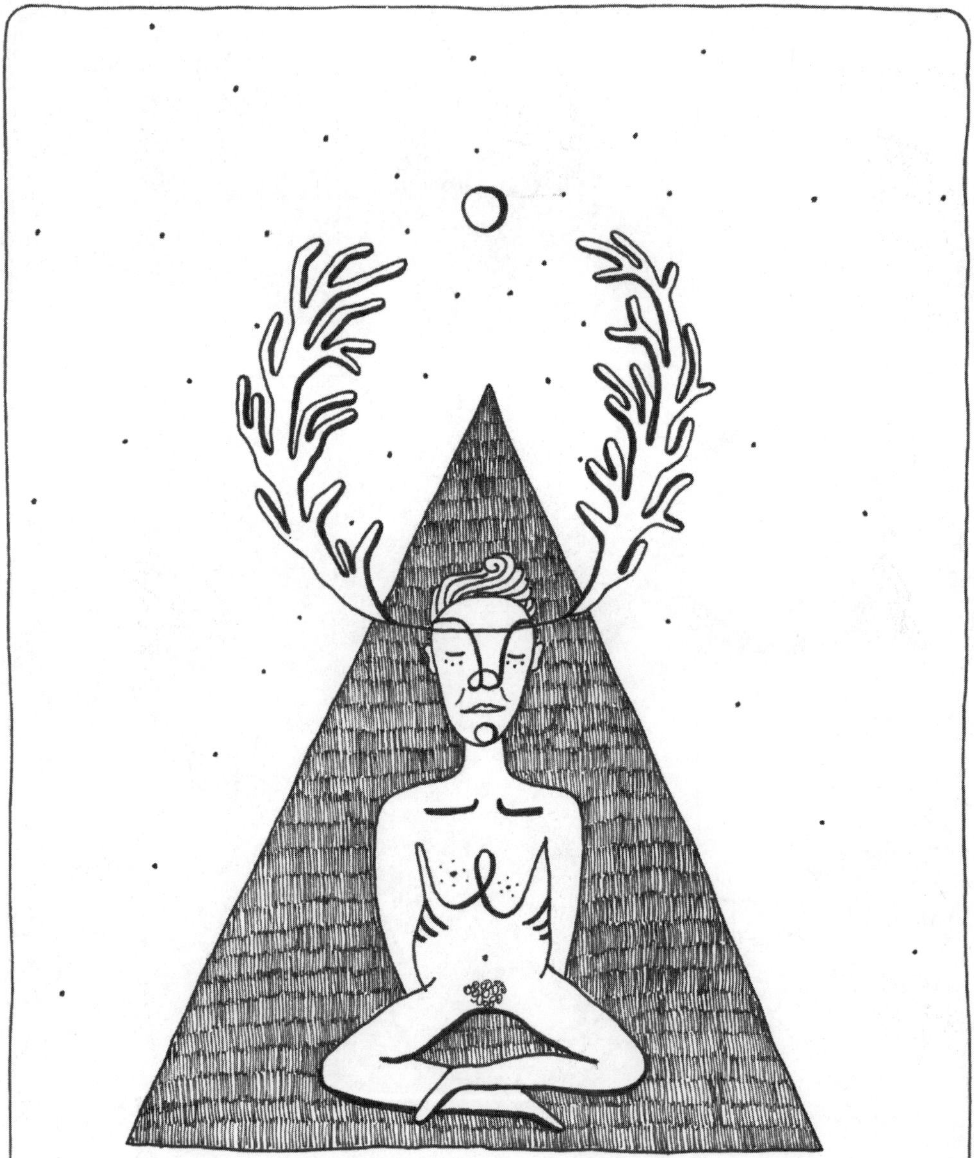

RELEASE

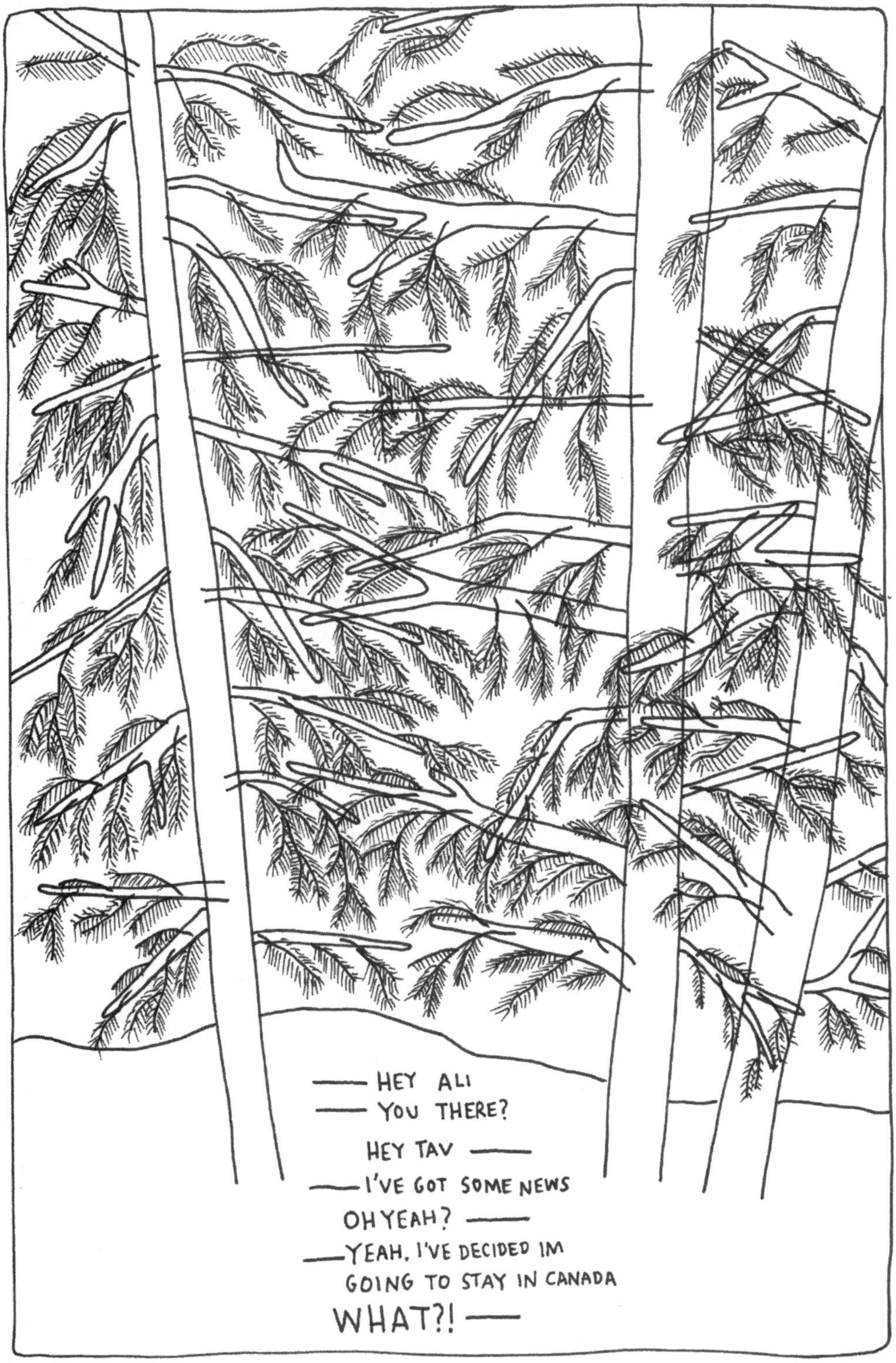
— HEY ALI
— YOU THERE?
HEY TAV —
— I'VE GOT SOME NEWS
OH YEAH? —
— YEAH. I'VE DECIDED IM GOING TO STAY IN CANADA
WHAT?! —

I MOVED IN WITH SOFIE

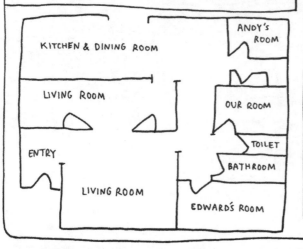

KITCHEN & DINING ROOM

ANDY'S ROOM

LIVING ROOM

OUR ROOM

TOILET

BATHROOM

ENTRY

LIVING ROOM

EDWARD'S ROOM

IT'S OK TO WAKE UP SAD

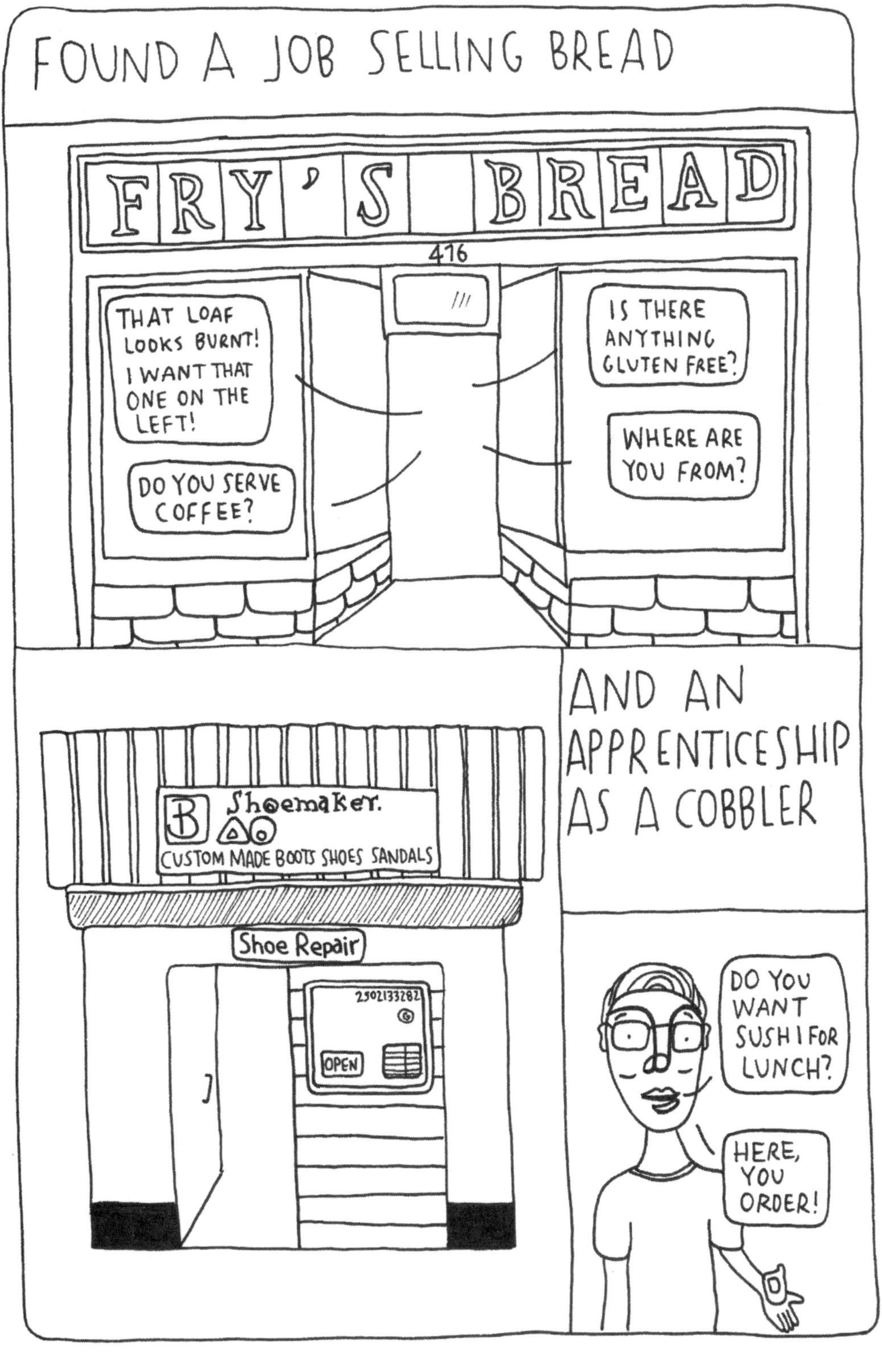
FOUND A JOB SELLING BREAD
FRY'S BREAD
416
THAT LOAF LOOKS BURNT! I WANT THAT ONE ON THE LEFT!
DO YOU SERVE COFFEE?
IS THERE ANYTHING GLUTEN FREE?
WHERE ARE YOU FROM?
AND AN APPRENTICESHIP AS A COBBLER
Shoemaker.
CUSTOM MADE BOOTS SHOES SANDALS
Shoe Repair
OPEN
DO YOU WANT SUSHI FOR LUNCH?
HERE, YOU ORDER!

IT WAS A LIFE DIVIDED IN TWO
SHOULD WE GO TO GOWLAN TODD?
DO YOU NEED ANYTHING FROM THE LOCAL GENERAL?
HOW MANY PEOPLE ARE COMING FOR SHABBAT?
WHAT ABOUT
LET'S WATCH A GHIBLI WITH LEAH & AUSTIN!
GO TO THE TALK
WANNA COME?
I'VE ORGANISED A SK
DATE WITH NOAH
GRAHAM & JOSH'S AND PLAY A BOARD GAME
LET'S GET BURGERS
HAVE YOU WATCHED THIS WEEKS Q&A?
2618

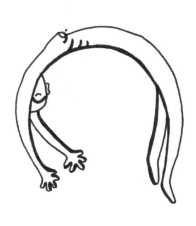

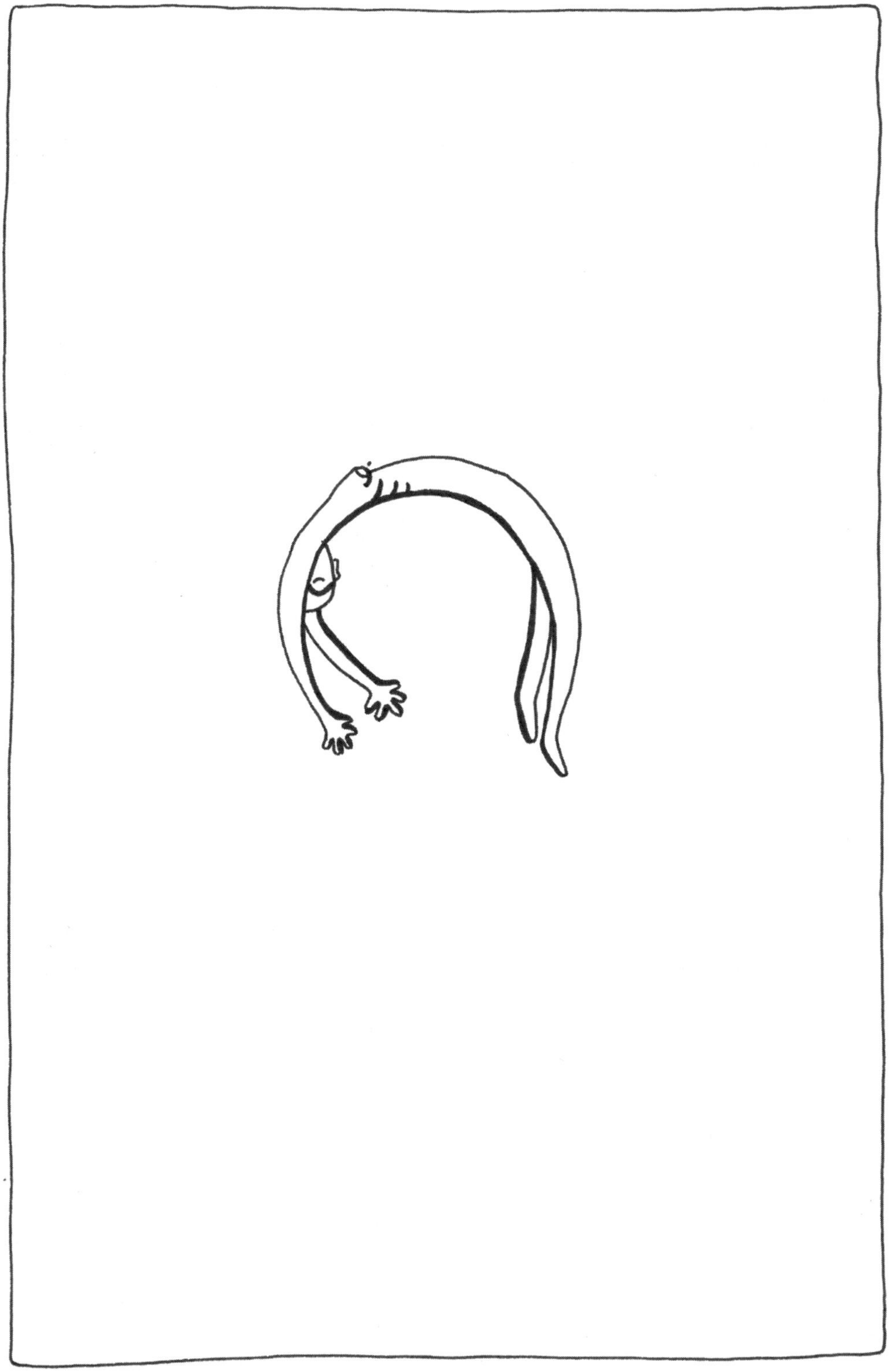

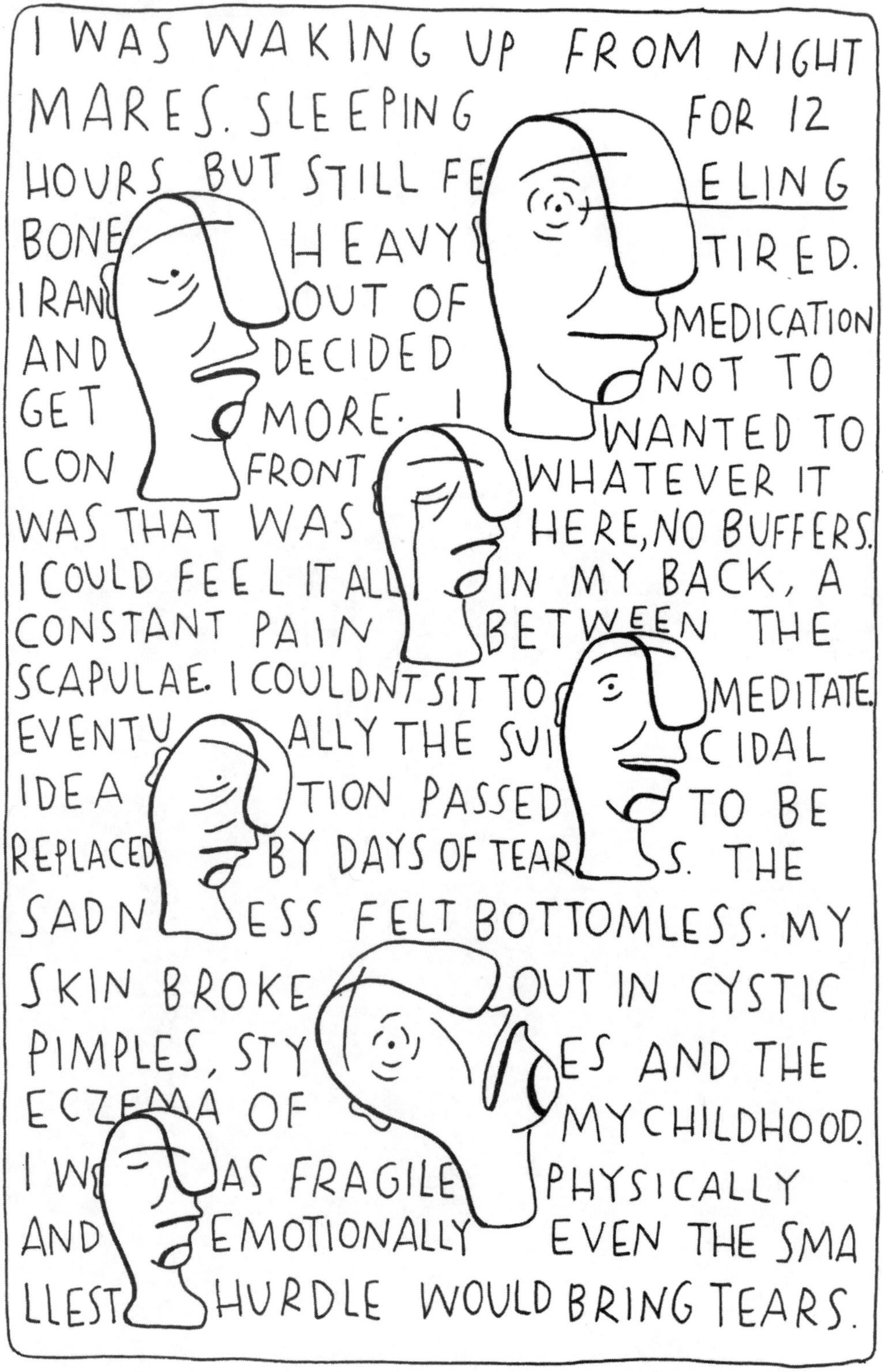
I WAS WAKING UP FROM NIGHT
MARES. SLEEPING FOR 12
HOURS BUT STILL FEELING
BONE HEAVY TIRED.
I RAN OUT OF MEDICATION
AND DECIDED NOT TO
GET MORE. I WANTED TO
CON FRONT WHATEVER IT
WAS THAT WAS HERE, NO BUFFERS.
I COULD FEEL IT ALL IN MY BACK, A
CONSTANT PAIN BETWEEN THE
SCAPULAE. I COULDNT SIT TO MEDITATE.
EVENTUALLY THE SUICIDAL
IDEATION PASSED TO BE
REPLACED BY DAYS OF TEARS. THE
SADNESS FELT BOTTOMLESS. MY
SKIN BROKE OUT IN CYSTIC
PIMPLES, STYES AND THE
ECZEMA OF MY CHILDHOOD.
I WAS FRAGILE PHYSICALLY
AND EMOTIONALLY EVEN THE SMA
LLEST HURDLE WOULD BRING TEARS.

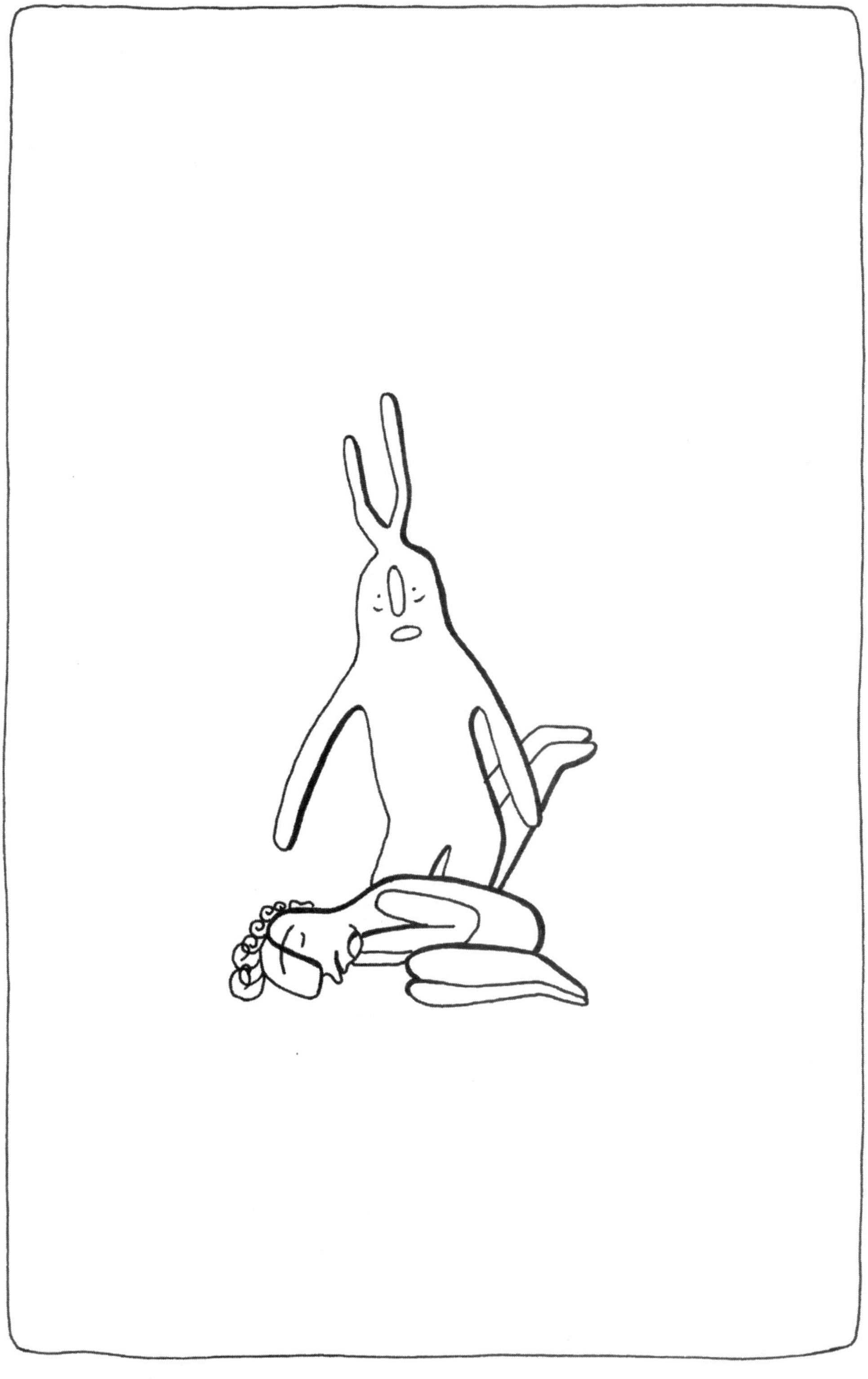

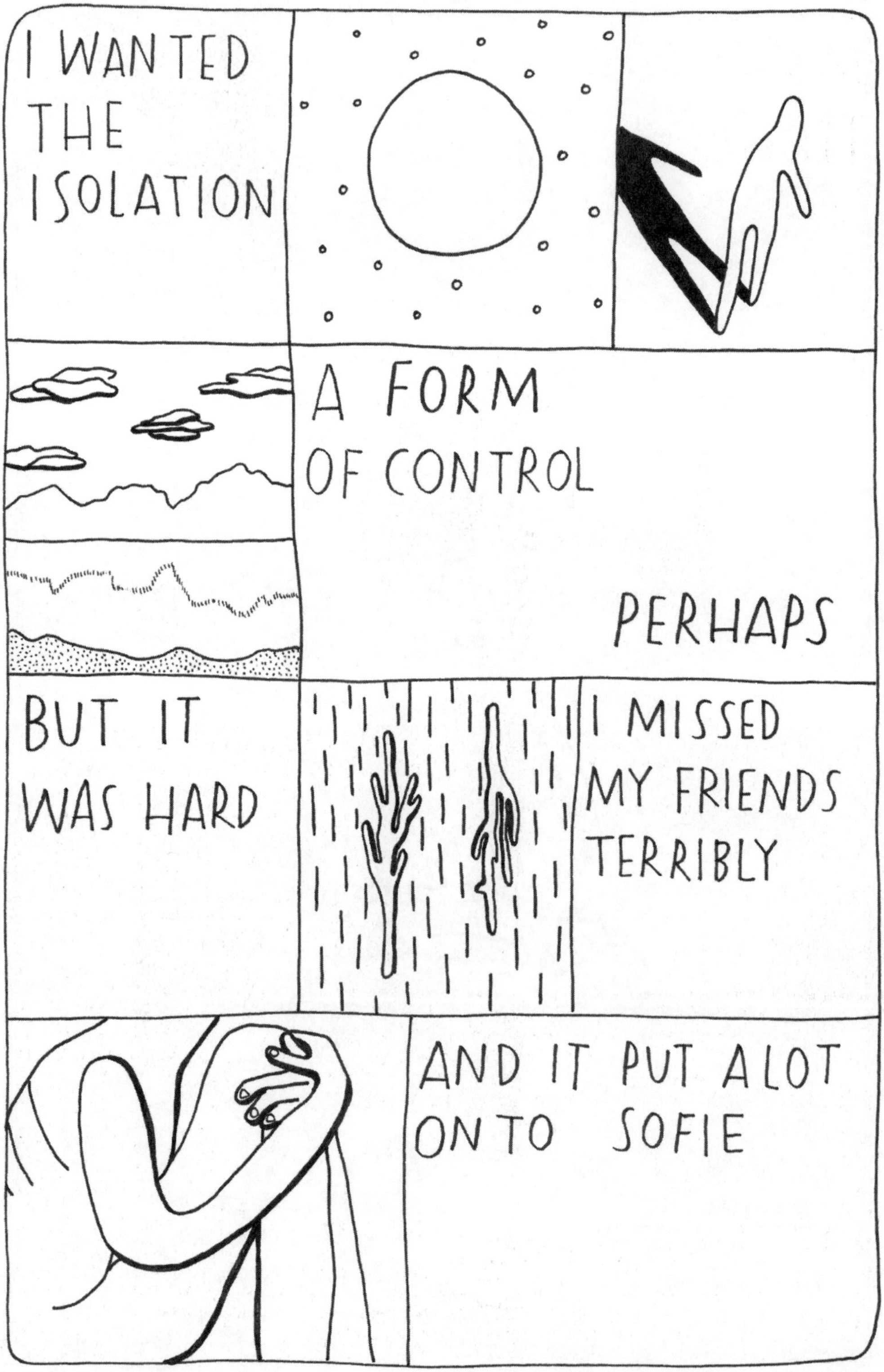
I WANTED THE ISOLATION
A FORM OF CONTROL
PERHAPS
BUT IT WAS HARD
I MISSED MY FRIENDS TERRIBLY
AND IT PUT ALOT ON TO SOFIE

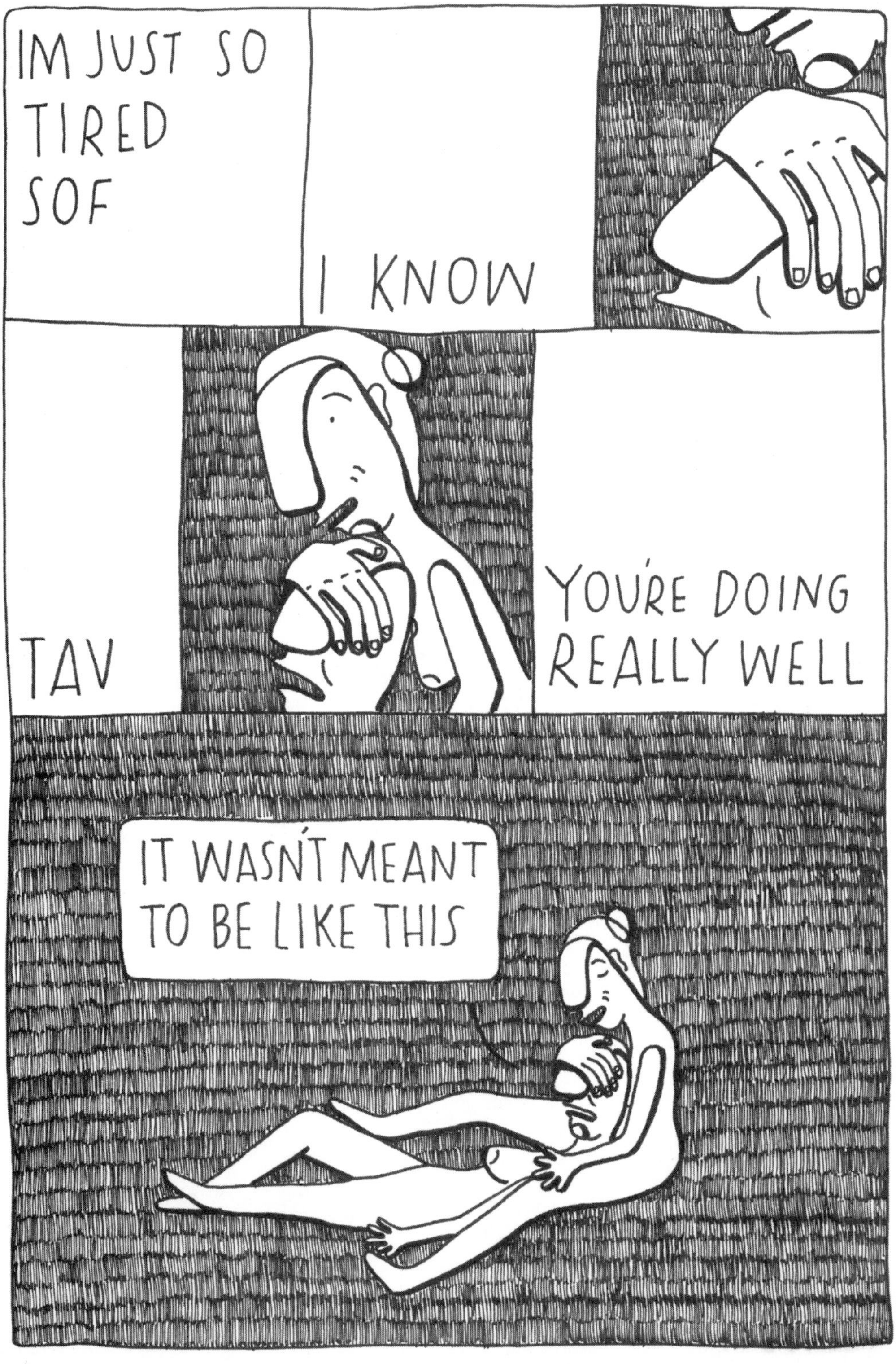
IM JUST SO TIRED SOF
I KNOW
TAV
YOU'RE DOING REALLY WELL
IT WASN'T MEANT TO BE LIKE THIS

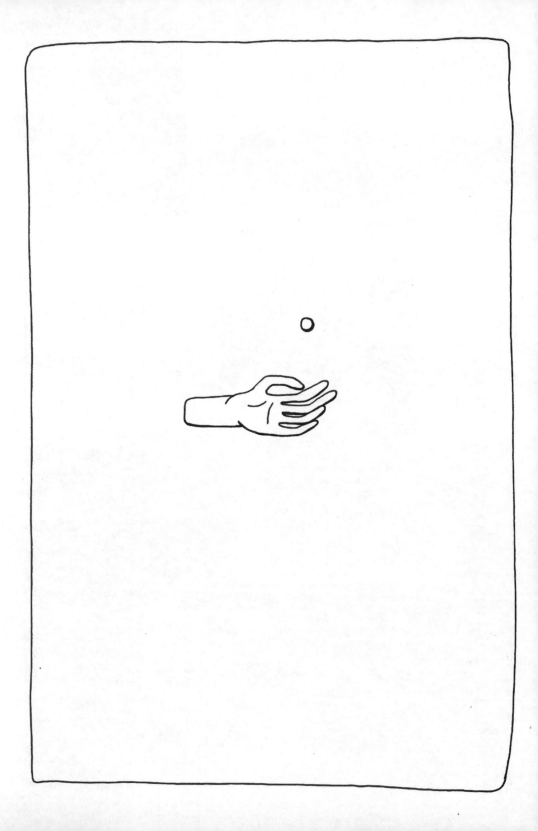

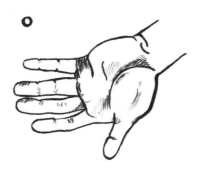

Tali, I'm worried I'm telling parts of this that aren't mine to tell... Like the quoted conversations?...

I don't know.

Tava saw the draft pages and said she got all teary.

I don't think "whose story is this?" is the right question. Like, once those words are in the air between you, I don't think one of you owns them.

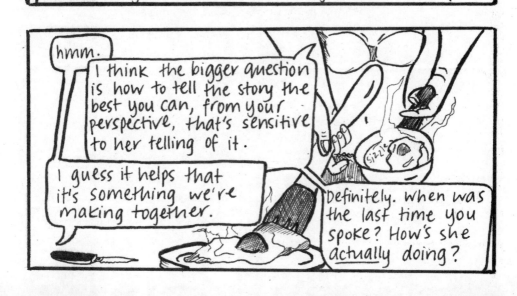

hmm.

I think the bigger question is how to tell the story the best you can, from your perspective, that's sensitive to her telling of it.

I guess it helps that it's something we're making together.

Definitely. When was the last time you spoke? How's she actually doing?

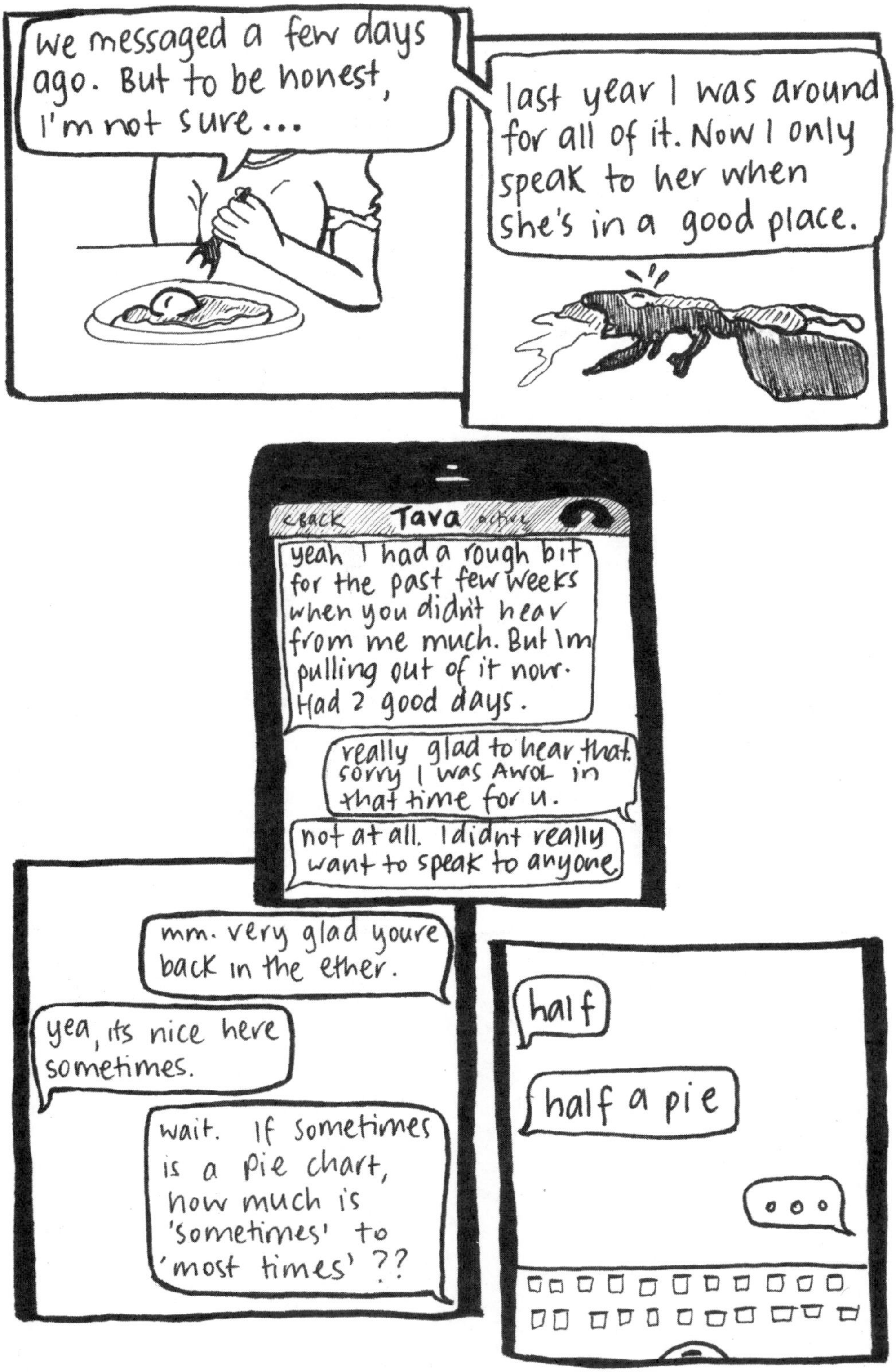
we messaged a few days ago. But to be honest, I'm not sure...
last year I was around for all of it. Now I only speak to her when she's in a good place.
BACK
Tava
yeah I had a rough bit for the past few weeks when you didn't hear from me much. But Im pulling out of it now. Had 2 good days.
really glad to hear that. sorry I was AWOL in that time for u.
not at all. I didnt really want to speak to anyone.
mm. very glad youre back in the ether.
yea, its nice here sometimes.
wait. If sometimes is a pie chart, how much is 'sometimes' to 'most times' ??
half
half a pie
...

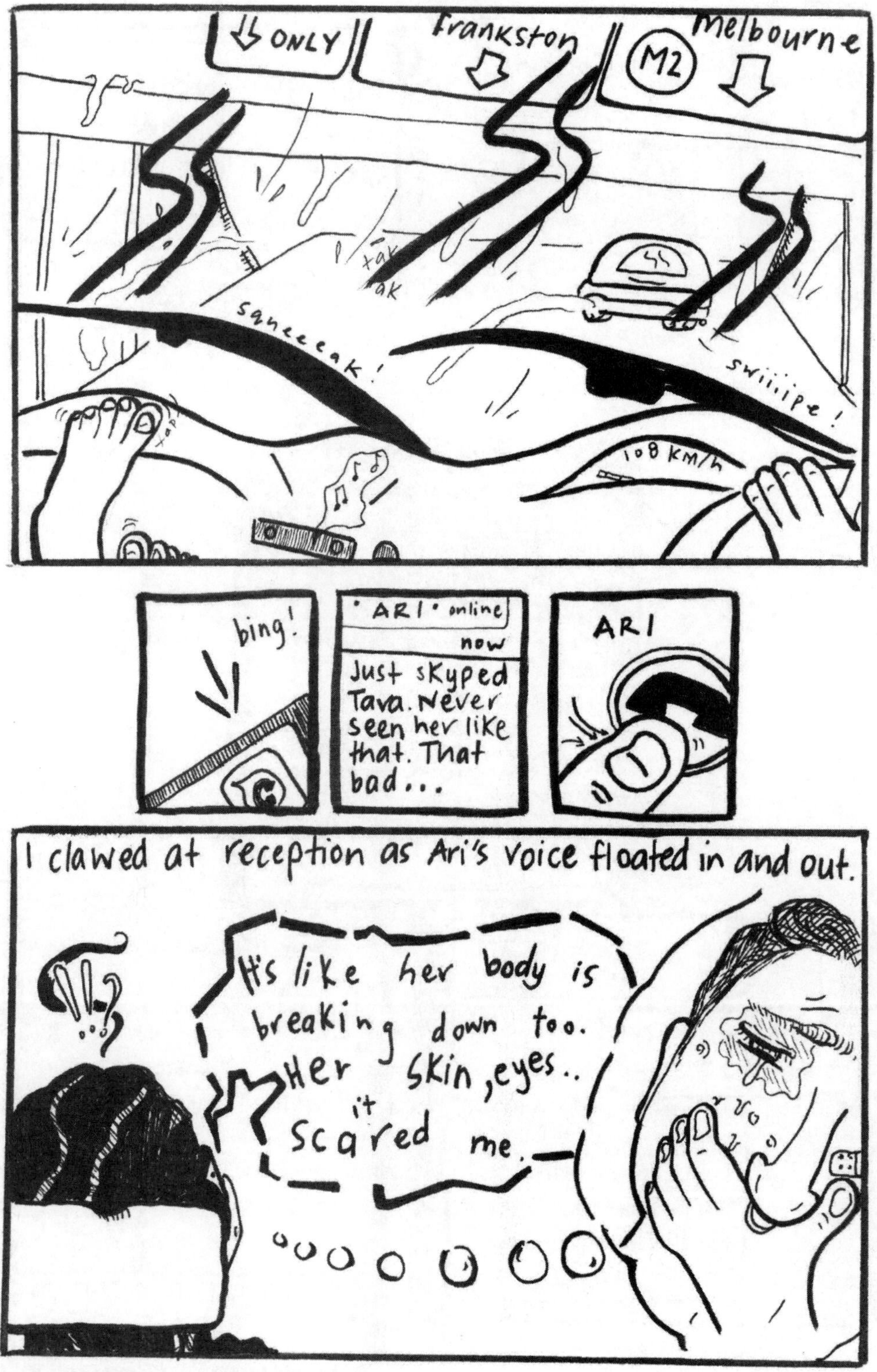
ONLY
Frankston
M2
Melbourne
tak
tak
squeeeeak!
swiiiipe!
108 KM/h
bing!
'ARI' online
now
Just skyped Tava. Never seen her like that. That bad...
ARI
I clawed at reception as Ari's voice floated in and out.
It's like her body is breaking down too. Her skin, eyes.. it scared me.

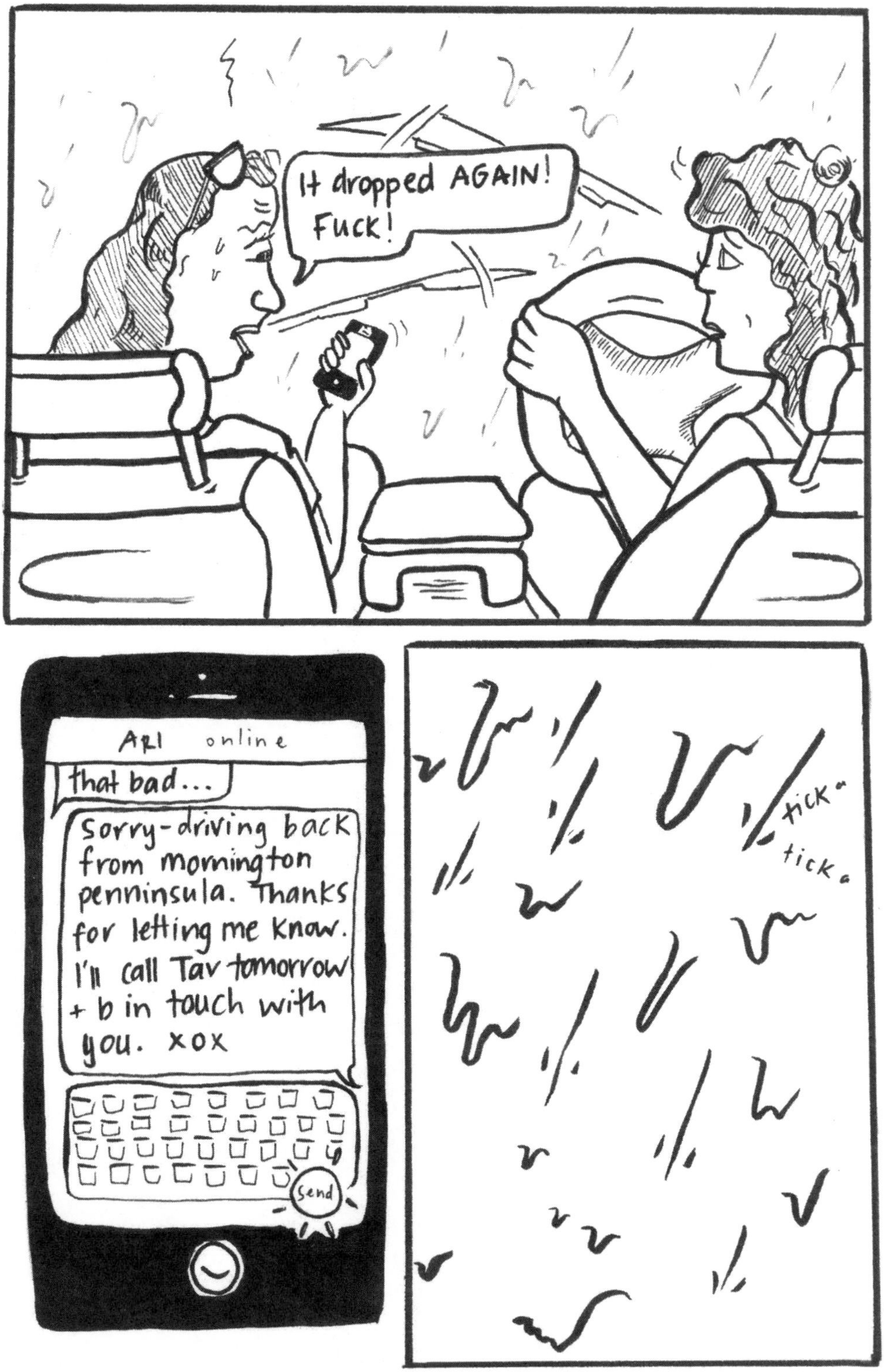
It dropped AGAIN! FUCK!
ARI online
that bad...
Sorry-driving back from mornington penninsula. Thanks for letting me know. I'll call Tav tomorrow + b in touch with you. xox
Send
tick
tick

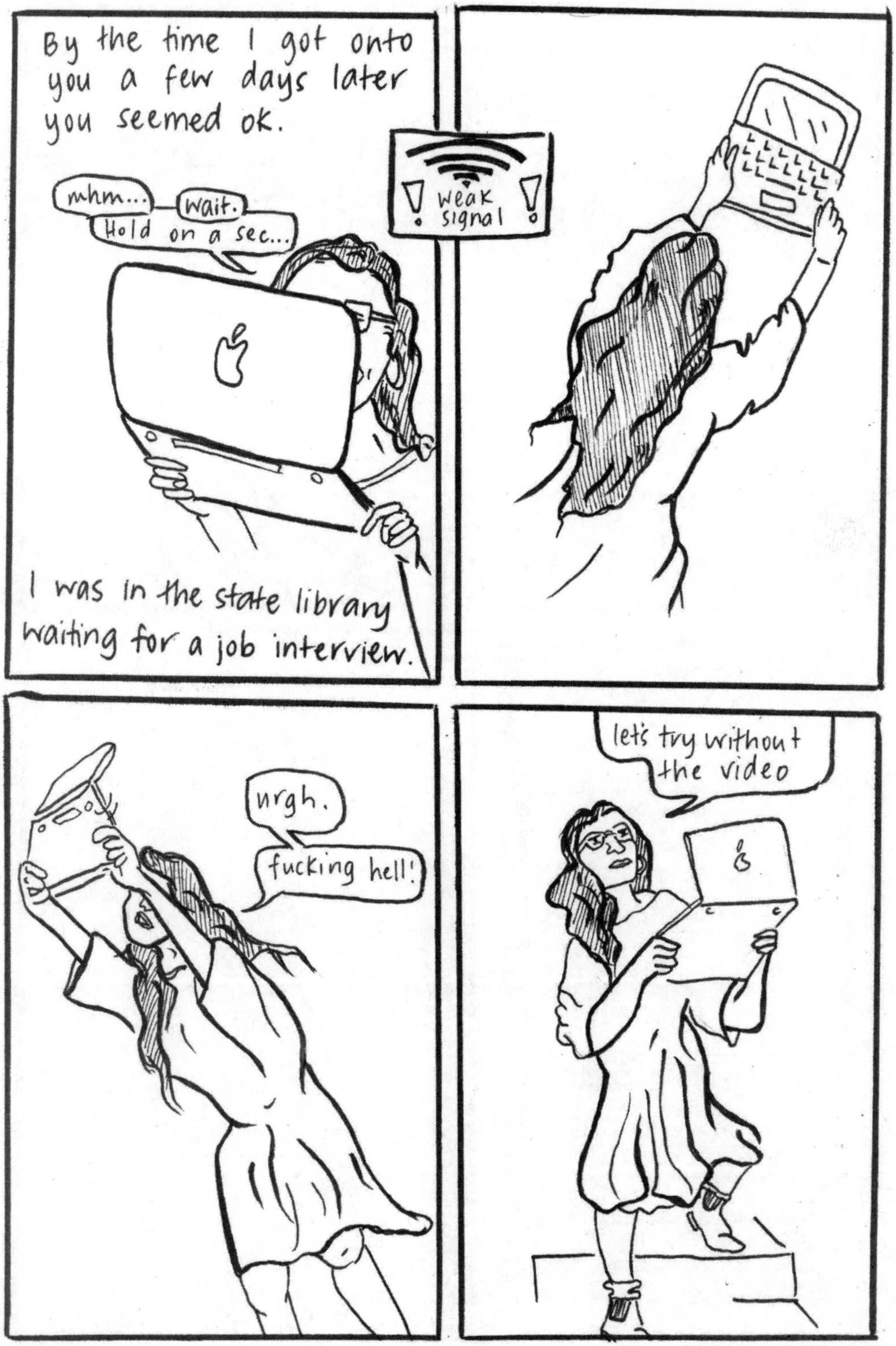
By the time I got onto you a few days later you seemed ok.
mhm...
wait.
Hold on a sec...
I was in the state library waiting for a job interview.
weak signal
urgh.
fucking hell!
let's try without the video

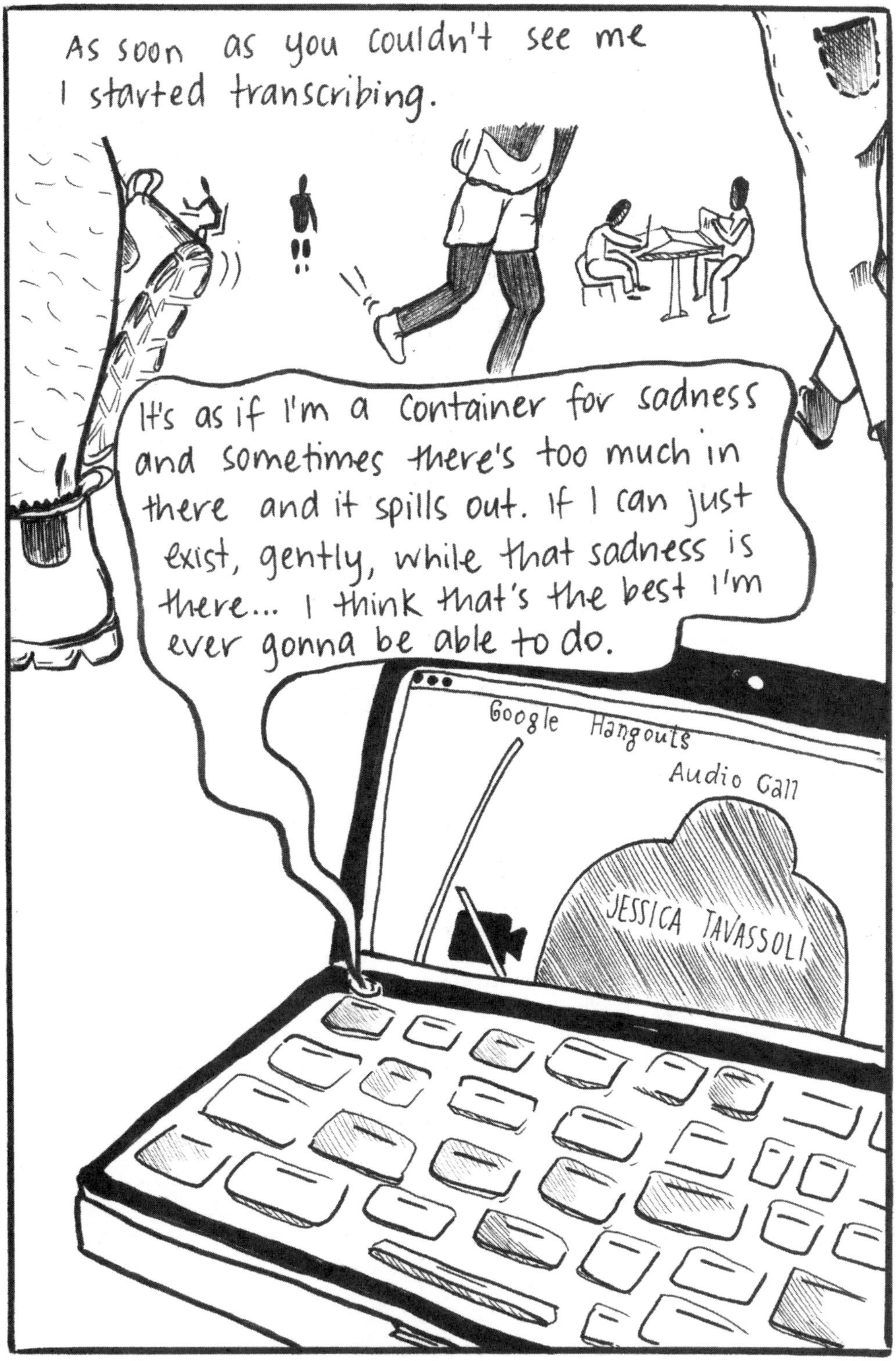
As soon as you couldn't see me I started transcribing.
It's as if I'm a container for sadness and sometimes there's too much in there and it spills out. If I can just exist, gently, while that sadness is there... I think that's the best I'm ever gonna be able to do.
Google Hangouts
Audio Call
JESSICA TAVASSOLI

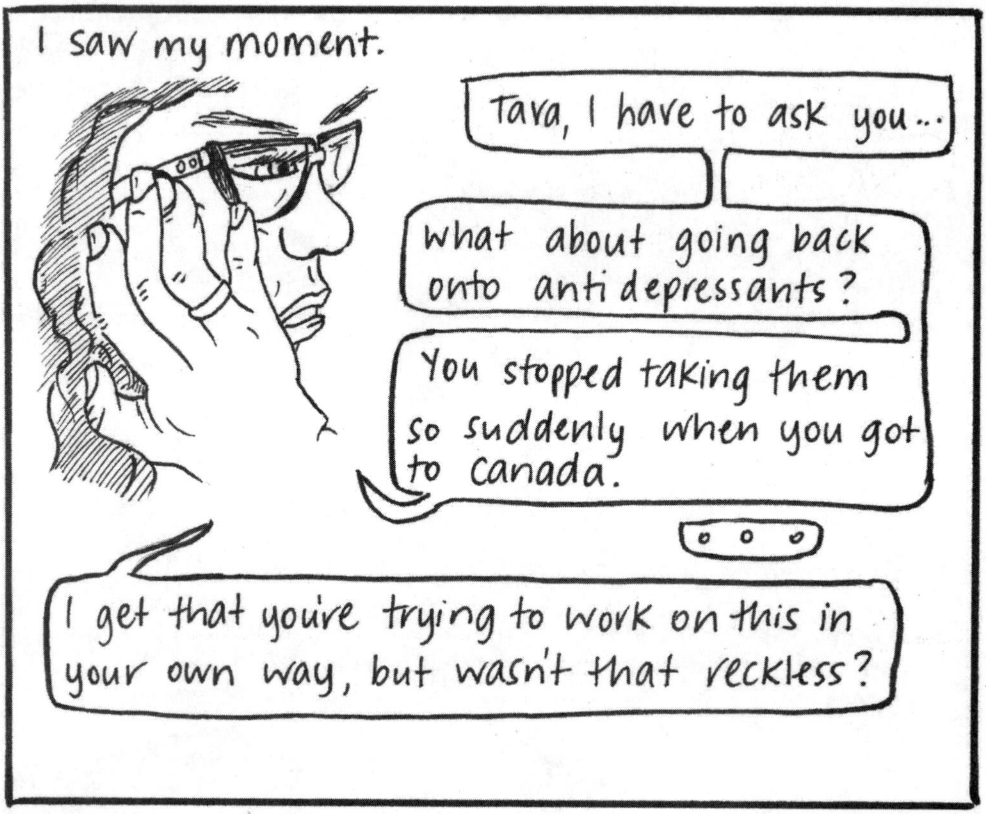
I saw my moment.
Tava, I have to ask you...
what about going back onto anti depressants?
You stopped taking them so suddenly when you got to canada.
o o o
I get that you're trying to work on this in your own way, but wasn't that reckless?

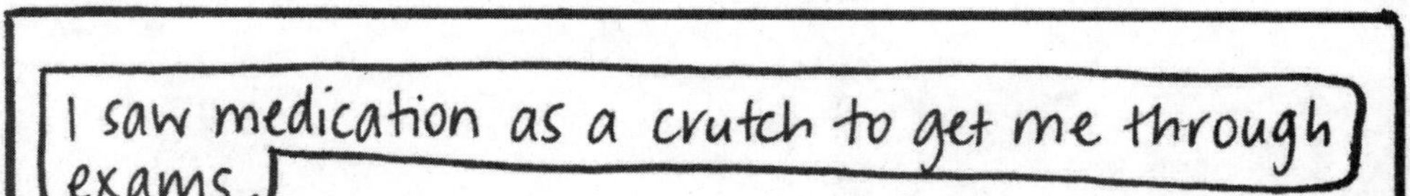
I saw medication as a crutch to get me through exams.
I admit it - it wasn't responsible the way I stepped off, without even talking to Anita.
Hangouts Audi
https://plus.google.com
TAVA
But I just don't want to swallow a manufactured chemical capsule twice a day.

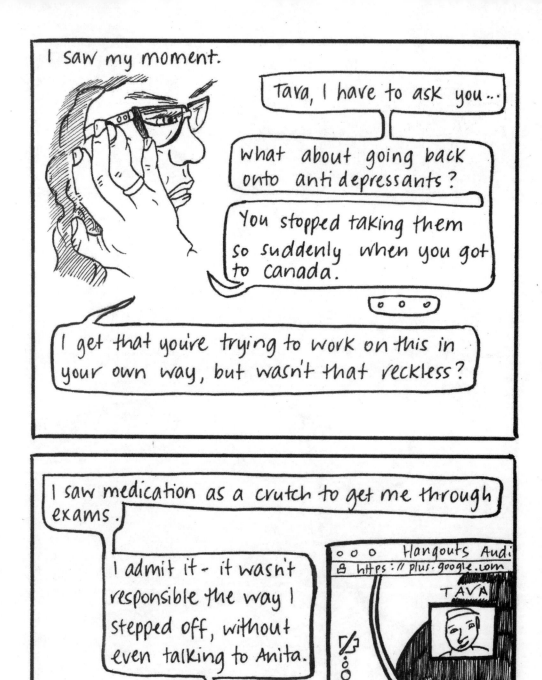

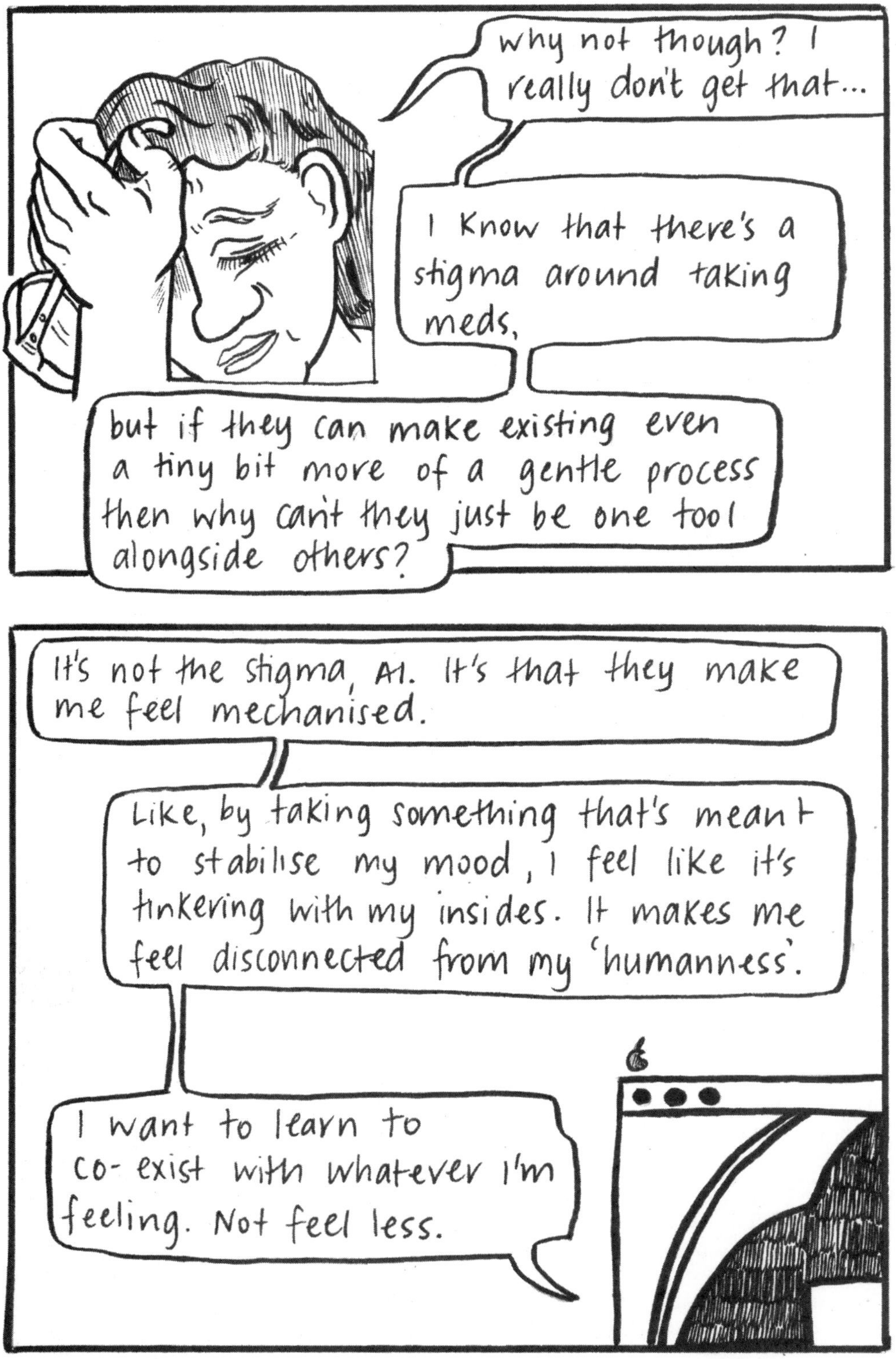
why not though? I really don't get that...
I Know that there's a stigma around taking meds.
but if they can make existing even a tiny bit more of a gentle process then why can't they just be one tool alongside others?
It's not the stigma, AI. It's that they make me feel mechanised.
Like, by taking something that's meant to stabilise my mood, I feel like it's tinkering with my insides. It makes me feel disconnected from my 'humanness'.
I want to learn to co-exist with whatever I'm feeling. Not feel less.

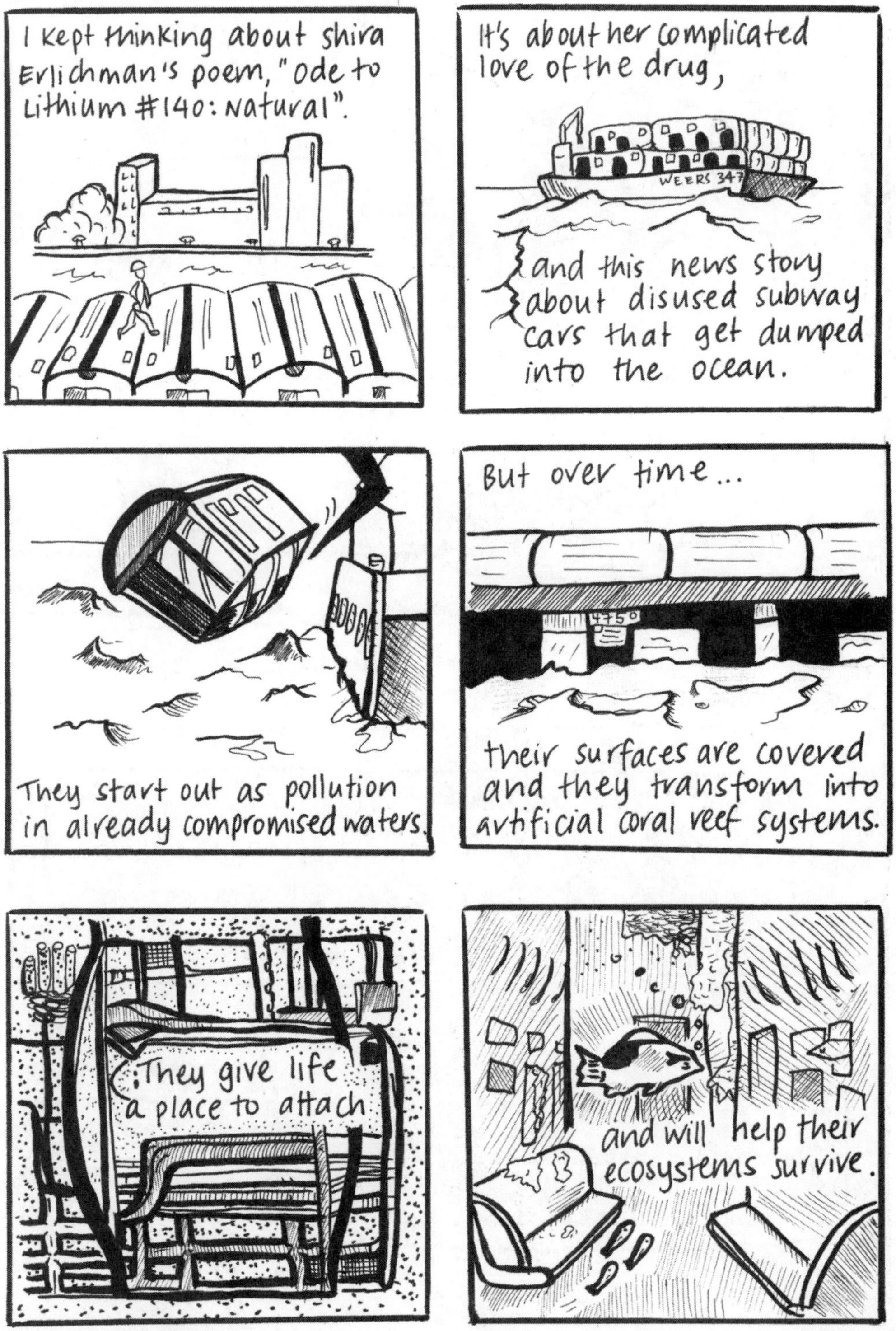
I kept thinking about Shira Erlichman's poem, "Ode to Lithium #140: Natural".
It's about her complicated love of the drug,
and this news story about disused subway cars that get dumped into the ocean.
WEERS 347
They start out as pollution in already compromised waters.
But over time...
4750
their surfaces are covered and they transform into artificial coral reef systems.
They give life a place to attach
and will help their ecosystems survive.

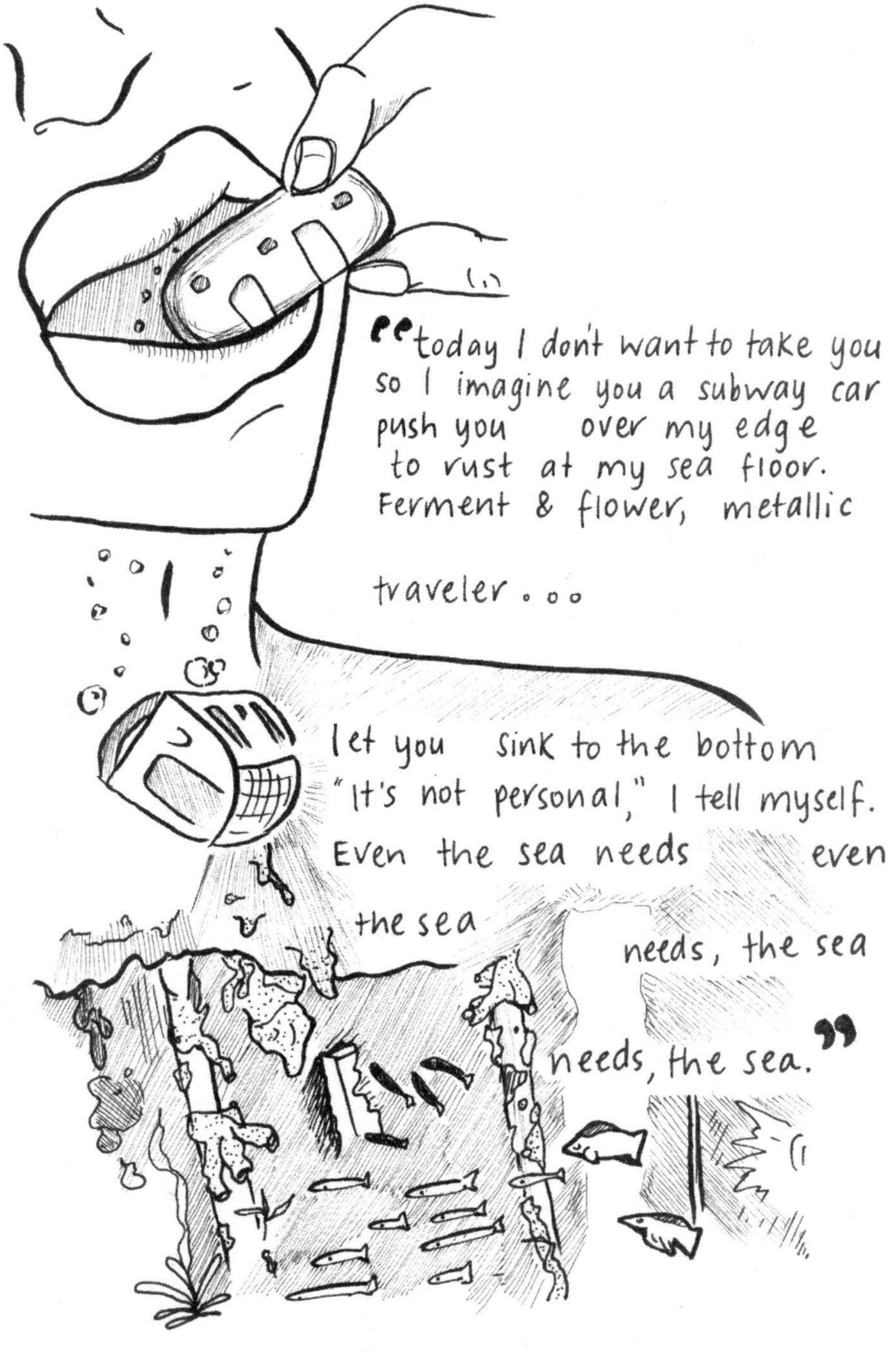
"today I don't want to take you
so I imagine you a subway car
push you over my edge
to rust at my sea floor.
Ferment & flower, metallic
traveler . . .
let you sink to the bottom
"It's not personal," I tell myself.
Even the sea needs even
the sea
needs, the sea
needs, the sea."

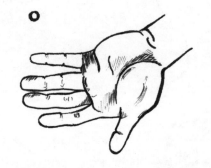

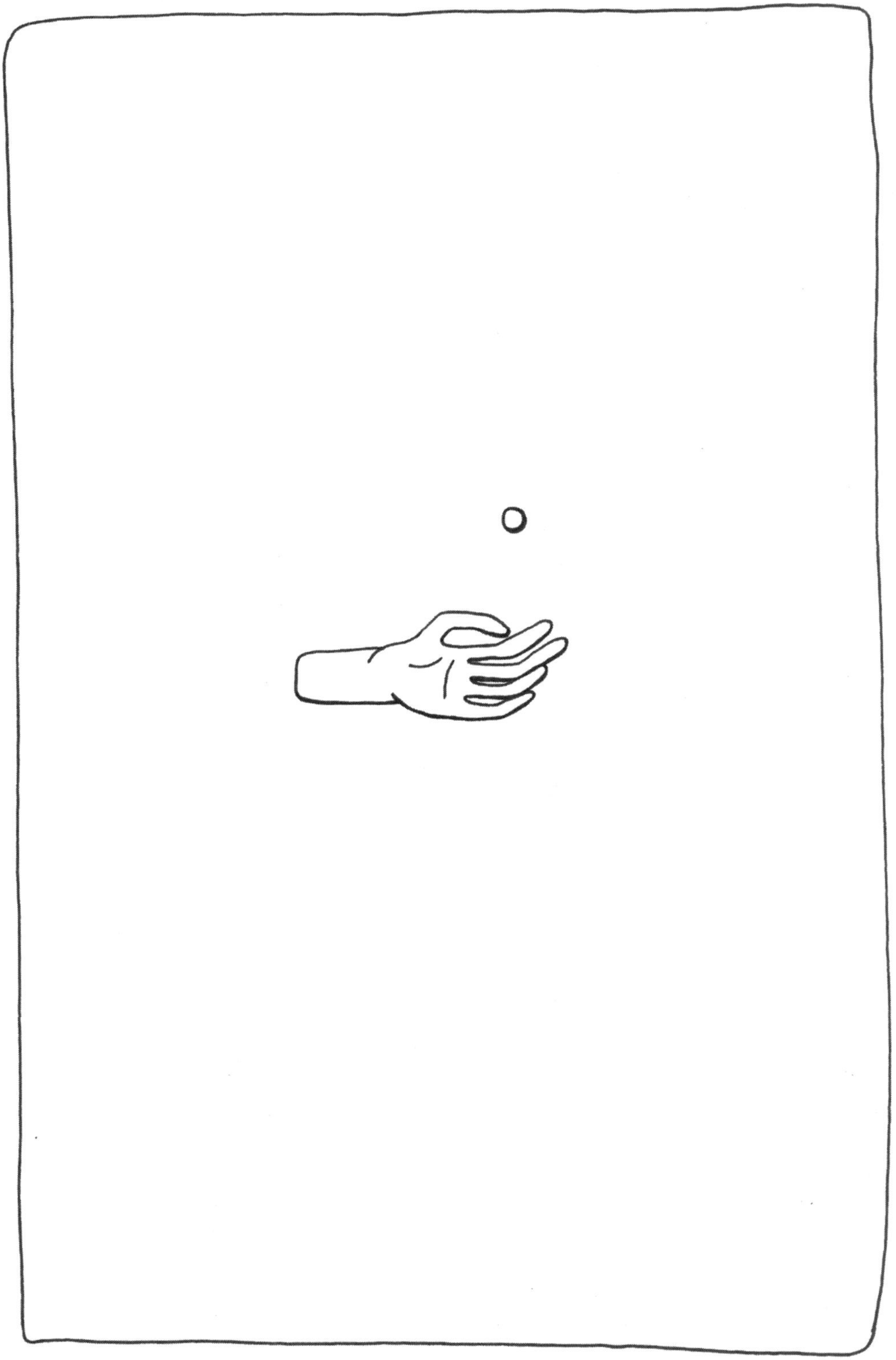

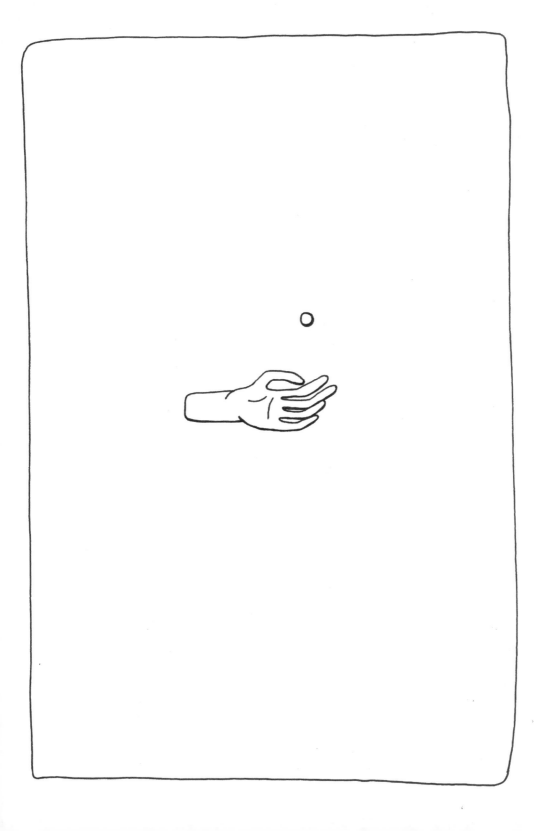

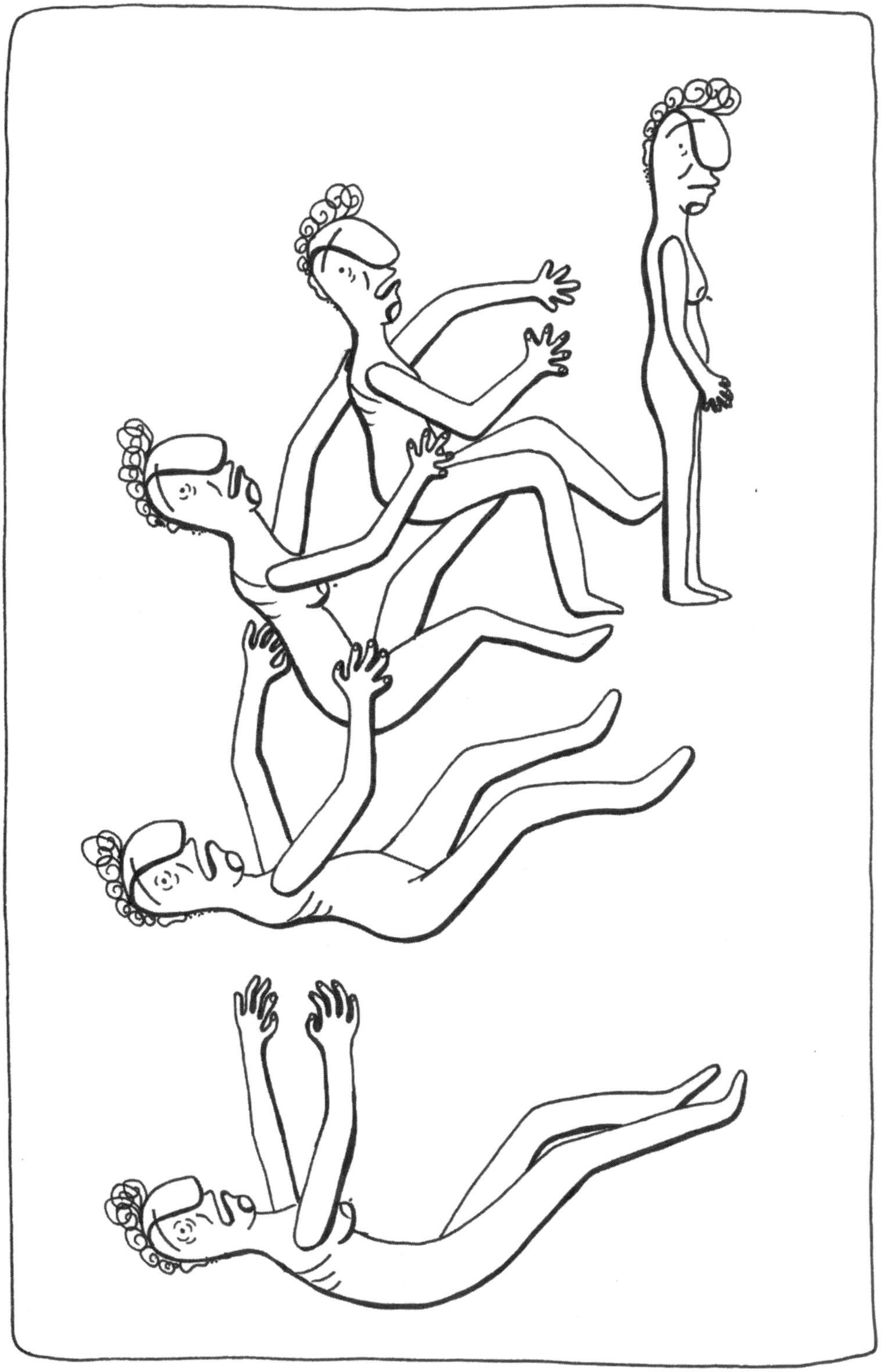

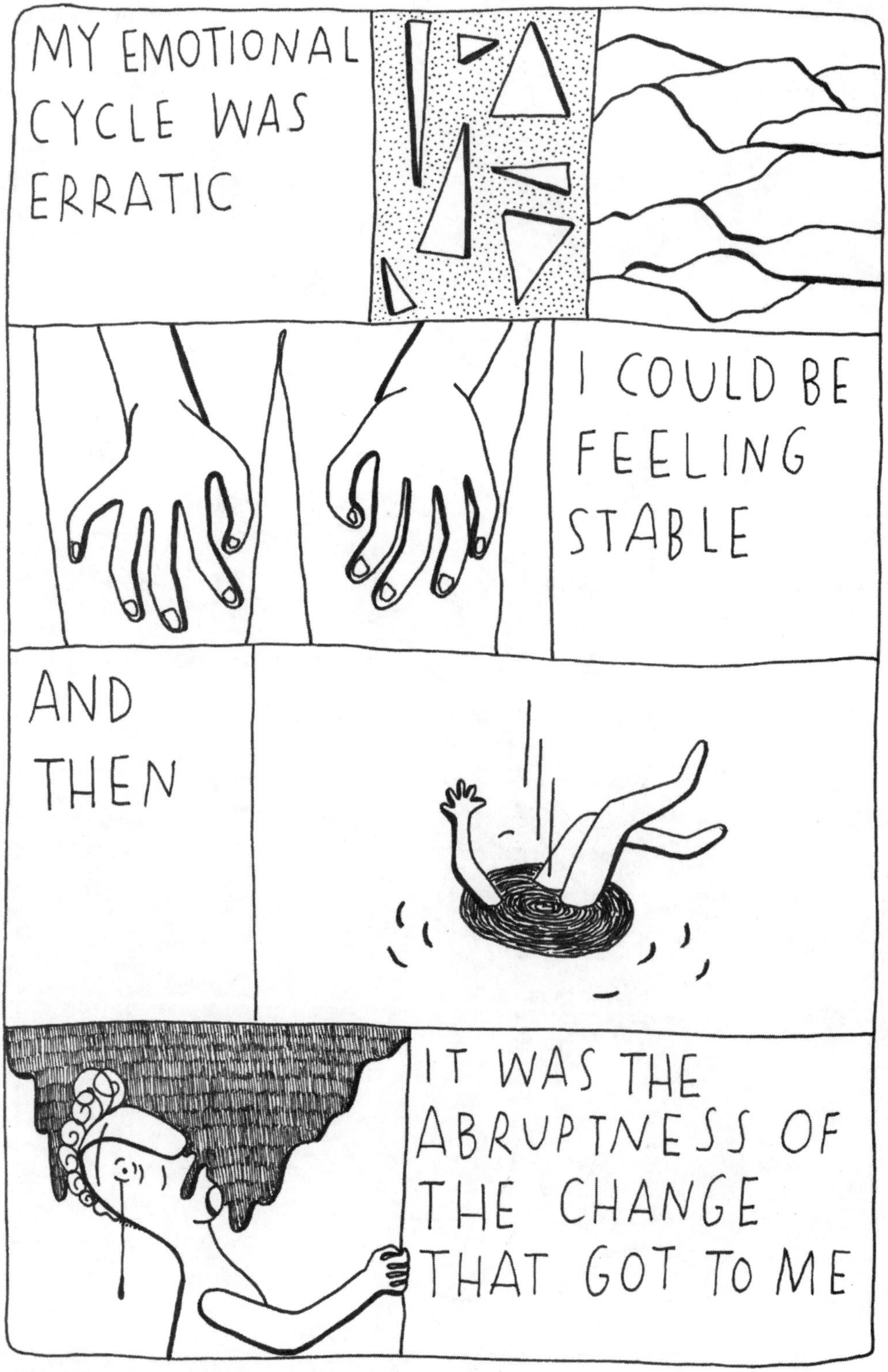
MY EMOTIONAL CYCLE WAS ERRATIC
I COULD BE FEELING STABLE
AND THEN
IT WAS THE ABRUPTNESS OF THE CHANGE THAT GOT TO ME

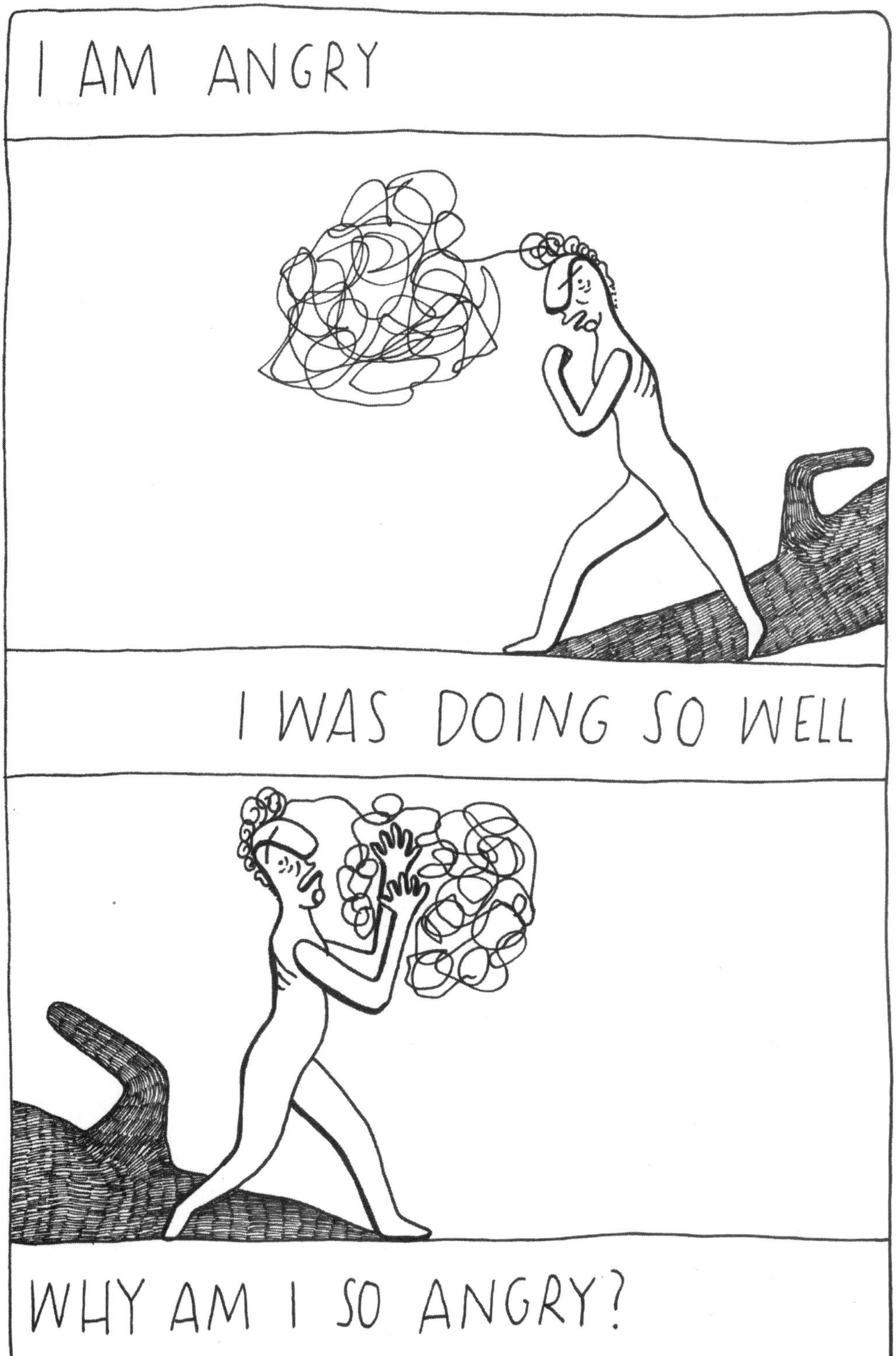
I AM ANGRY
I WAS DOING SO WELL
WHY AM I SO ANGRY?

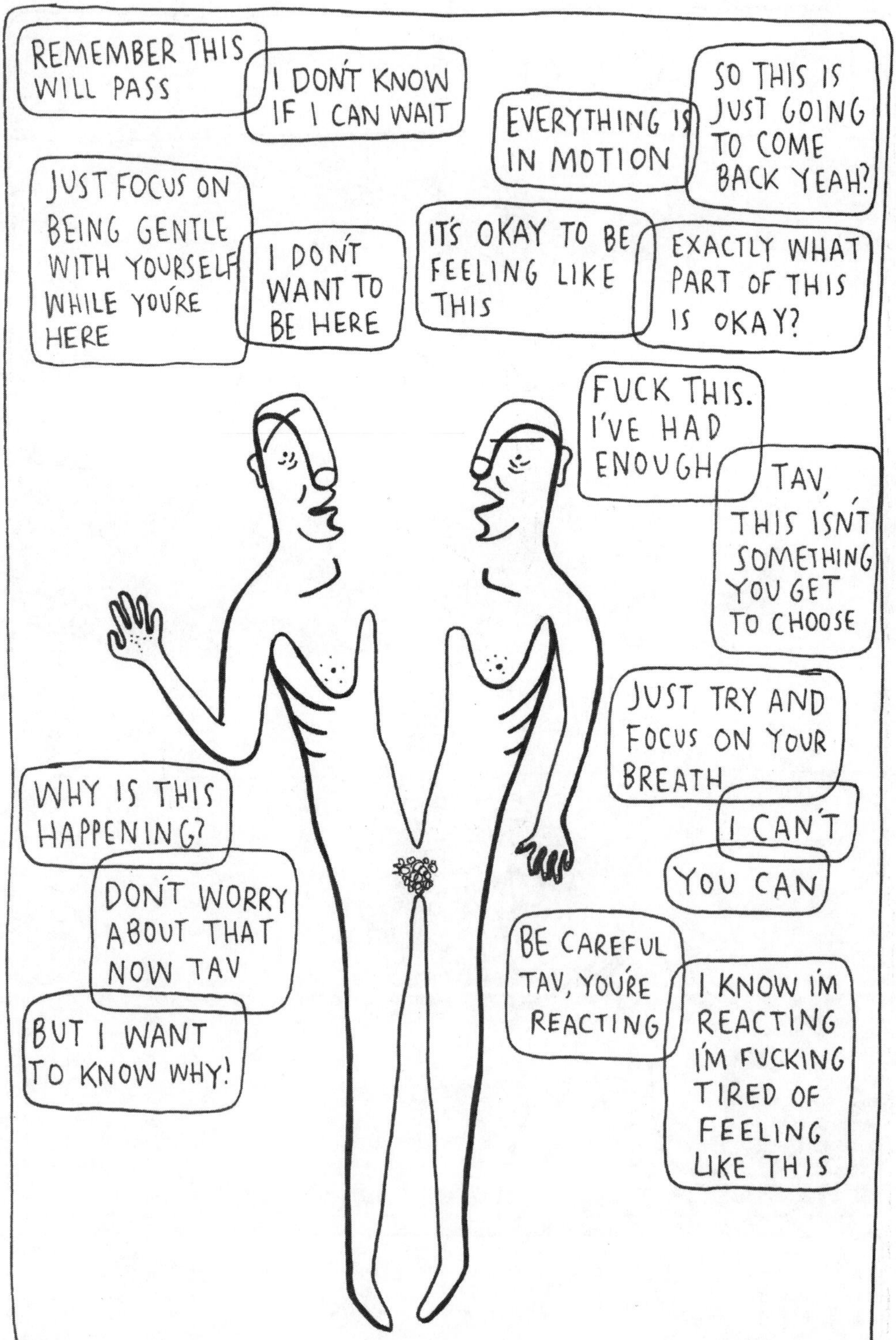
REMEMBER THIS WILL PASS
I DON'T KNOW IF I CAN WAIT
EVERYTHING IS IN MOTION
SO THIS IS JUST GOING TO COME BACK YEAH?
JUST FOCUS ON BEING GENTLE WITH YOURSELF WHILE YOU'RE HERE
I DON'T WANT TO BE HERE
IT'S OKAY TO BE FEELING LIKE THIS
EXACTLY WHAT PART OF THIS IS OKAY?
FUCK THIS. I'VE HAD ENOUGH
TAV, THIS ISN'T SOMETHING YOU GET TO CHOOSE
JUST TRY AND FOCUS ON YOUR BREATH
I CAN'T
YOU CAN
WHY IS THIS HAPPENING?
DON'T WORRY ABOUT THAT NOW TAV
BUT I WANT TO KNOW WHY!
BE CAREFUL TAV, YOU'RE REACTING
I KNOW I'M REACTING I'M FUCKING TIRED OF FEELING LIKE THIS

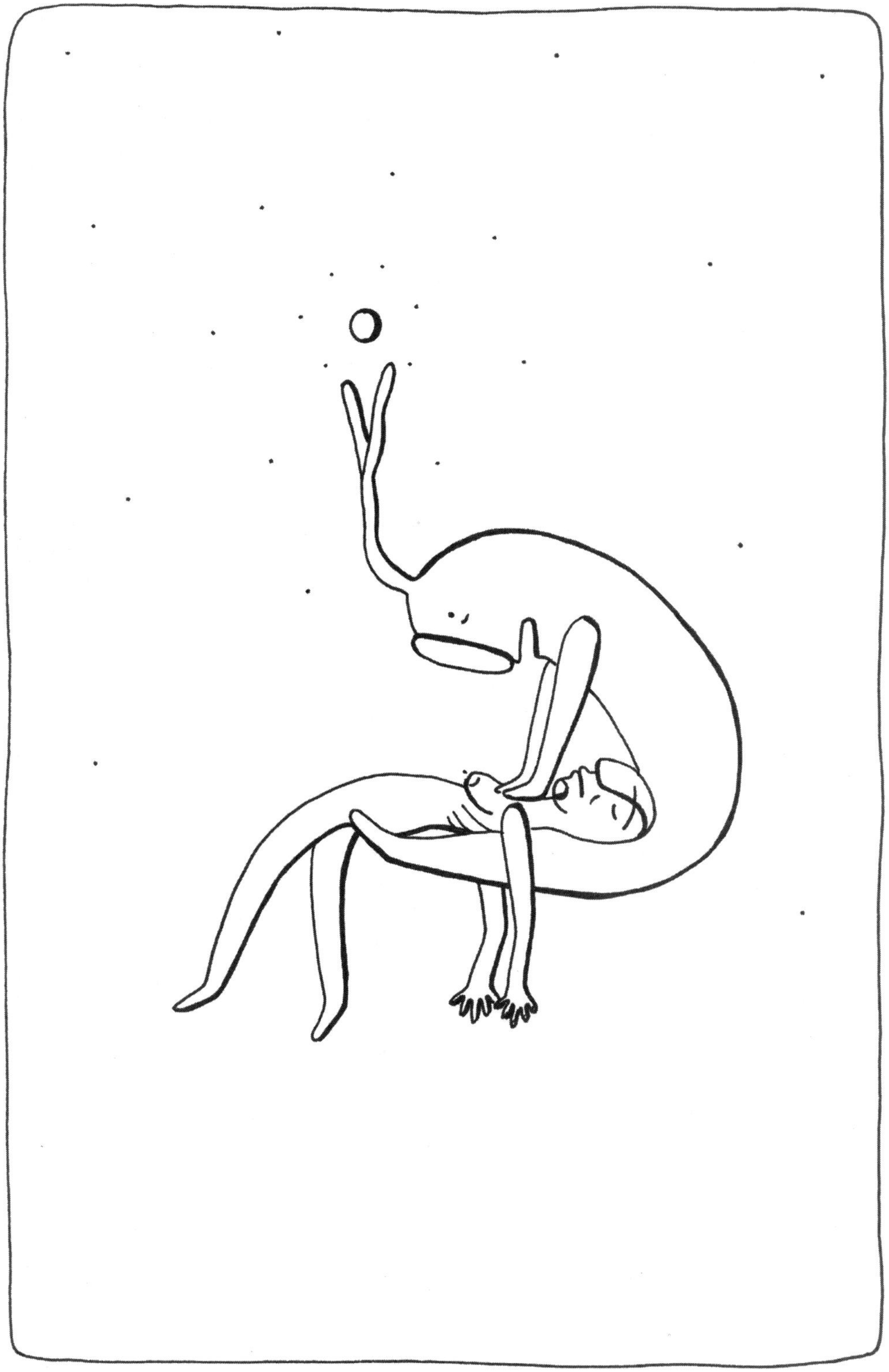

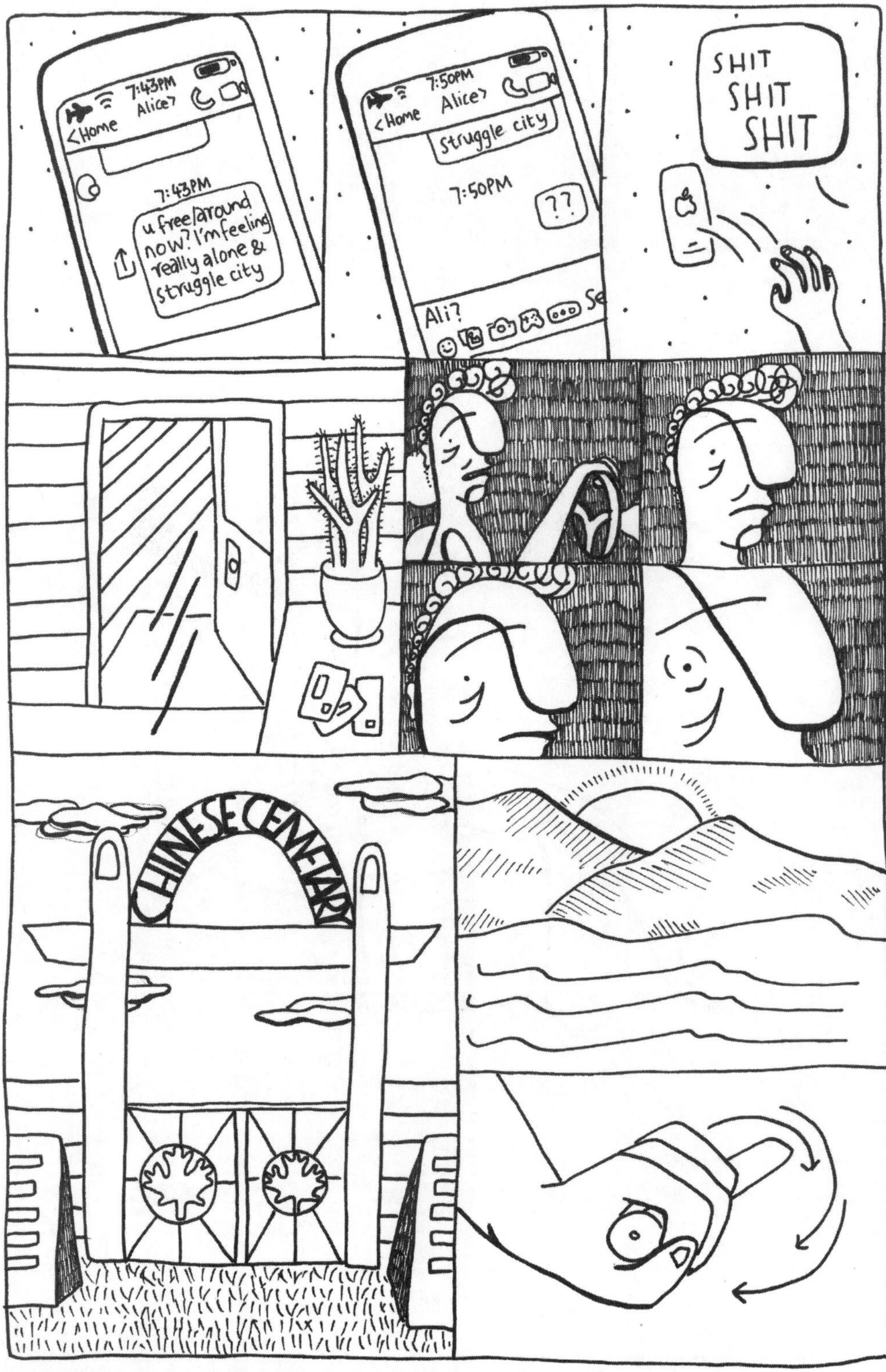

7:43PM
<Home
Alice>
7:43PM
u free/around now? I'm feeling really alone & struggle city
7:50PM
<Home
Alice>
struggle city
7:50PM
??
Ali?
SHIT SHIT SHIT
CHINESE CEMETARY

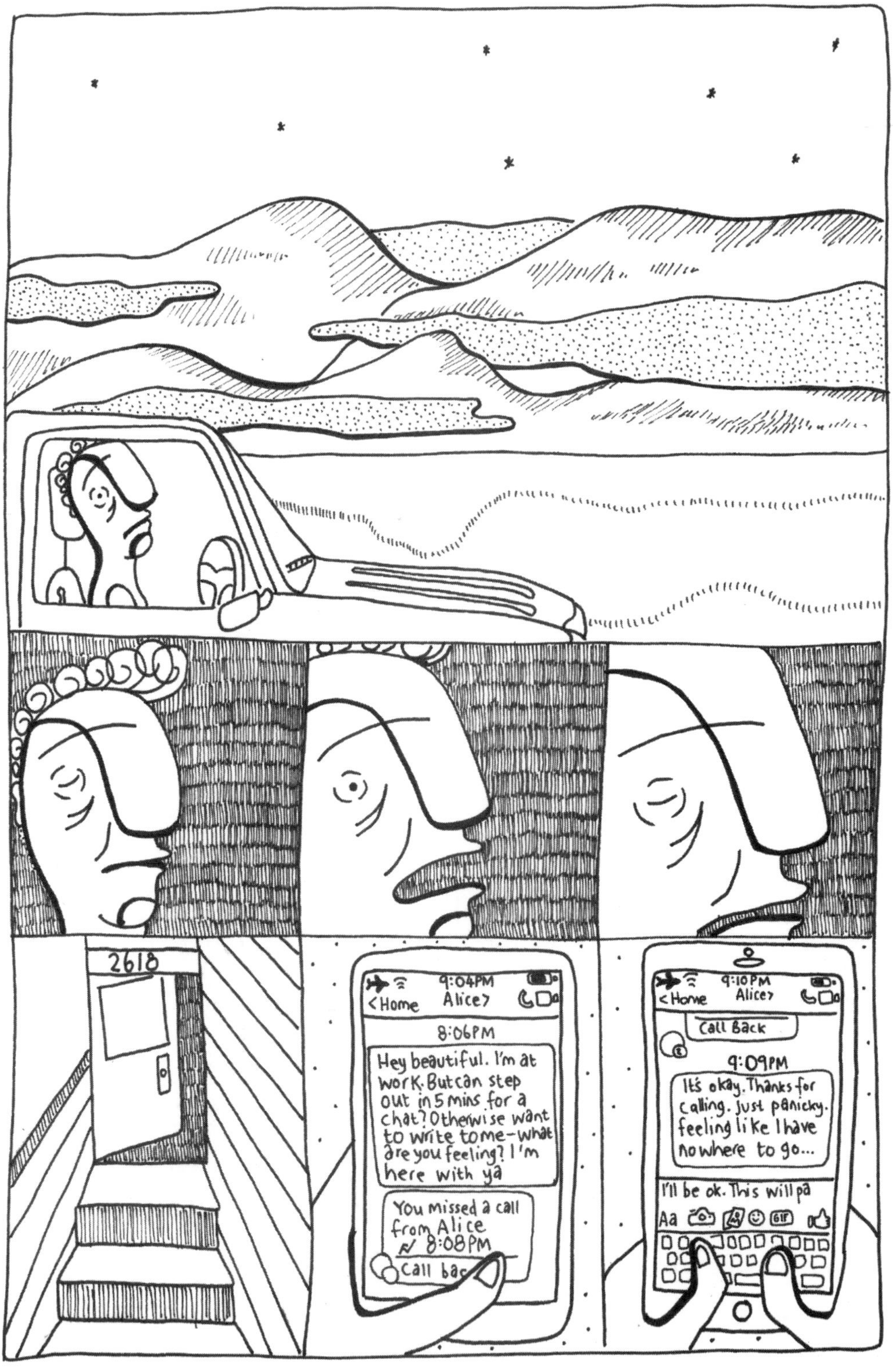
2618
9:04PM
<Home
Alice>
8:06PM
Hey beautiful. I'm at work. But can step out in 5 mins for a chat? Otherwise want to write to me - what are you feeling? I'm here with ya
You missed a call from Alice
8:08PM
Call bac
9:10PM
<Home
Alice>
Call Back
9:09PM
It's okay. Thanks for calling. Just panicky. feeling like I have nowhere to go...
I'll be ok. This will pa
Aa
GIF

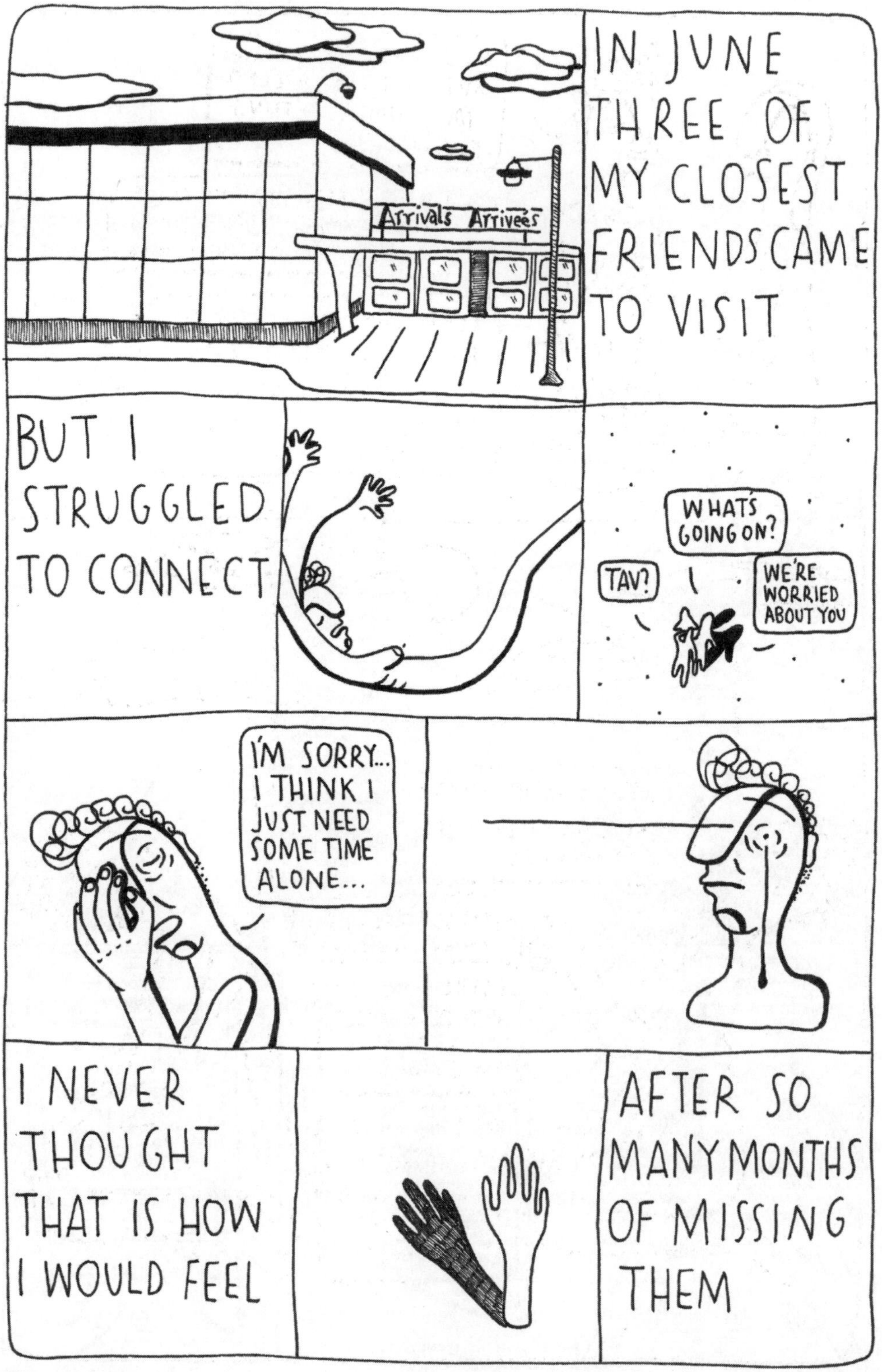

IN JUNE THREE OF MY CLOSEST FRIENDS CAME TO VISIT
Arrivals Arrivées
BUT I STRUGGLED TO CONNECT
WHAT'S GOING ON?
TAV?
WE'RE WORRIED ABOUT YOU
I'M SORRY... I THINK I JUST NEED SOME TIME ALONE...
I NEVER THOUGHT THAT IS HOW I WOULD FEEL
AFTER SO MANY MONTHS OF MISSING THEM

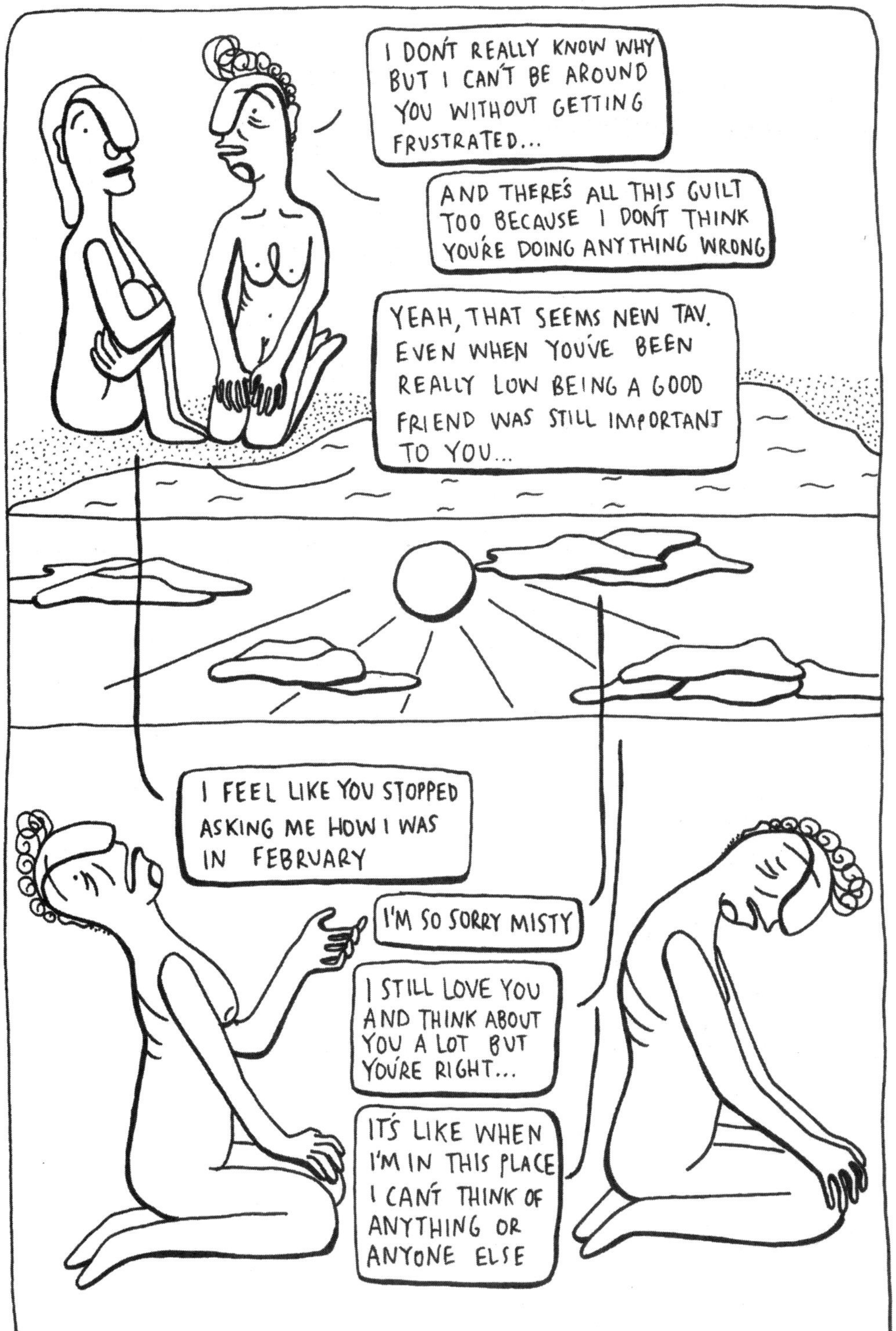
I DON'T REALLY KNOW WHY BUT I CAN'T BE AROUND YOU WITHOUT GETTING FRUSTRATED...
AND THERE'S ALL THIS GUILT TOO BECAUSE I DON'T THINK YOU'RE DOING ANYTHING WRONG
YEAH, THAT SEEMS NEW TAV. EVEN WHEN YOU'VE BEEN REALLY LOW BEING A GOOD FRIEND WAS STILL IMPORTANT TO YOU...
I FEEL LIKE YOU STOPPED ASKING ME HOW I WAS IN FEBRUARY
I'M SO SORRY MISTY
I STILL LOVE YOU AND THINK ABOUT YOU A LOT BUT YOU'RE RIGHT...
IT'S LIKE WHEN I'M IN THIS PLACE I CAN'T THINK OF ANYTHING OR ANYONE ELSE

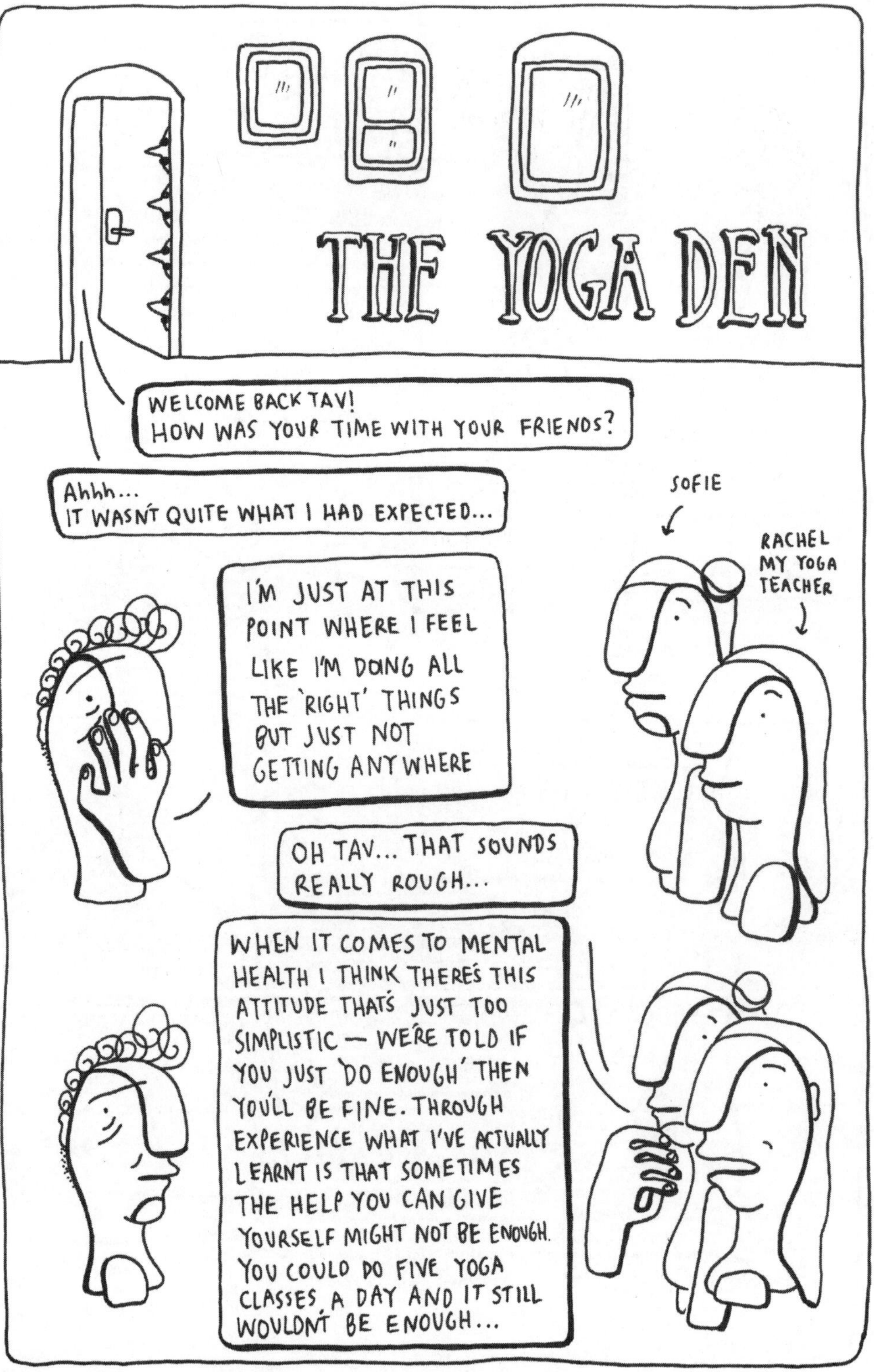
THE YOGA DEN
WELCOME BACK TAV! HOW WAS YOUR TIME WITH YOUR FRIENDS?
Ahhh... IT WASN'T QUITE WHAT I HAD EXPECTED...
SOFIE
RACHEL MY YOGA TEACHER
I'M JUST AT THIS POINT WHERE I FEEL LIKE I'M DOING ALL THE 'RIGHT' THINGS BUT JUST NOT GETTING ANYWHERE
OH TAV... THAT SOUNDS REALLY ROUGH...
WHEN IT COMES TO MENTAL HEALTH I THINK THERE'S THIS ATTITUDE THAT'S JUST TOO SIMPLISTIC — WE'RE TOLD IF YOU JUST 'DO ENOUGH' THEN YOU'LL BE FINE. THROUGH EXPERIENCE WHAT I'VE ACTUALLY LEARNT IS THAT SOMETIMES THE HELP YOU CAN GIVE YOURSELF MIGHT NOT BE ENOUGH. YOU COULD DO FIVE YOGA CLASSES A DAY AND IT STILL WOULDN'T BE ENOUGH...

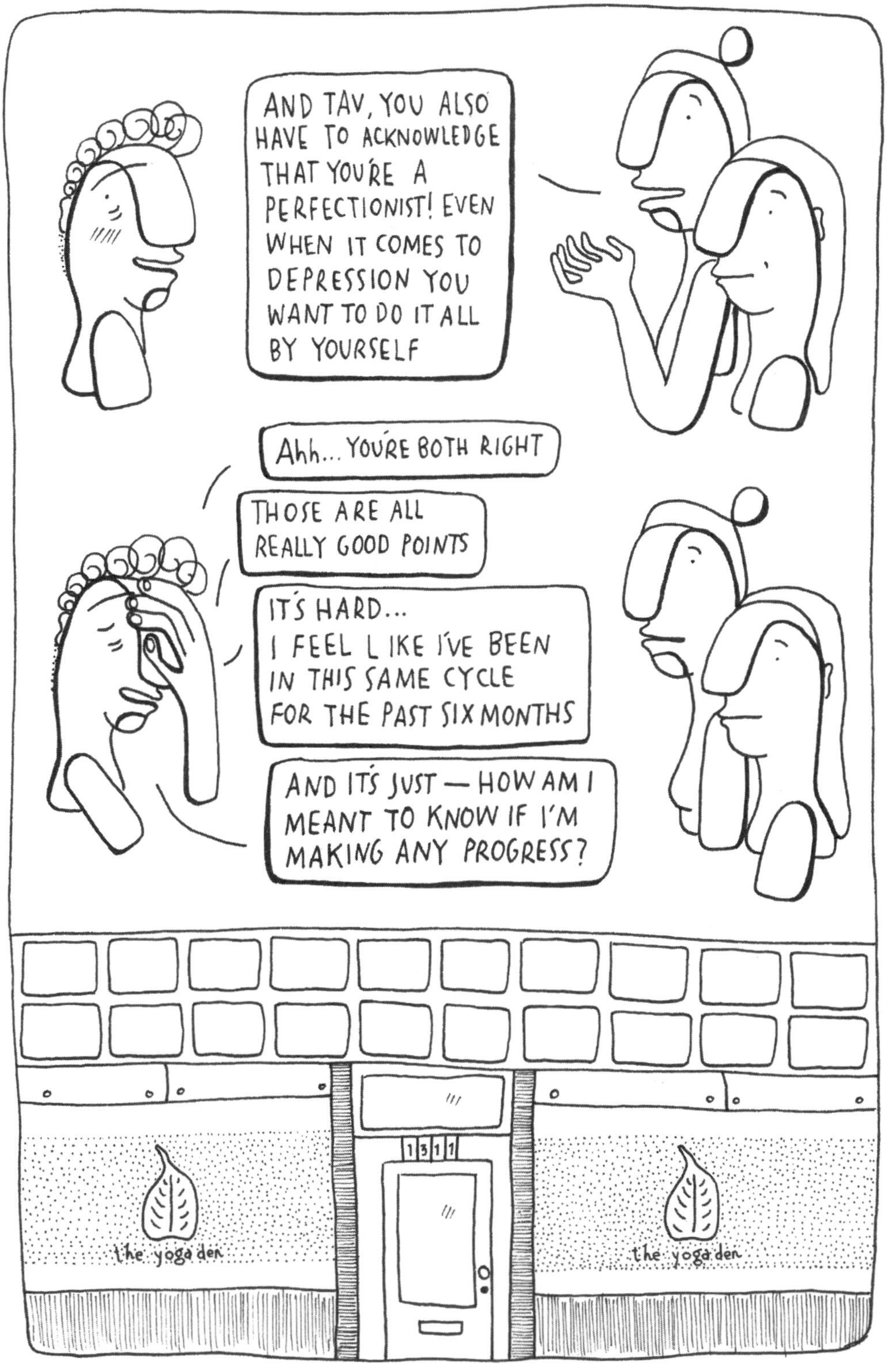
AND TAV, YOU ALSO HAVE TO ACKNOWLEDGE THAT YOU'RE A PERFECTIONIST! EVEN WHEN IT COMES TO DEPRESSION YOU WANT TO DO IT ALL BY YOURSELF
Ahh... YOU'RE BOTH RIGHT
THOSE ARE ALL REALLY GOOD POINTS
IT'S HARD... I FEEL LIKE I'VE BEEN IN THIS SAME CYCLE FOR THE PAST SIX MONTHS
AND IT'S JUST — HOW AM I MEANT TO KNOW IF I'M MAKING ANY PROGRESS?
1311
the yoga den
the yoga den

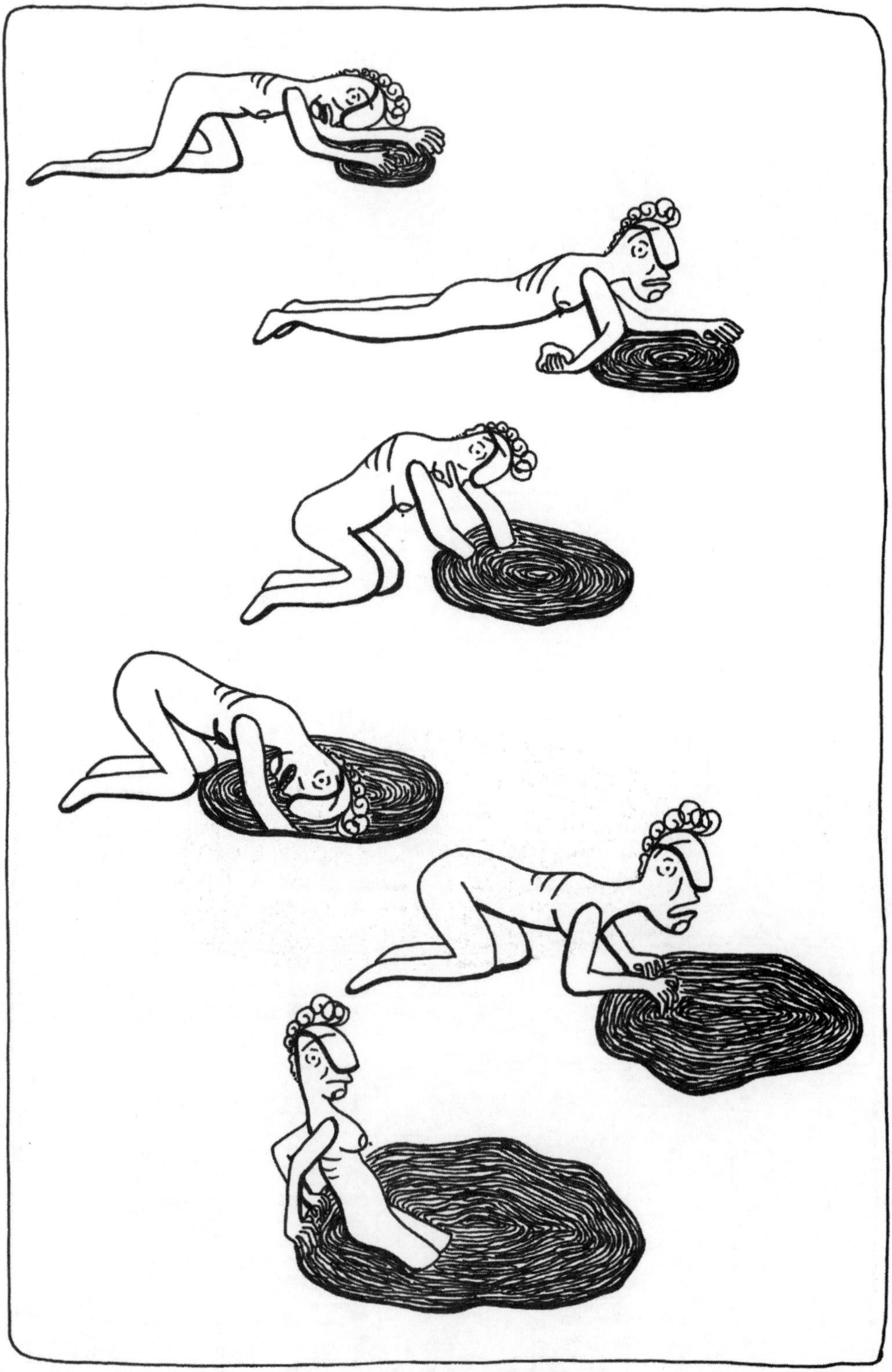

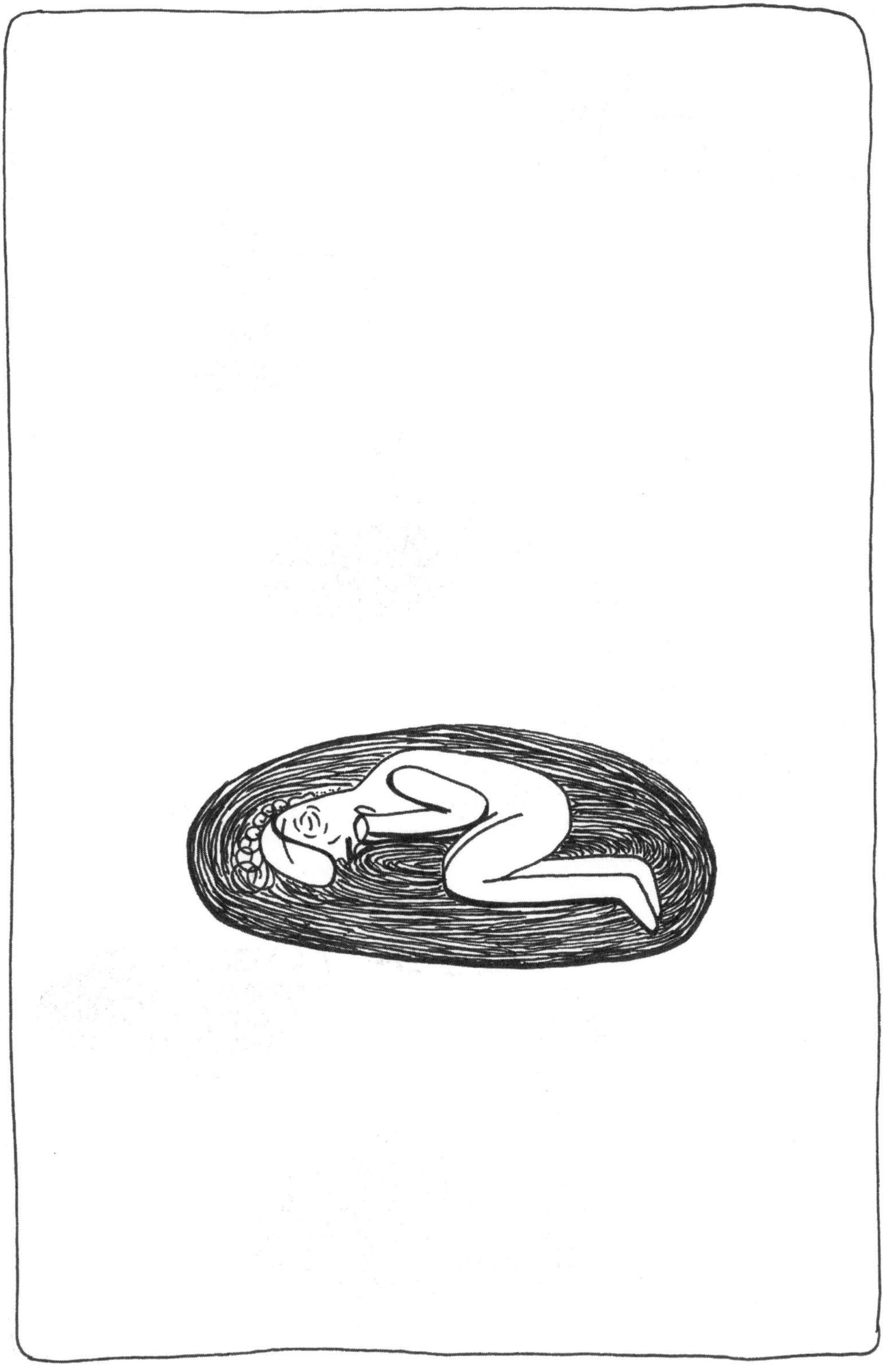

DEPRESSION   CARRIES BAGGAGE/
MEDICALLY, WE DON'T UNDERSTAND IT   WELL/

IT DOESN'T FIT NEATLY INTO DEFINITION/

WITH DEPRESSION , IT'S PERSONAL
                   A REFLECTION OF YOU
                   YOUR ABILITY TO COPE, TO BE RESILIENT
                                             OR NOT/
              A WEAKNESS
                 THAT IS ONLY SOMETIMES JUSTIFIED
 I REMEMBER/
 MY PARENTS TELLING ME "YOU THINK TOO MUCH
                         THAT'S WHY YOU'RE SO SAD"

AND THERE'S THE PART OF ME

                                 WHO BELIEVES/

   BUT ALL THAT IS
   BASED ON TWO PREMISES/
ONE. THAT FEELINGS ARE CONTROLLABLE
TWO. THAT AS A YOUNG, OTHERWISE HEALTHY, PRIVILEGED HUMAN
      I SHOULDN'T FEEL DEPRESSED
THEREFORE   I MUST BE DOING SOMETHING WRONG
        OR   THERE MUST BE SOMETHING WRONG
                                   WITH ME/

 I THINK/
 THIS IS WHAT DRIVES
 MY RELENTLESS SELF ANALYSIS

 IF   I CAN JUST FIGURE OUT WHY

 THEN   I COULD FIX

                           MY SELF

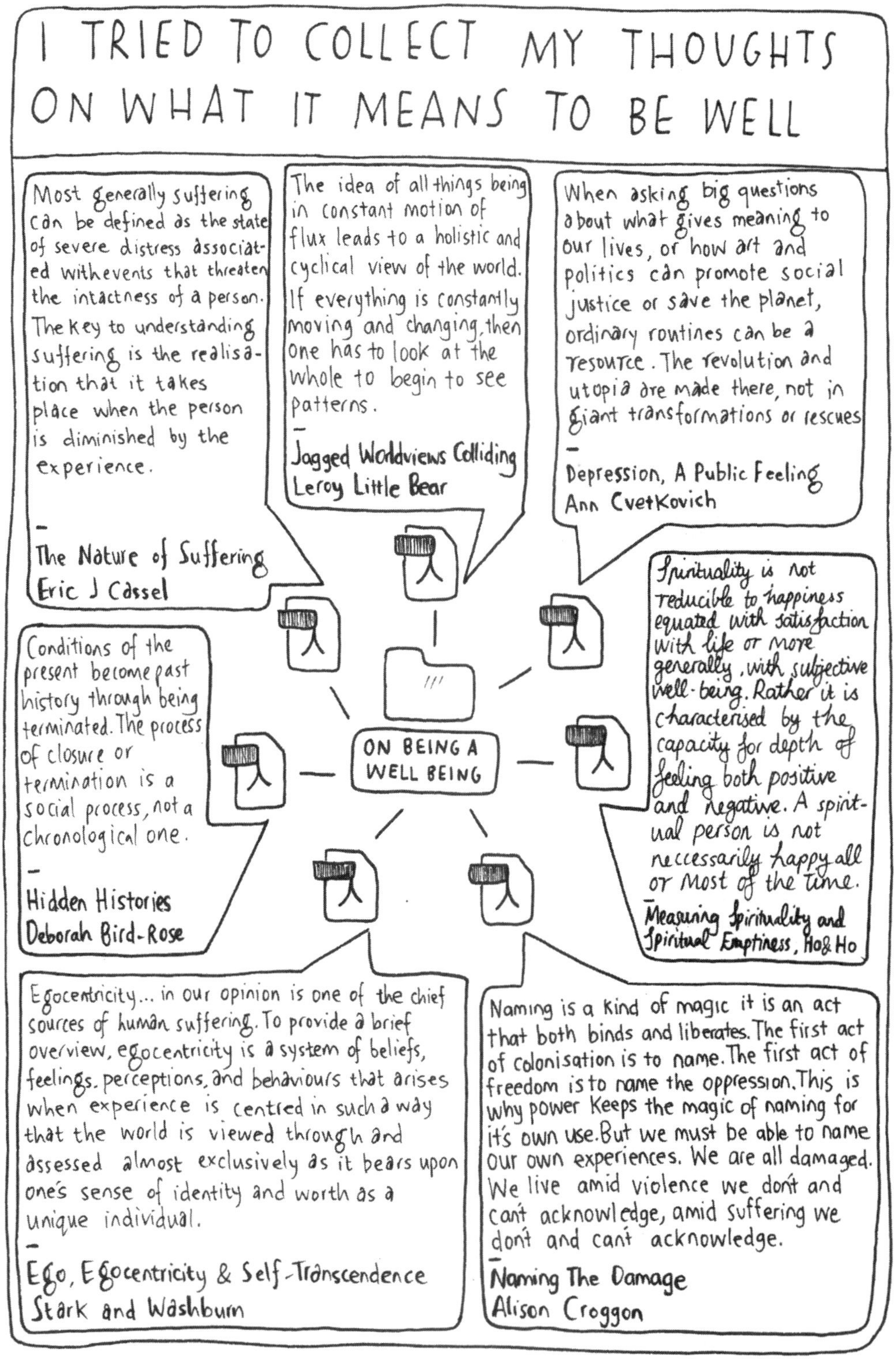

I TRIED TO COLLECT MY THOUGHTS ON WHAT IT MEANS TO BE WELL
Most generally suffering can be defined as the state of severe distress associated with events that threaten the intactness of a person. The key to understanding suffering is the realisation that it takes place when the person is diminished by the experience. — The Nature of Suffering Eric J Cassel
The idea of all things being in constant motion of flux leads to a holistic and cyclical view of the world. If everything is constantly moving and changing, then one has to look at the whole to begin to see patterns. — Jagged Worldviews Colliding Leroy Little Bear
When asking big questions about what gives meaning to our lives, or how art and politics can promote social justice or save the planet, ordinary routines can be a resource. The revolution and utopia are made there, not in giant transformations or rescues — Depression, A Public Feeling Ann Cvetkovich
Conditions of the present become past history through being terminated. The process of closure or termination is a social process, not a chronological one. — Hidden Histories Deborah Bird-Rose
ON BEING A WELL BEING
Spirituality is not reducible to happiness equated with satisfaction with life or more generally, with subjective well-being. Rather it is characterised by the capacity for depth of feeling both positive and negative. A spiritual person is not neccessarily happy all or most of the time. — Measuring Spirituality and Spiritual Emptiness, Ho & Ho
Egocentricity... in our opinion is one of the chief sources of human suffering. To provide a brief overview, egocentricity is a system of beliefs, feelings, perceptions, and behaviours that arises when experience is centred in such a way that the world is viewed through and assessed almost exclusively as it bears upon one's sense of identity and worth as a unique individual. — Ego, Egocentricity & Self-Transcendence Stark and Washburn
Naming is a kind of magic it is an act that both binds and liberates. The first act of colonisation is to name. The first act of freedom is to name the oppression. This is why power keeps the magic of naming for it's own use. But we must be able to name our own experiences. We are all damaged. We live amid violence we don't and can't acknowledge, amid suffering we don't and can't acknowledge. — Naming The Damage Alison Croggon

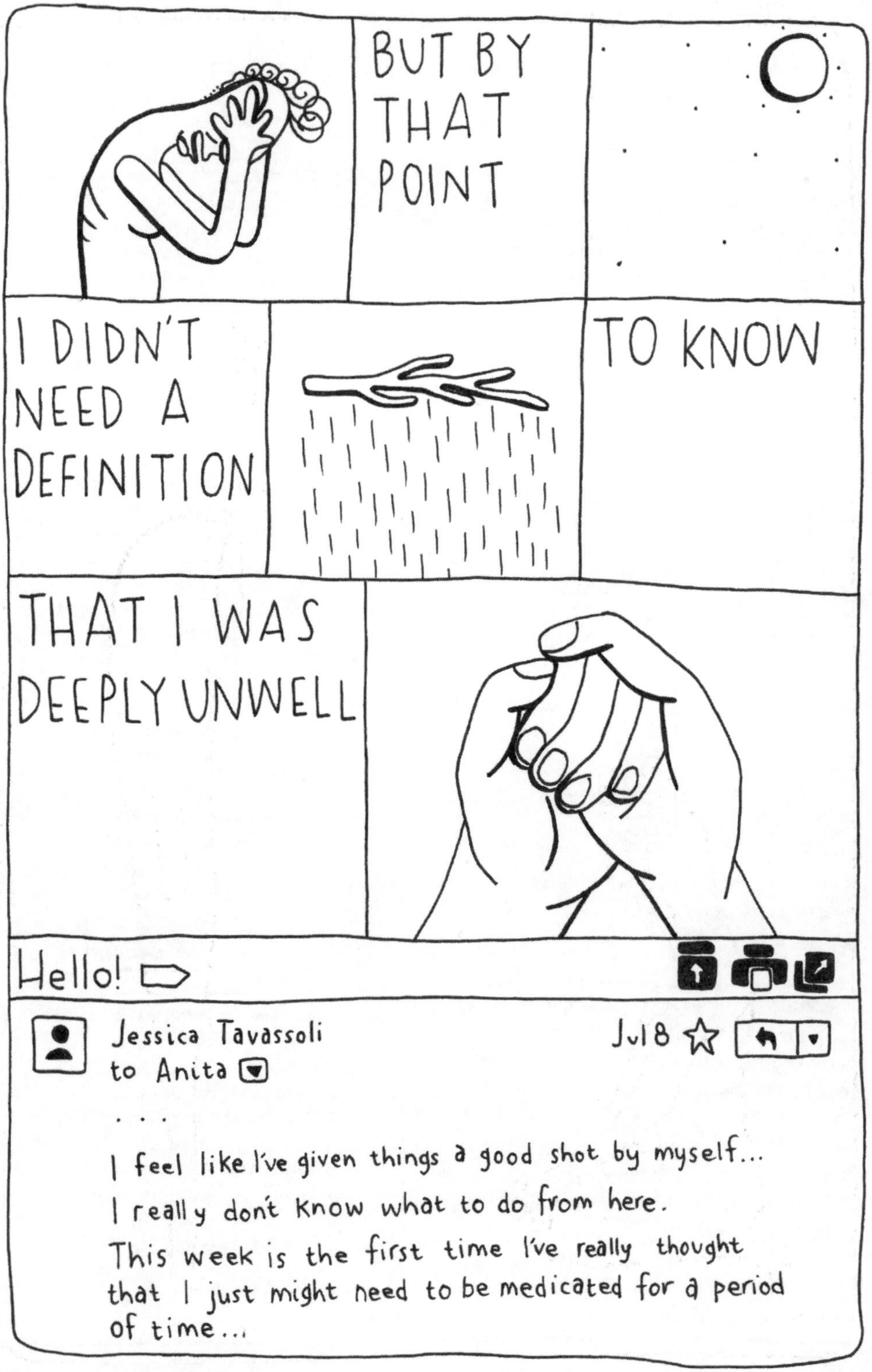
BUT BY THAT POINT
I DIDN'T NEED A DEFINITION
TO KNOW
THAT I WAS DEEPLY UNWELL
Hello!
Jessica Tavassoli
to Anita
Jul 8
. . .
I feel like I've given things a good shot by myself...
I really don't know what to do from here.
This week is the first time I've really thought that I just might need to be medicated for a period of time...

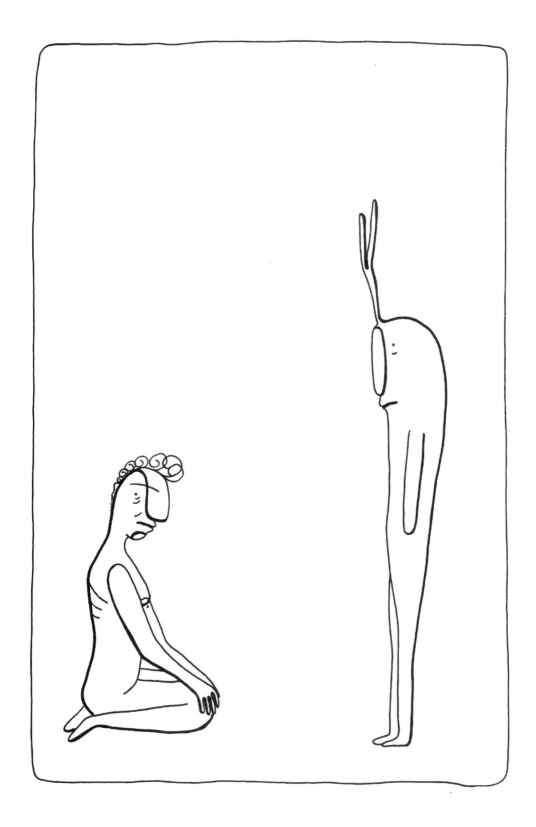

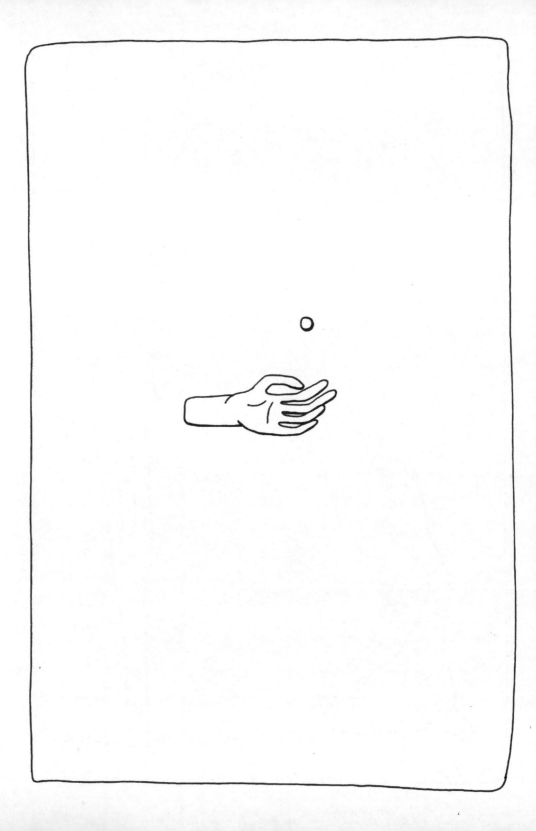

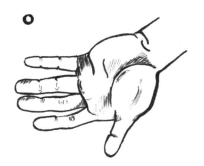

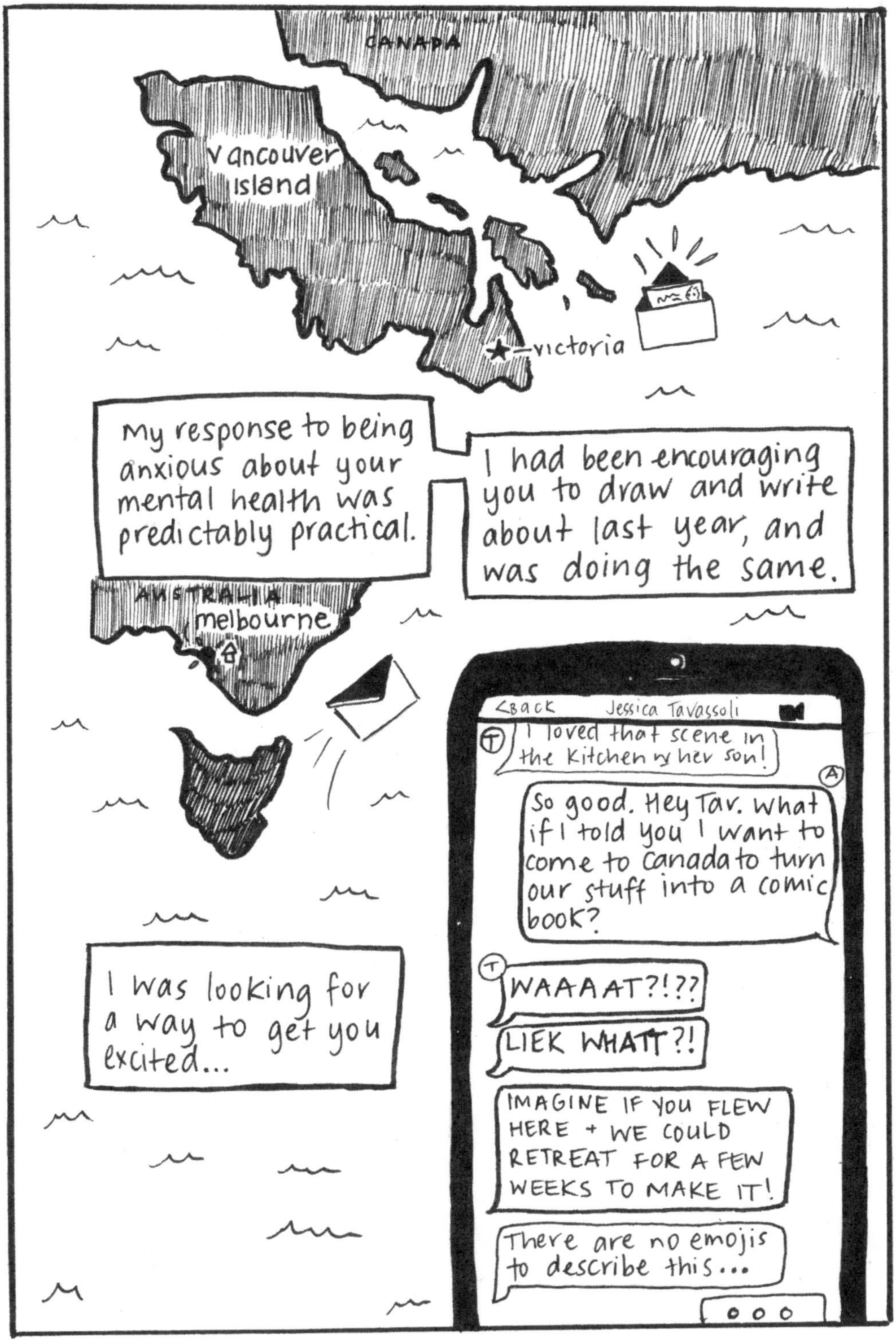

CANADA
Vancouver Island
Victoria
My response to being anxious about your mental health was predictably practical.
I had been encouraging you to draw and write about last year, and was doing the same.
AUSTRALIA
Melbourne
<Back
Jessica Tavassoli
T
I loved that scene in the kitchen w/ her son!
A
So good. Hey Tav. What if I told you I want to come to Canada to turn our stuff into a comic book?
I was looking for a way to get you excited...
T
WAAAAT?!??
LIEK WHATT?!
IMAGINE IF YOU FLEW HERE + WE COULD RETREAT FOR A FEW WEEKS TO MAKE IT!
There are no emojis to describe this...

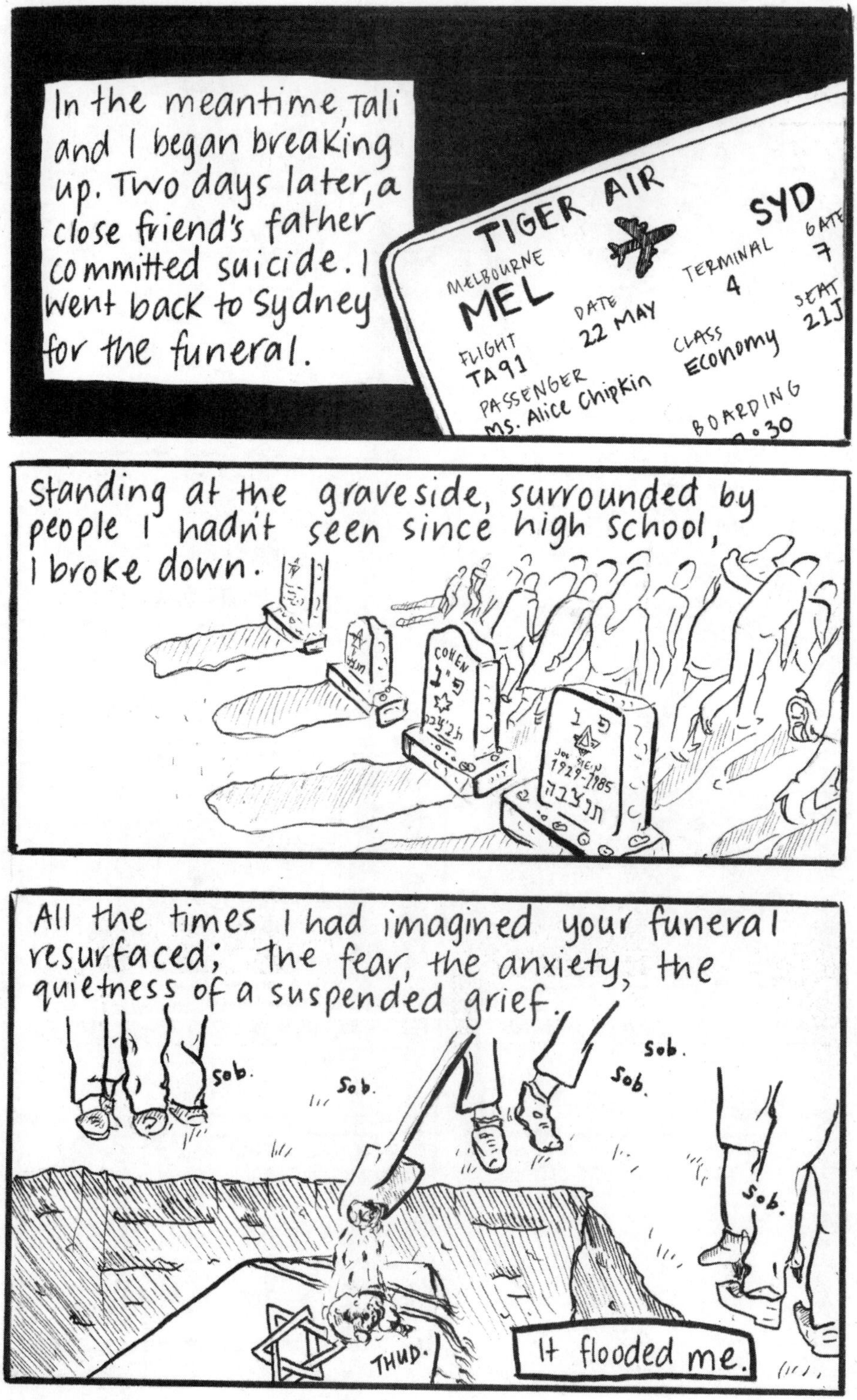
In the meantime, Tali and I began breaking up. Two days later, a close friend's father committed suicide. I went back to Sydney for the funeral.
TIGER AIR
MELBOURNE
MEL
SYD
TERMINAL
4
GATE
7
DATE
22 MAY
SEAT
21J
FLIGHT
TA91
CLASS
Economy
PASSENGER
Ms. Alice Chipkin
BOARDING
Standing at the graveside, surrounded by people I hadn't seen since high school, I broke down.
COHEN
1929-1985
All the times I had imagined your funeral resurfaced; the fear, the anxiety, the quietness of a suspended grief.
sob.
Sob.
Sob.
Sob.
Sob.
THUD.
It flooded me.

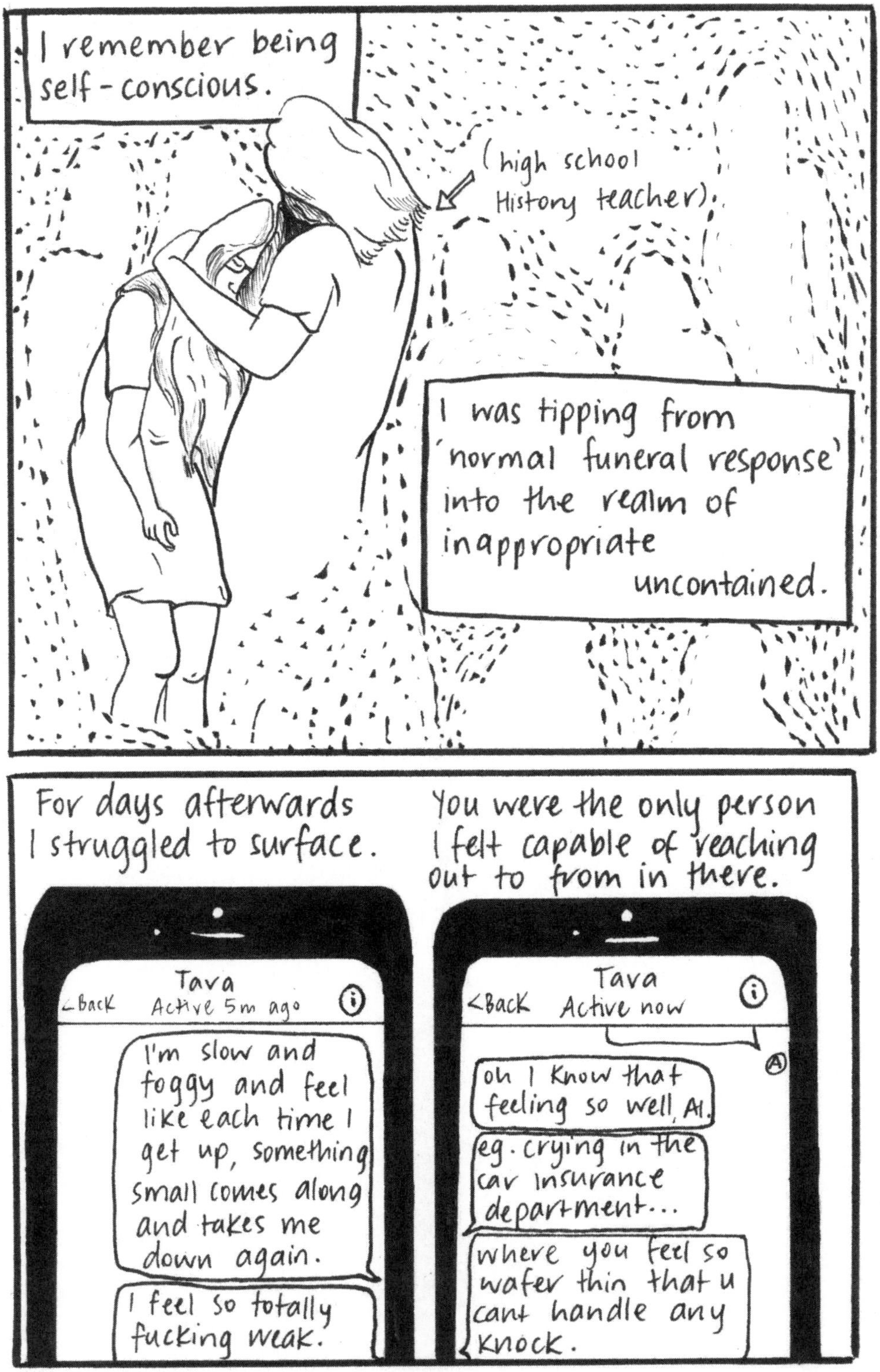
I remember being self-conscious.
(high school History teacher)
I was tipping from 'normal funeral response' into the realm of inappropriate uncontained.
For days afterwards I struggled to surface.
<Back
Tava
Active 5m ago
I'm slow and foggy and feel like each time I get up, something small comes along and takes me down again.
I feel so totally fucking weak.
You were the only person I felt capable of reaching out to from in there.
<Back
Tava
Active now
oh I know that feeling so well, Al.
eg. crying in the car insurance department...
where you feel so wafer thin that u cant handle any knock.

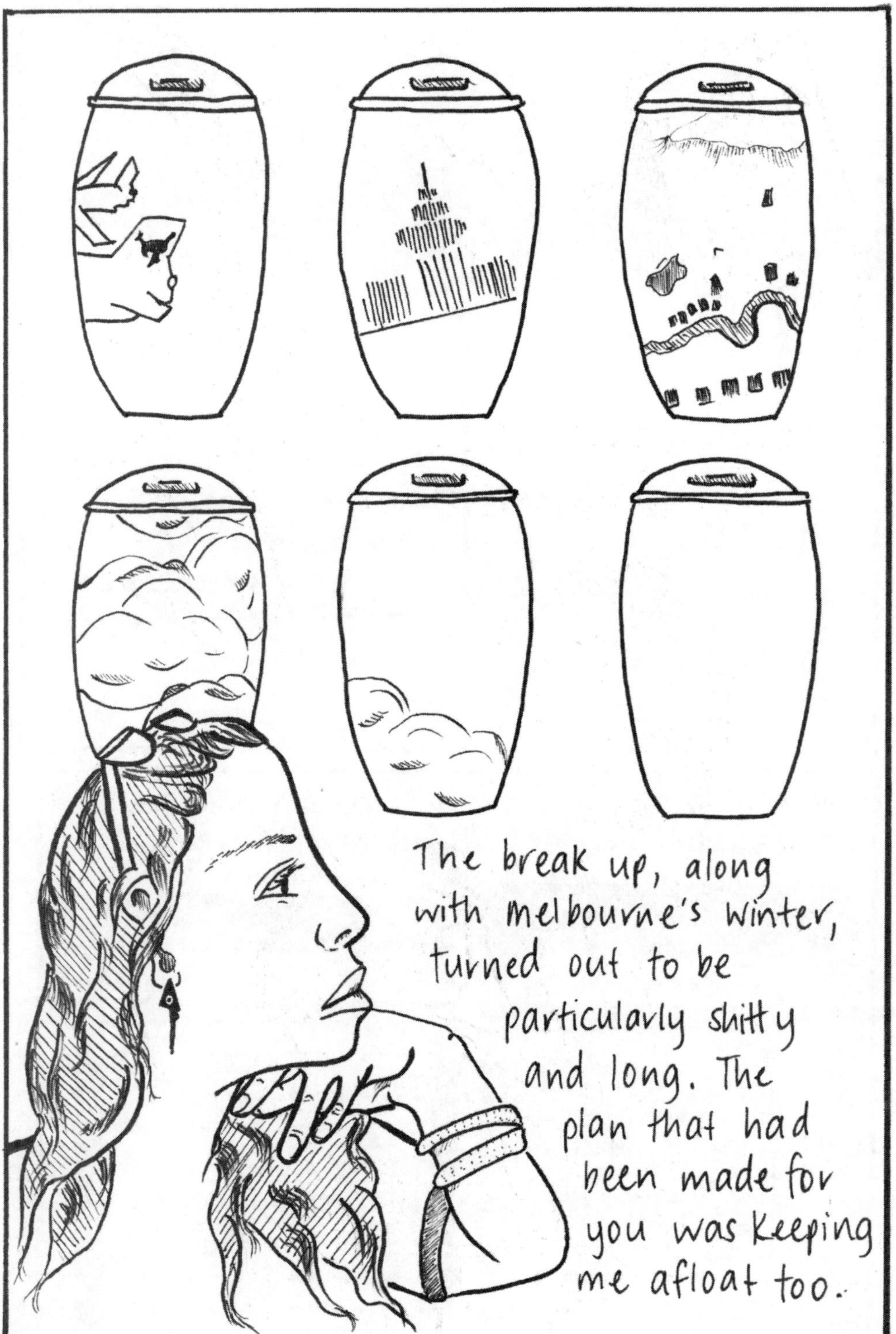
The break up, along with melbourne's winter, turned out to be particularly shitty and long. The plan that had been made for you was keeping me afloat too.

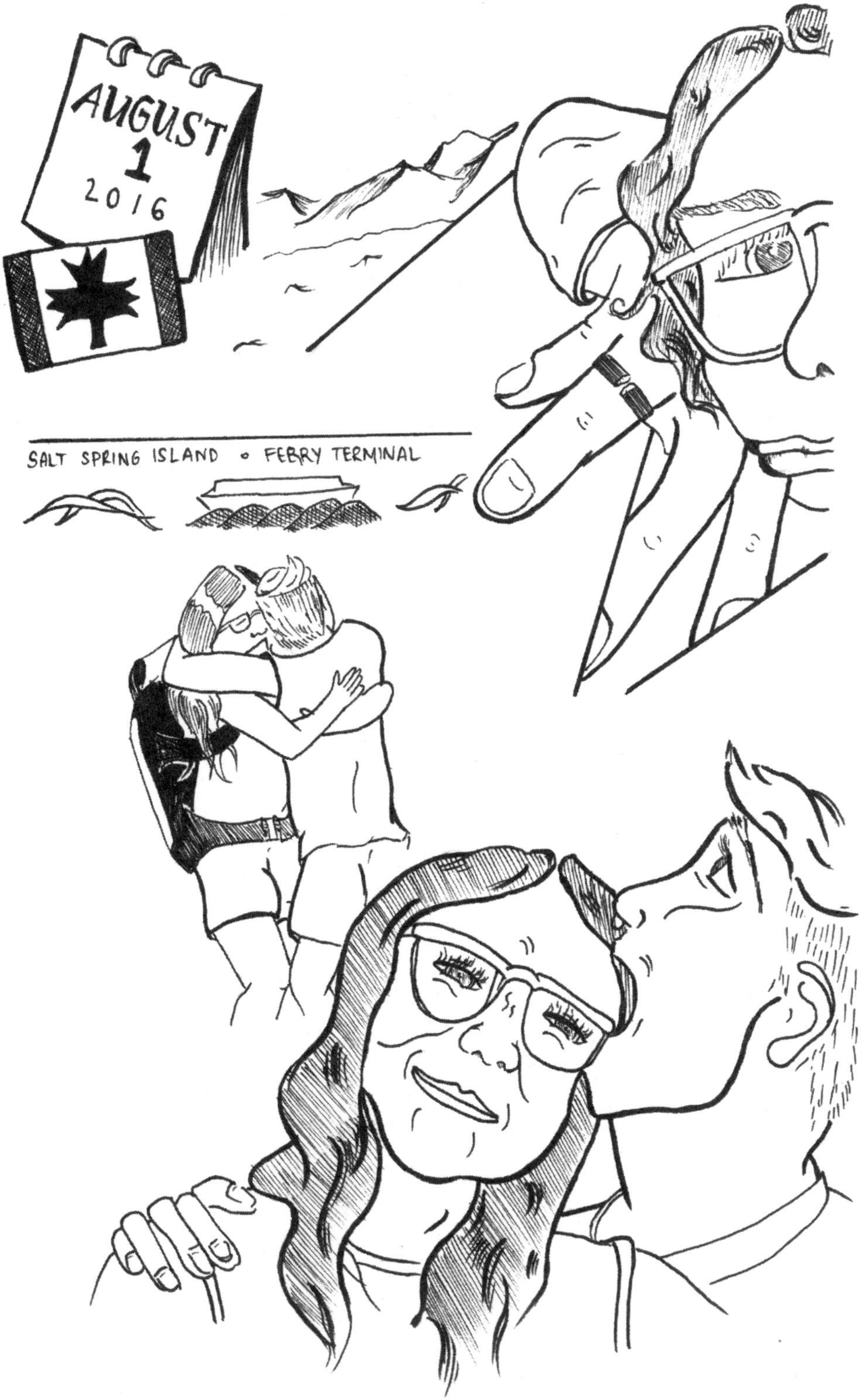
AUGUST
1
2016
SALT SPRING ISLAND ∘ FERRY TERMINAL

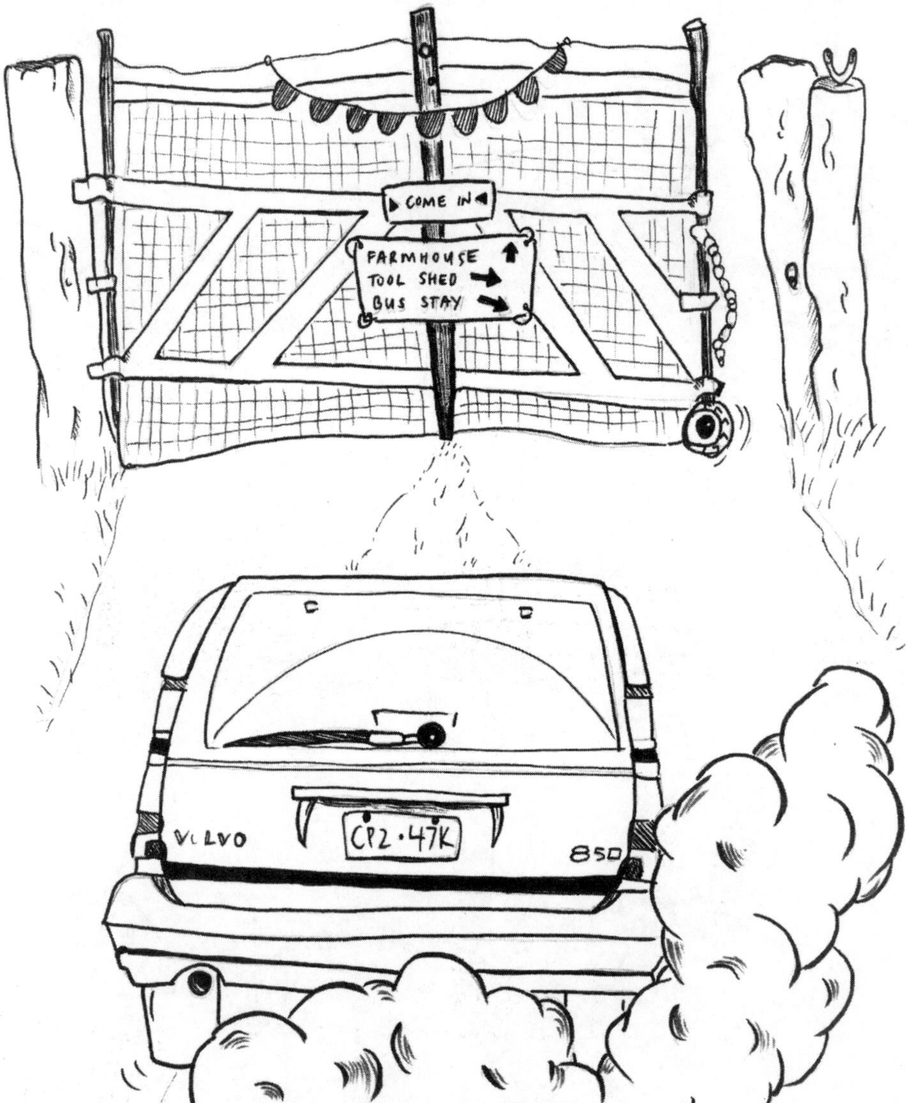
COME IN
FARMHOUSE
TOOL SHED
BUS STAY
CP2·47K
850

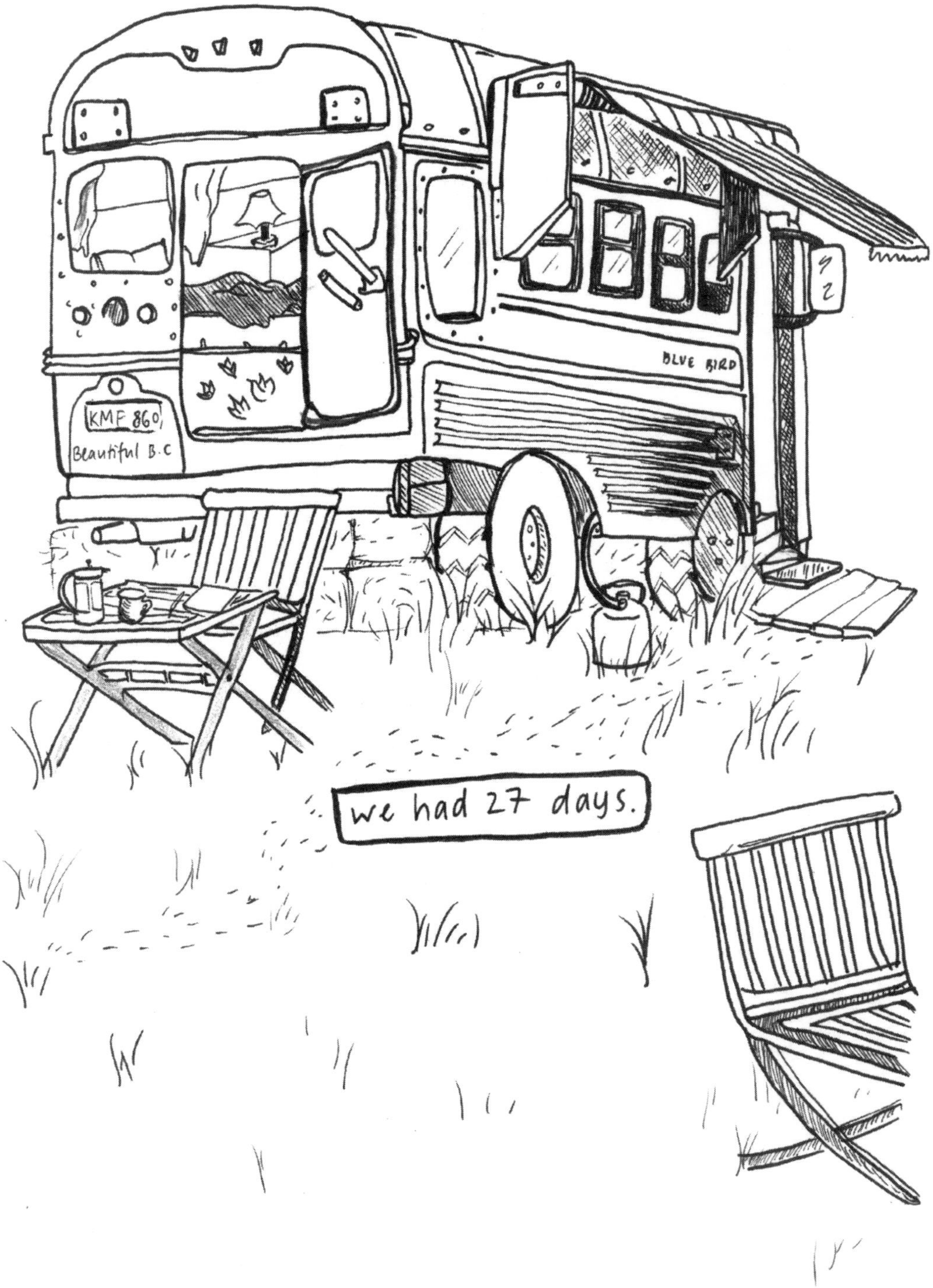
KMF 860
Beautiful B.C
BLVE BIRD
we had 27 days.

BREATHINGS

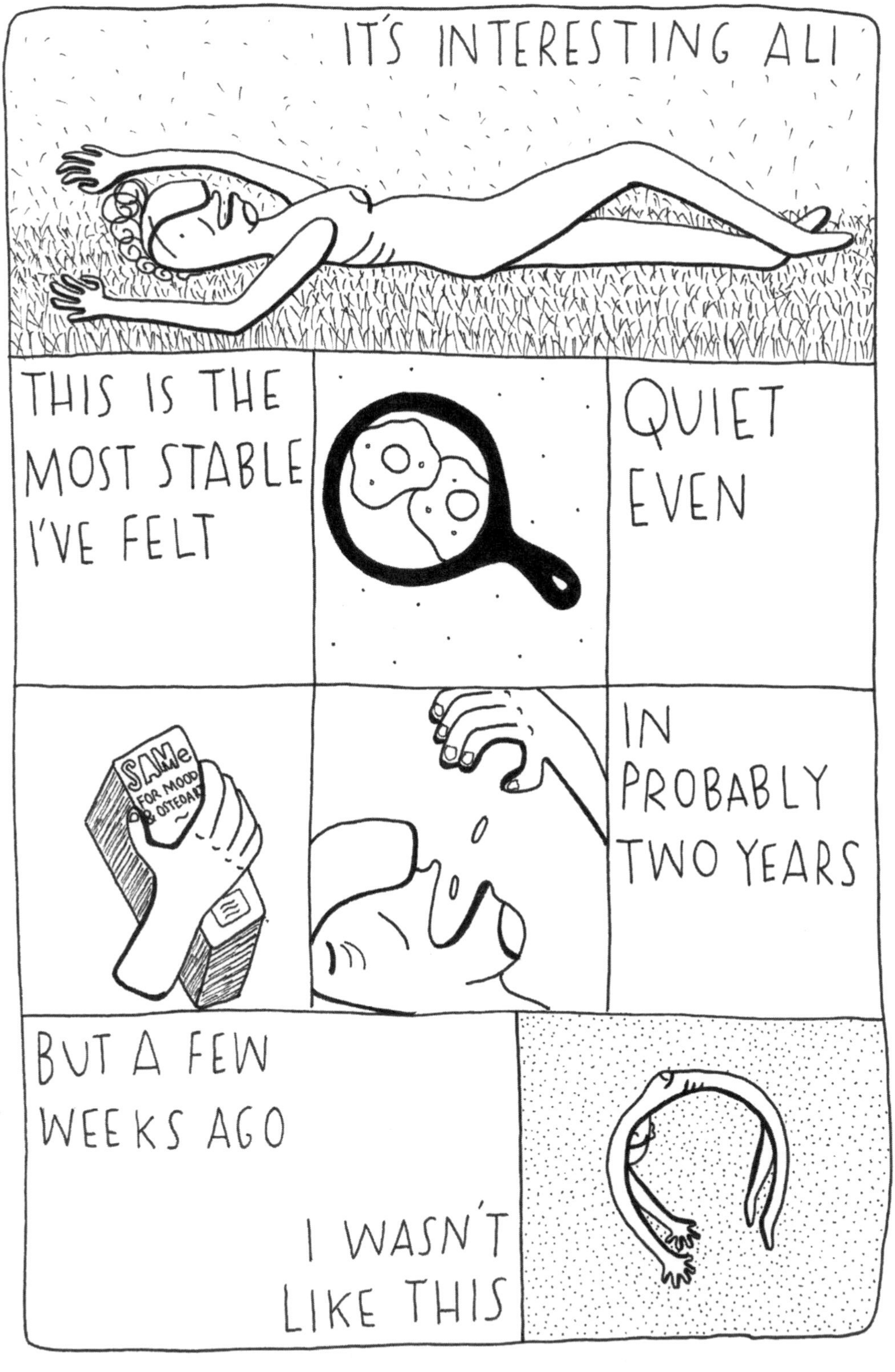
IT'S INTERESTING ALI
THIS IS THE MOST STABLE I'VE FELT
SAMe
FOR MOOD & OSTEOAR
QUIET EVEN
IN PROBABLY TWO YEARS
BUT A FEW WEEKS AGO
I WASN'T LIKE THIS

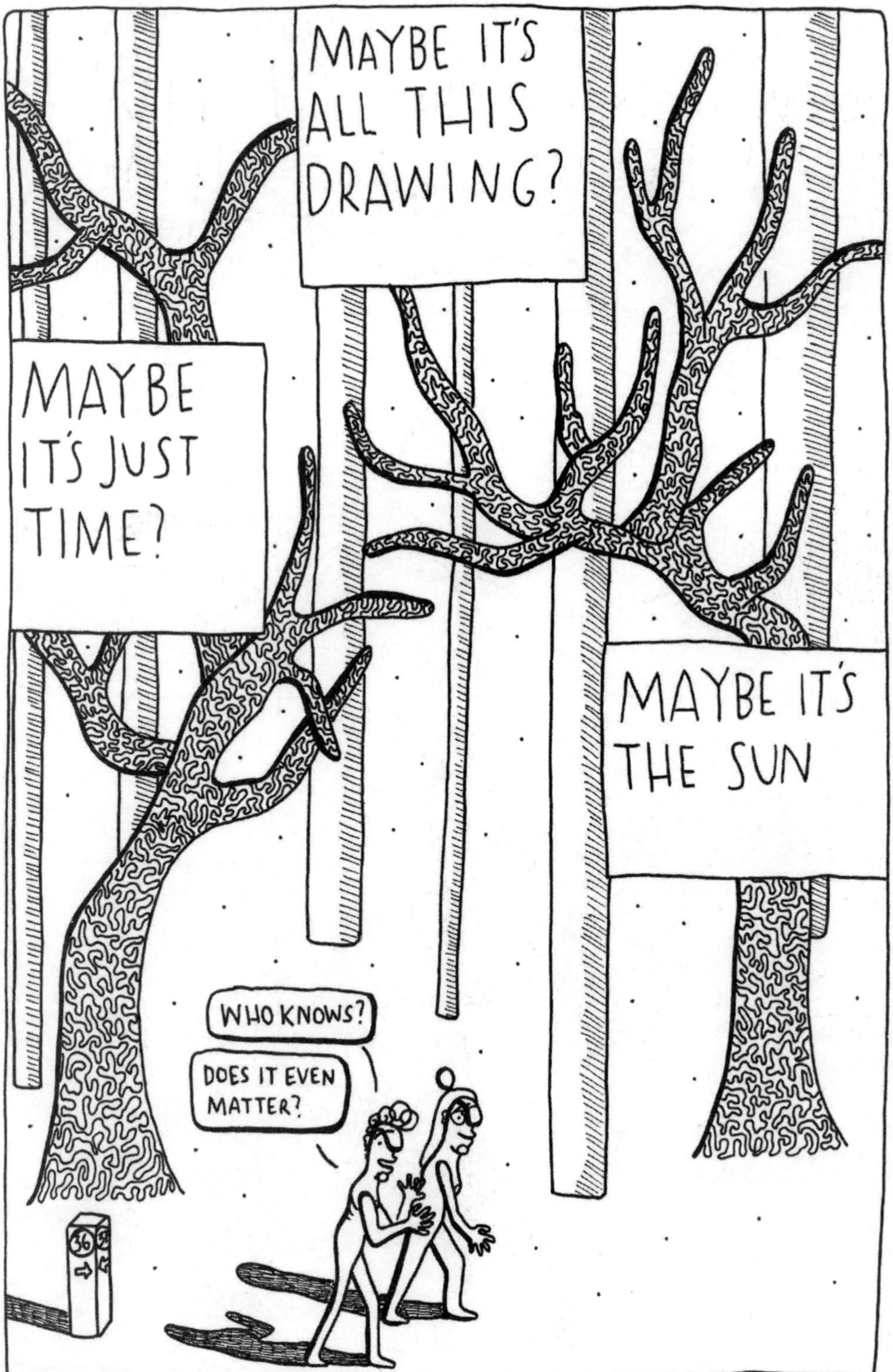
MAYBE IT'S ALL THIS DRAWING?
MAYBE IT'S JUST TIME?
MAYBE IT'S THE SUN
WHO KNOWS?
DOES IT EVEN MATTER?
36

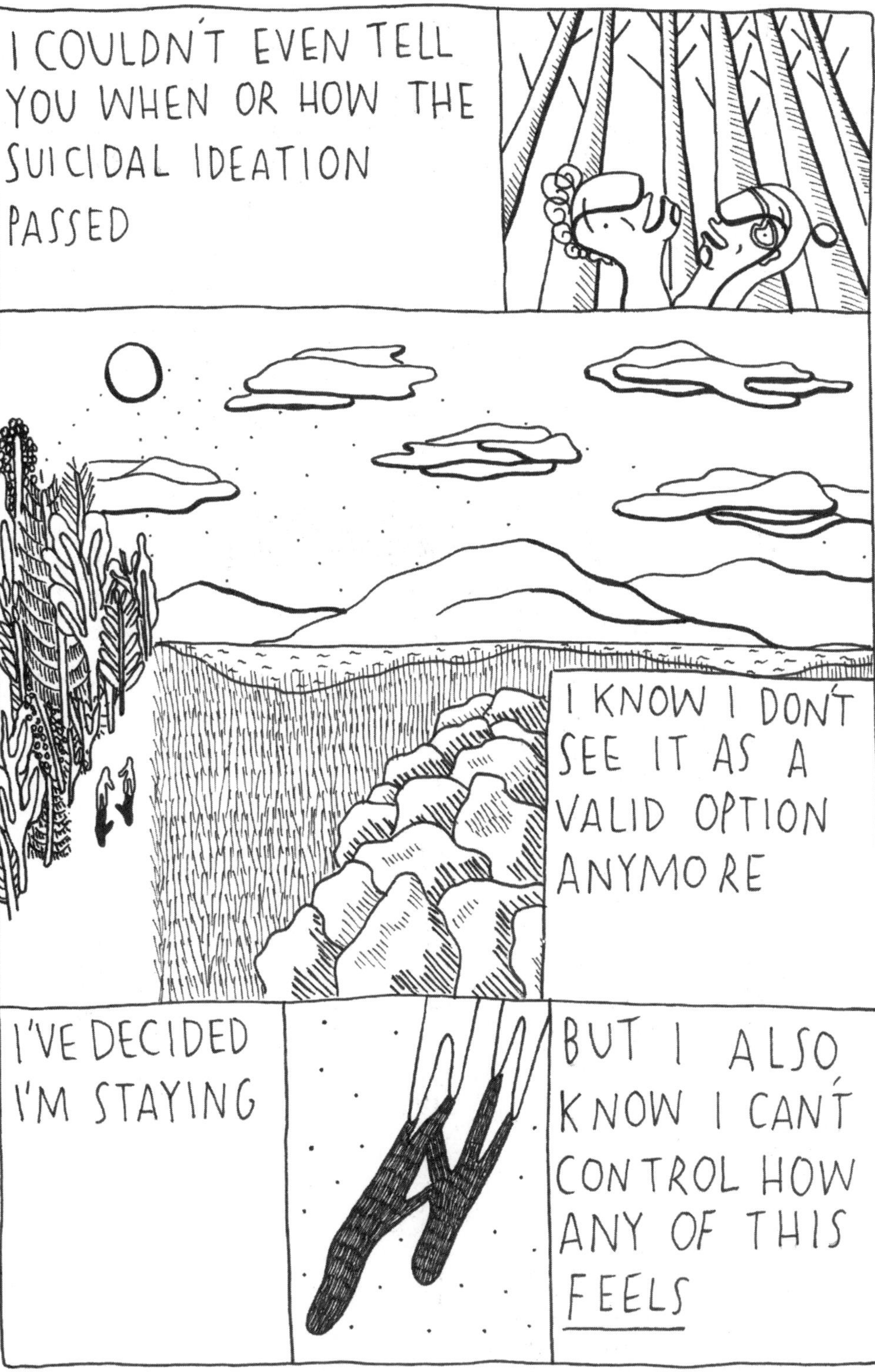
I COULDN'T EVEN TELL YOU WHEN OR HOW THE SUICIDAL IDEATION PASSED
I KNOW I DON'T SEE IT AS A VALID OPTION ANYMORE
I'VE DECIDED I'M STAYING
BUT I ALSO KNOW I CAN'T CONTROL HOW ANY OF THIS FEELS

I'M GRATEFUL

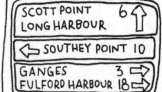

SCOTT POINT 6 ↑
LONG HARBOUR
← SOUTHEY POINT 10
GANGES 3 →
FULFORD HARBOUR 18 →

THAT AT LEAST FOR NOW

SOME OF THE INTENSITY HAS SUBSIDED

IT'S A RELIEF

BUT I DON'T SEE IT AS MUCH MORE THAN THAT

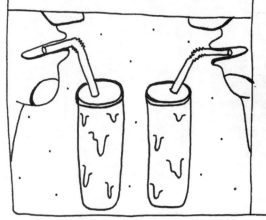

5:31 PM
< Home   Kate >
Active Now

I think those feelings might always be there

You can live with them and still choose life / think your life is worth something

Feeling suicidal is not proof of anything aside from the fact that you feel it

Like it's not a statement of how unwell you are

I think its what we do with it that will matter

Type a message...
Aa 📷 😀 GIF ••• 👍

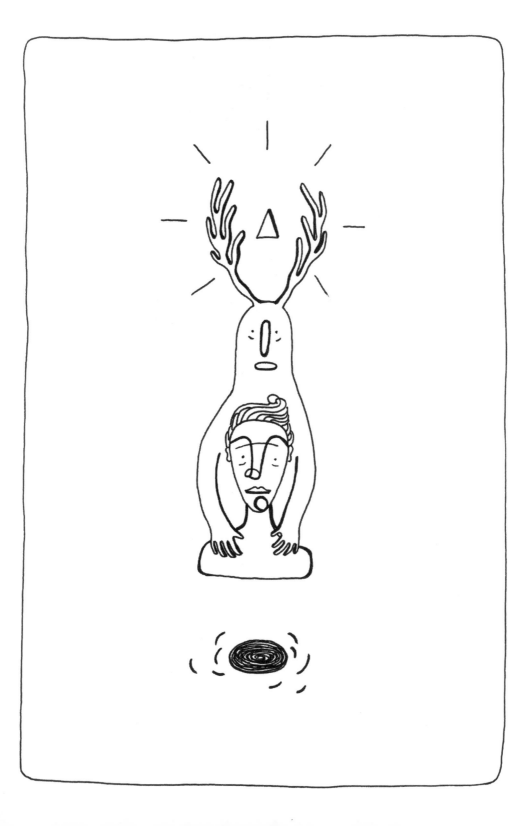

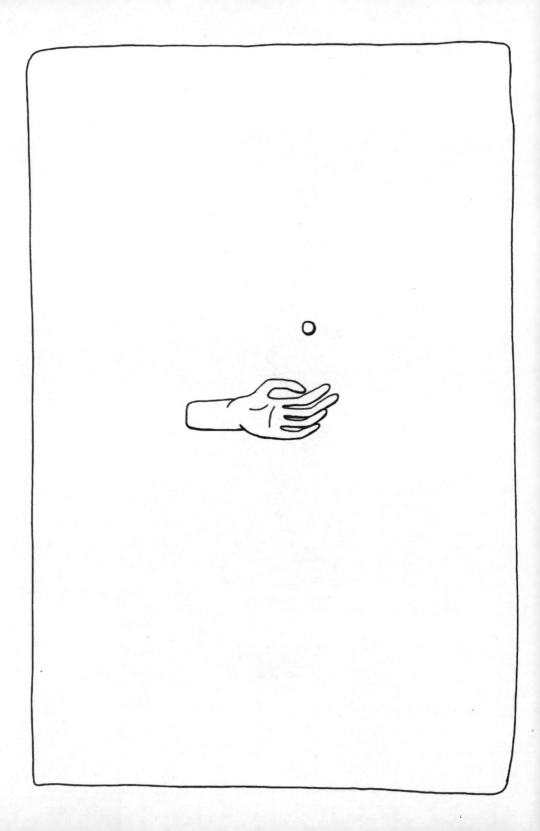

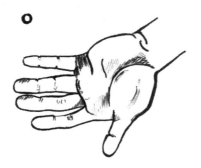

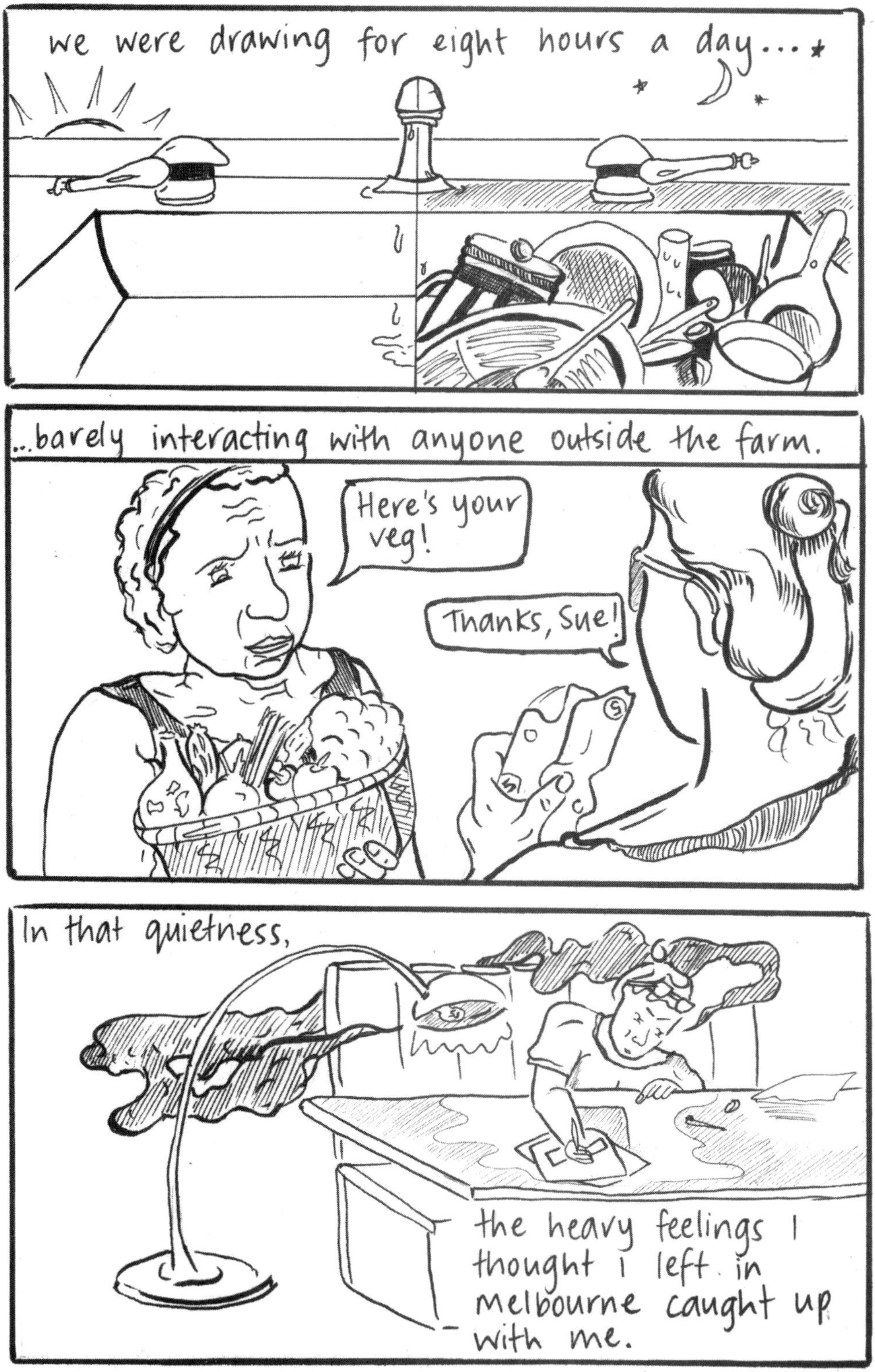
we were drawing for eight hours a day...
...barely interacting with anyone outside the farm.
Here's your veg!
Thanks, Sue!
In that quietness,
the heavy feelings I thought I left in Melbourne caught up with me.

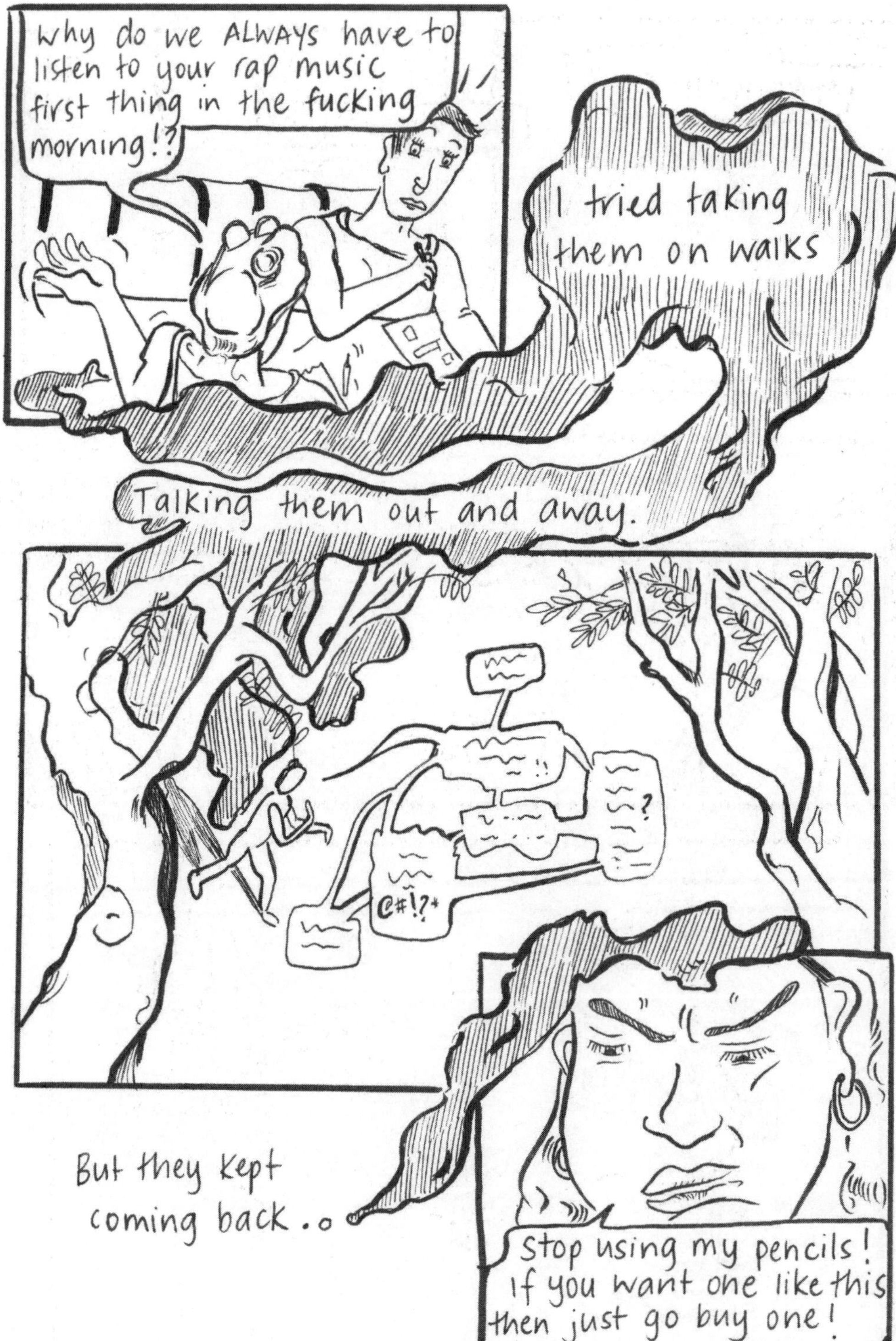
why do we ALWAYS have to listen to your rap music first thing in the fucking morning!?
I tried taking them on walks
Talking them out and away.
@#!?*
But they kept coming back..
Stop using my pencils! If you want one like this then just go buy one!

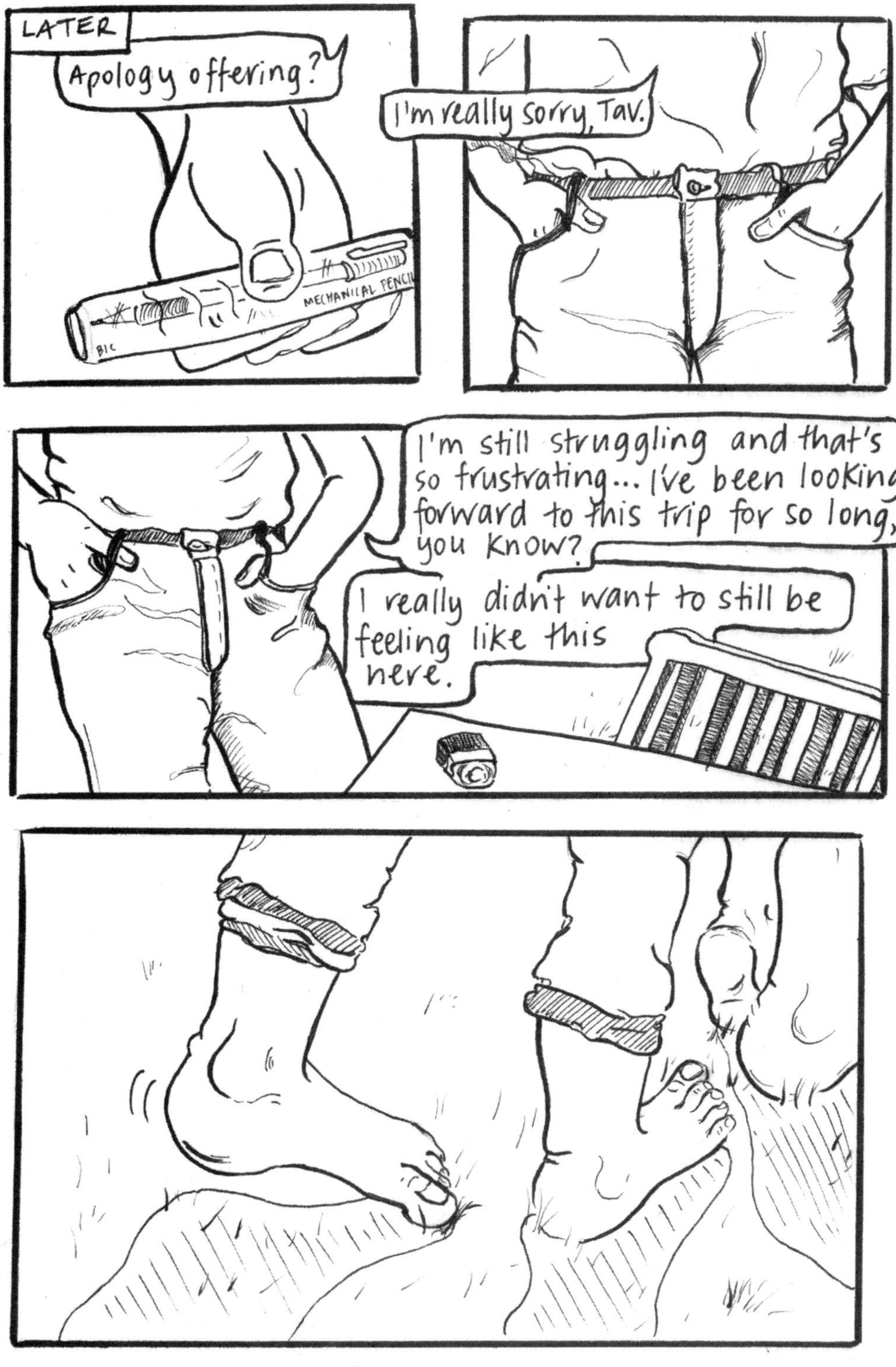
LATER
Apology offering?
MECHANICAL PENCIL
BIC
I'm really sorry, Tav.
I'm still struggling and that's so frustrating... I've been looking forward to this trip for so long, you know?
I really didn't want to still be feeling like this here.

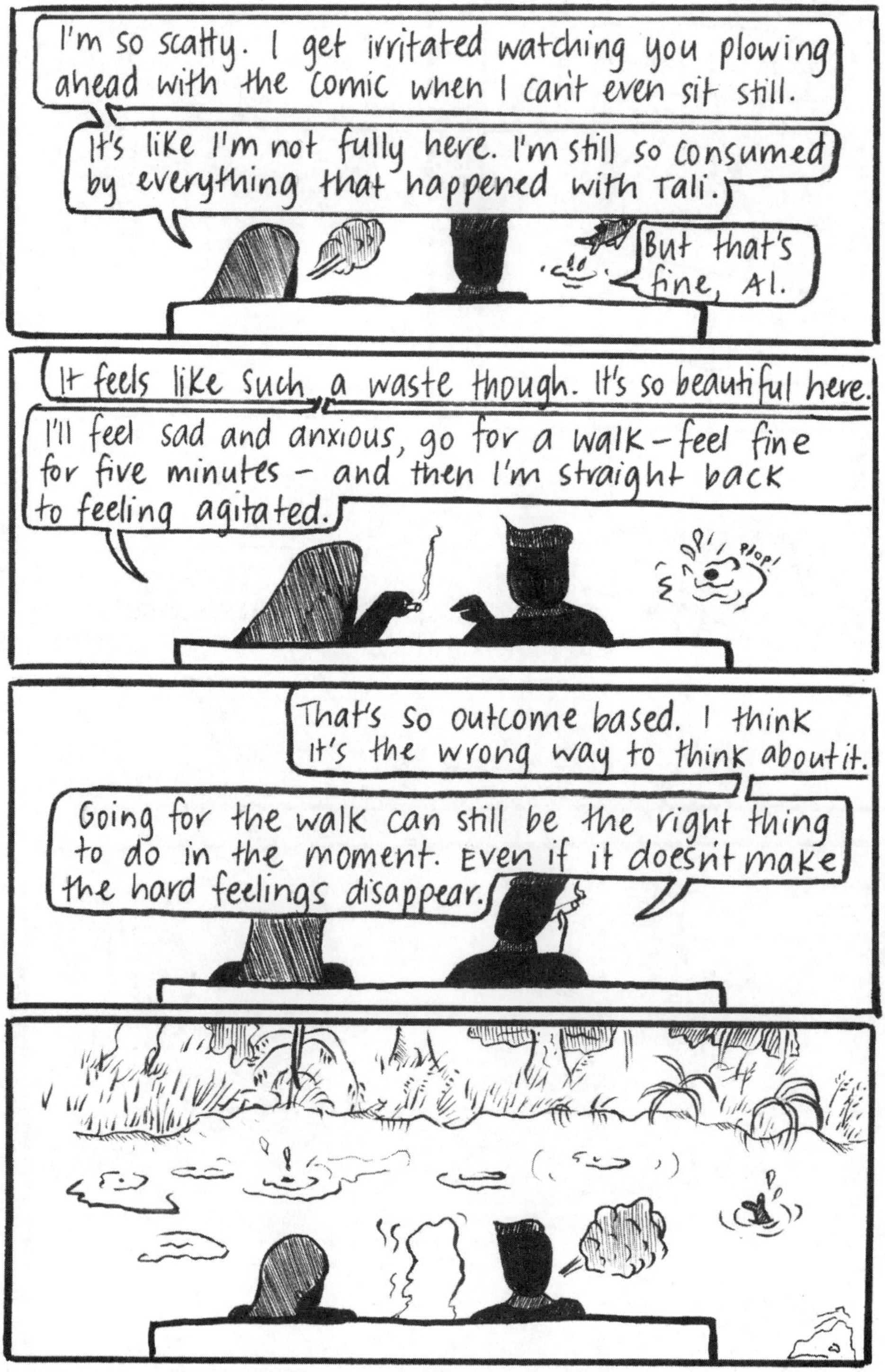
I'm so scatty. I get irritated watching you plowing ahead with the comic when I can't even sit still.
It's like I'm not fully here. I'm still so consumed by everything that happened with Tali.
But that's fine, Al.
It feels like such a waste though. It's so beautiful here.
I'll feel sad and anxious, go for a walk - feel fine for five minutes - and then I'm straight back to feeling agitated.
Plop!
That's so outcome based. I think it's the wrong way to think about it.
Going for the walk can still be the right thing to do in the moment. Even if it doesn't make the hard feelings disappear.

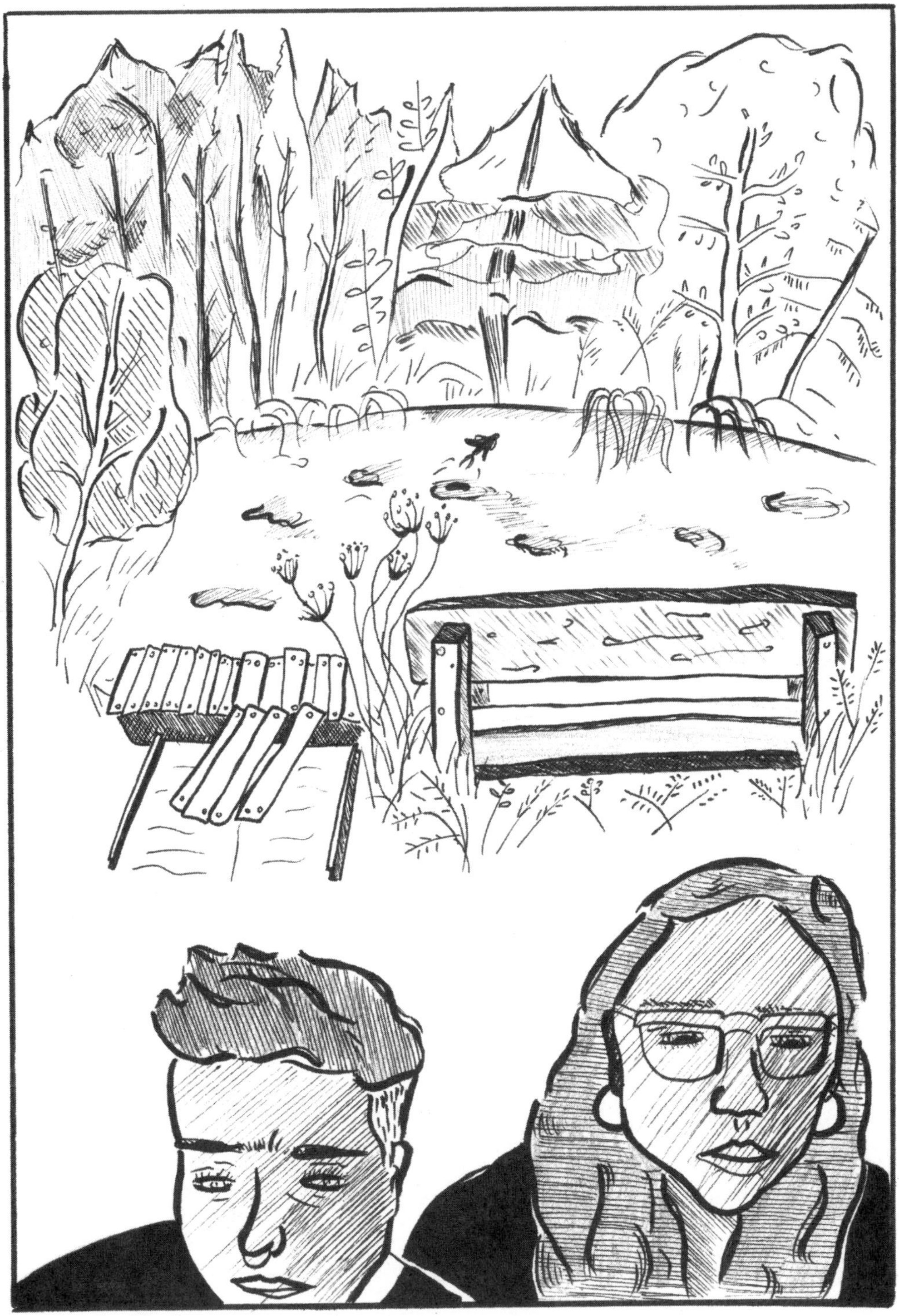

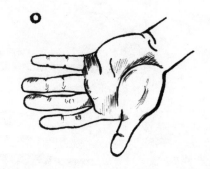

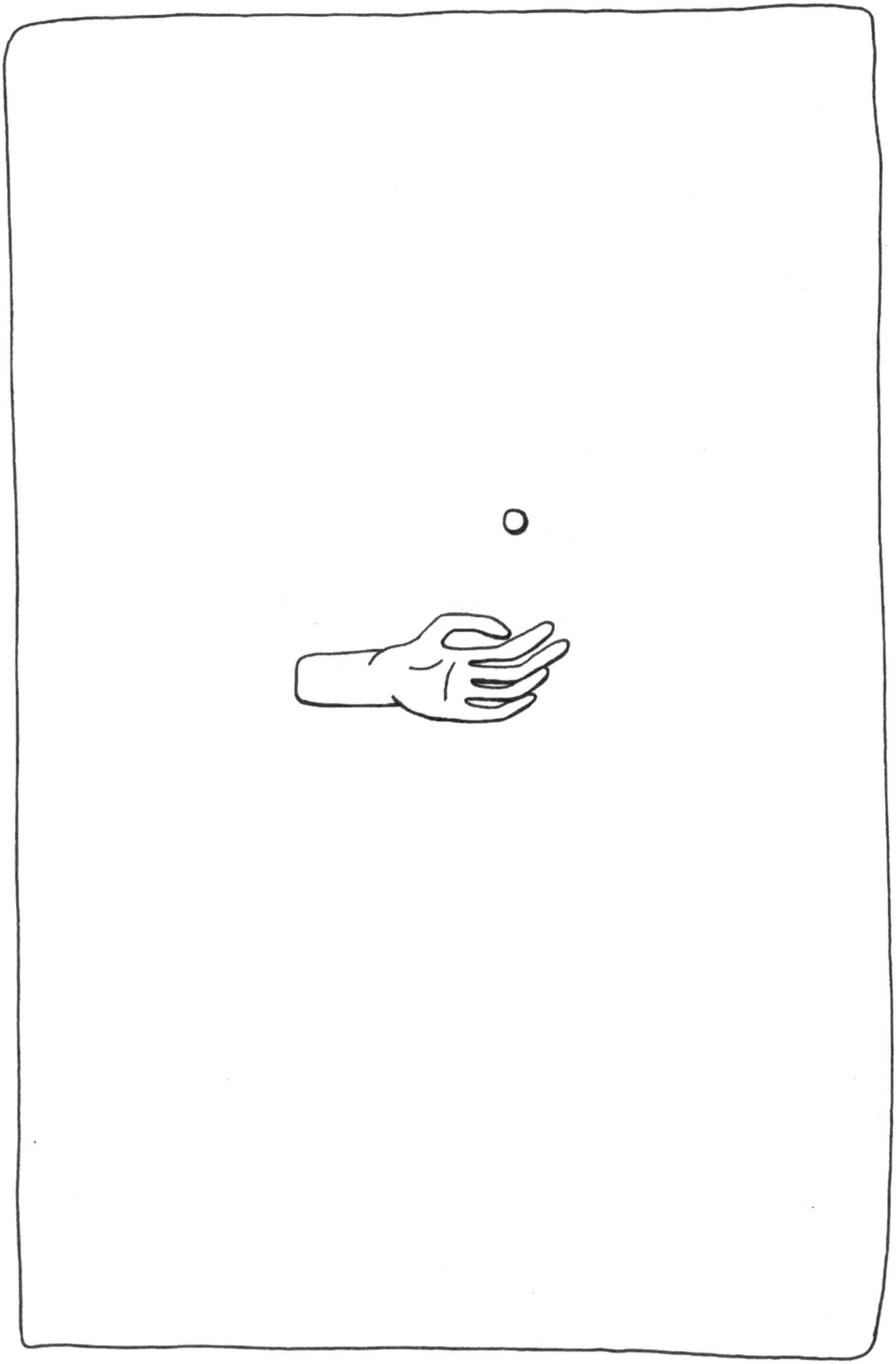

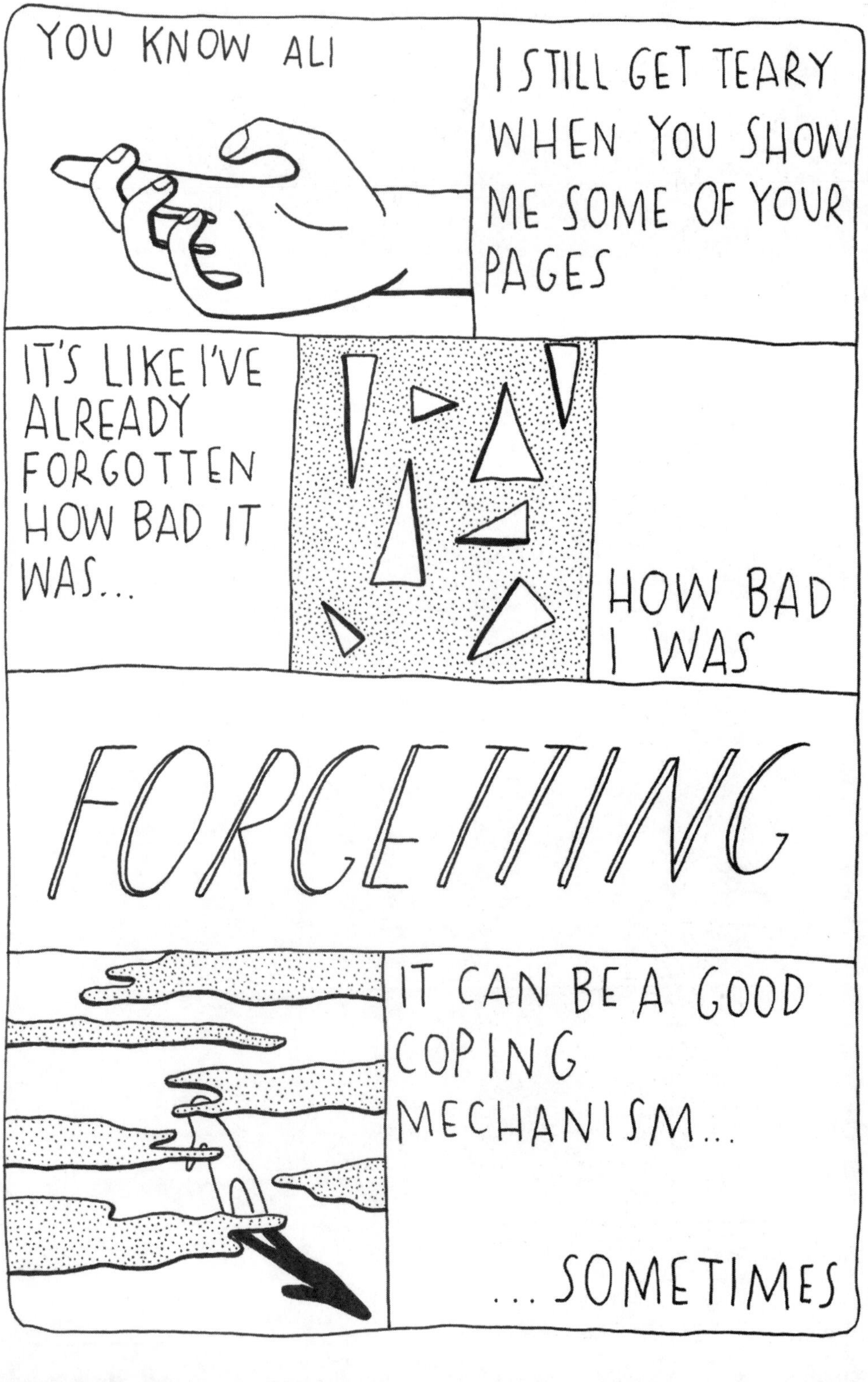
YOU KNOW ALI
I STILL GET TEARY WHEN YOU SHOW ME SOME OF YOUR PAGES
IT'S LIKE I'VE ALREADY FORGOTTEN HOW BAD IT WAS...
HOW BAD I WAS
FORGETTING
IT CAN BE A GOOD COPING MECHANISM...
...SOMETIMES

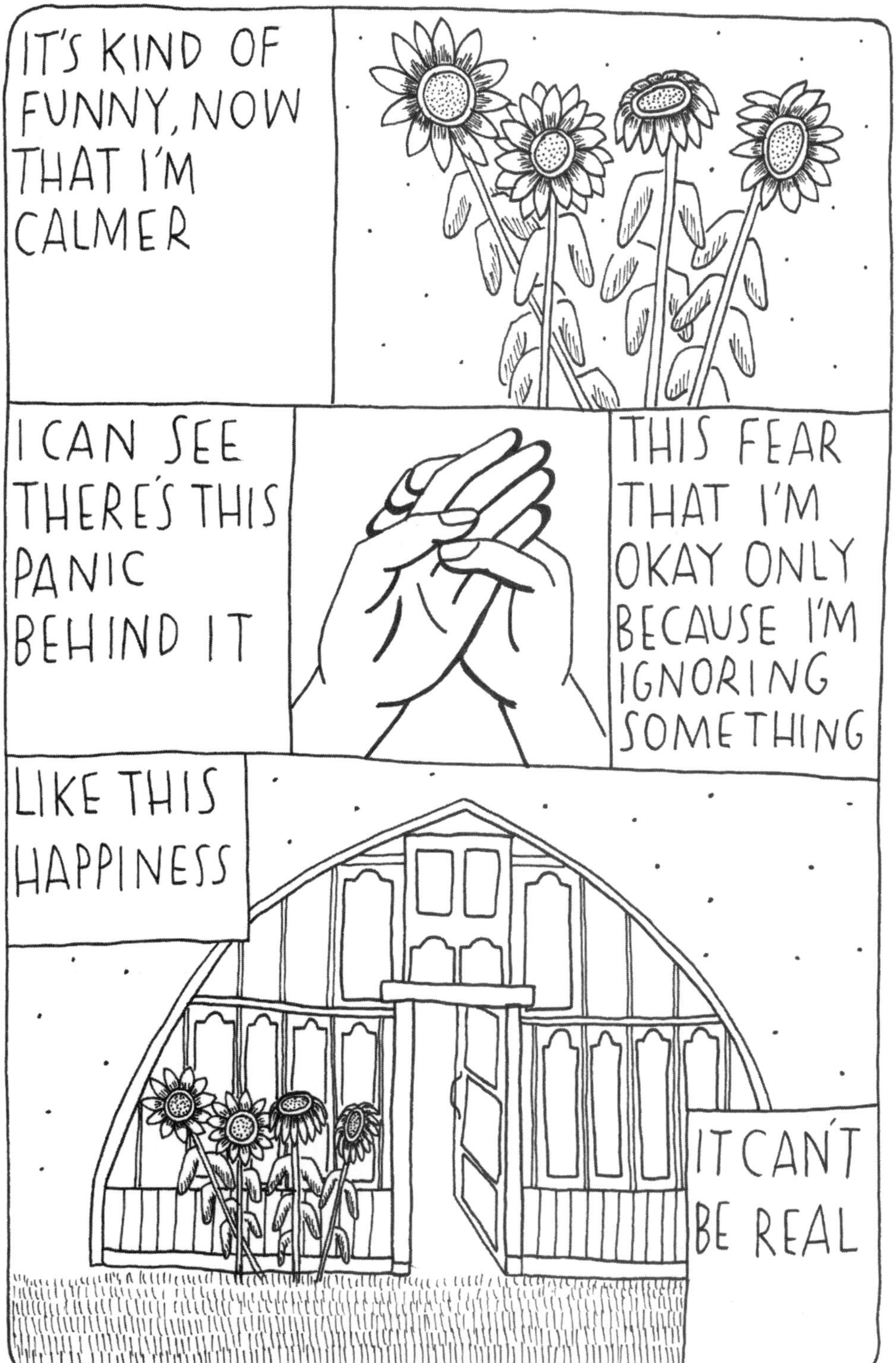
IT'S KIND OF FUNNY, NOW THAT I'M CALMER
I CAN SEE THERE'S THIS PANIC BEHIND IT
THIS FEAR THAT I'M OKAY ONLY BECAUSE I'M IGNORING SOMETHING
LIKE THIS HAPPINESS
IT CAN'T BE REAL

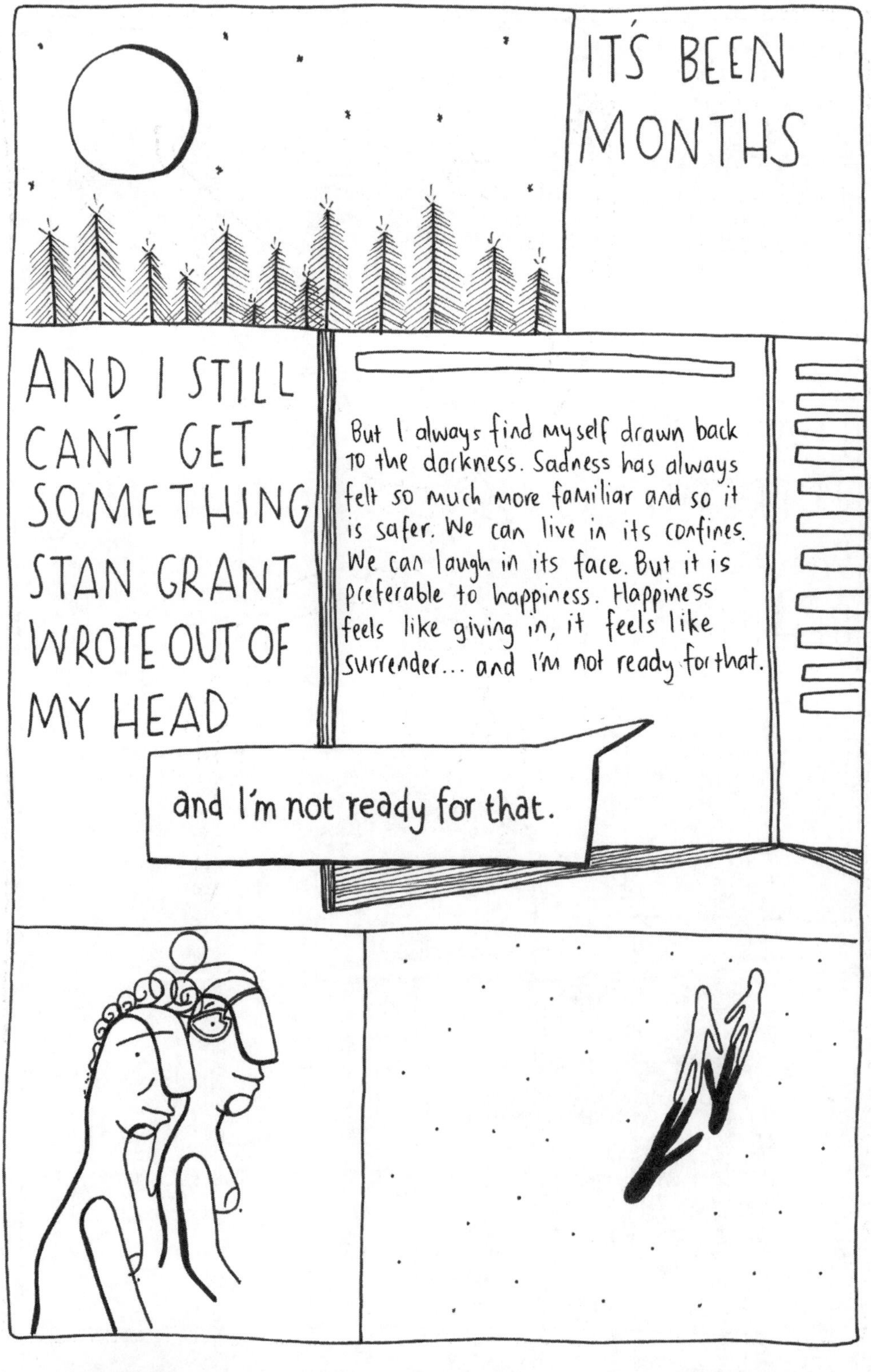
ITS BEEN MONTHS
AND I STILL CAN'T GET SOMETHING STAN GRANT WROTE OUT OF MY HEAD
But I always find myself drawn back to the darkness. Sadness has always felt so much more familiar and so it is safer. We can live in its confines. We can laugh in its face. But it is preferable to happiness. Happiness feels like giving in, it feels like surrender... and I'm not ready for that.
and I'm not ready for that.

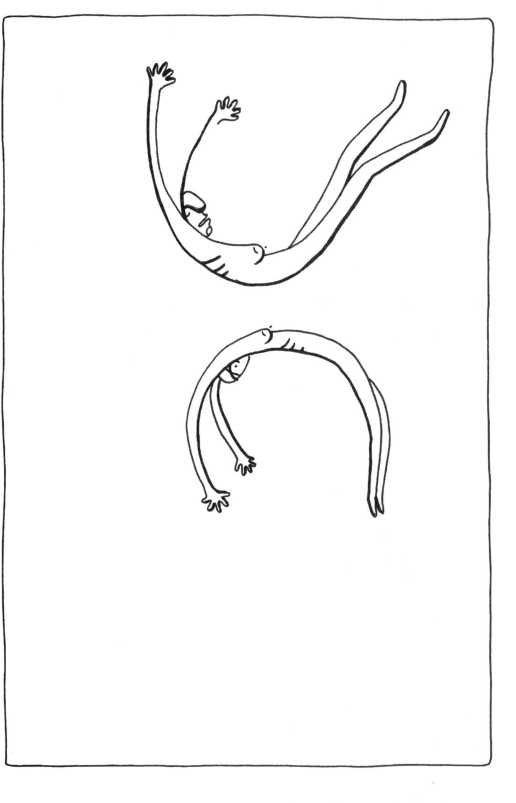

CLOSINGS

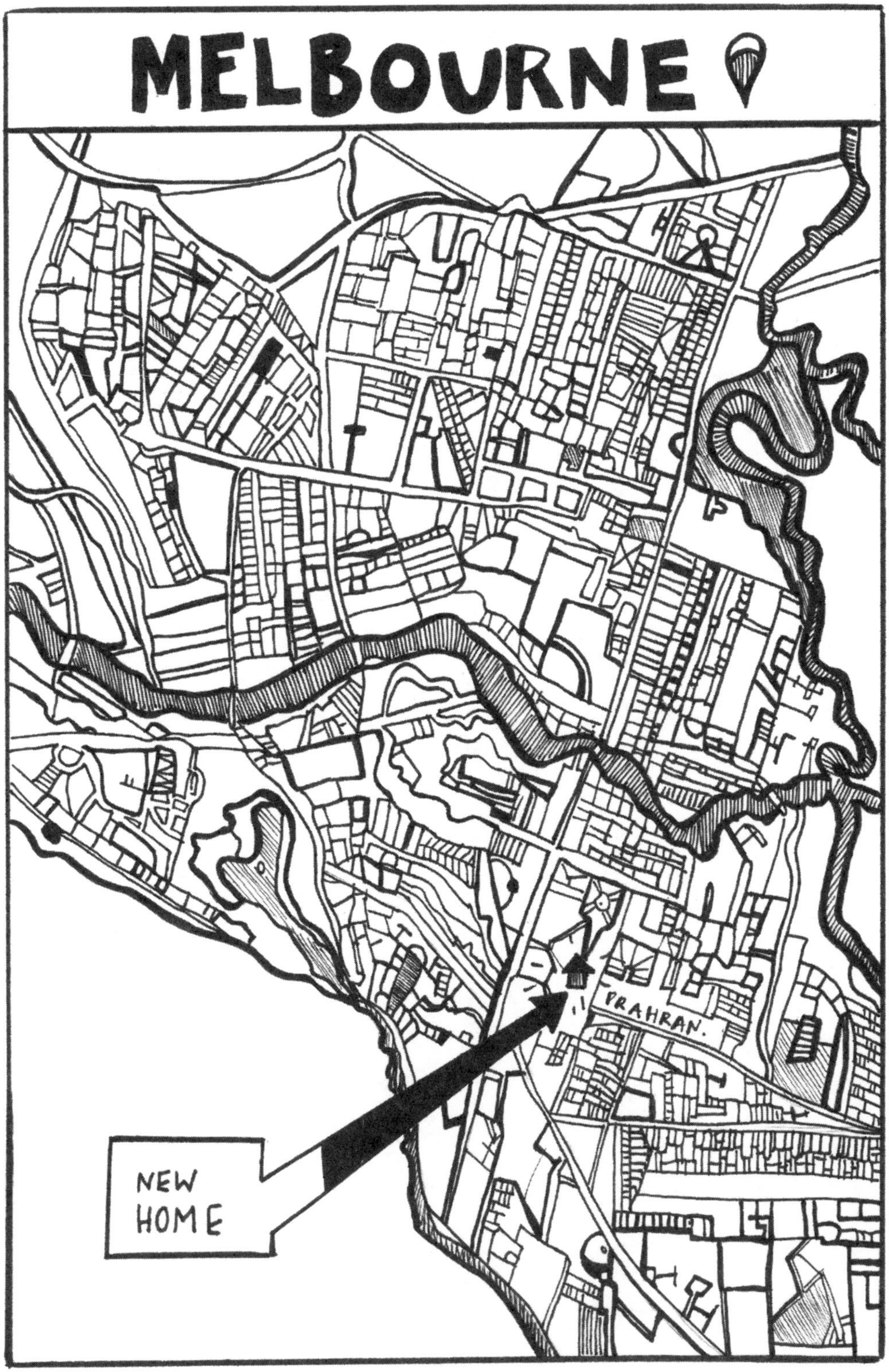
MELBOURNE
PRAHRAN.
NEW HOME

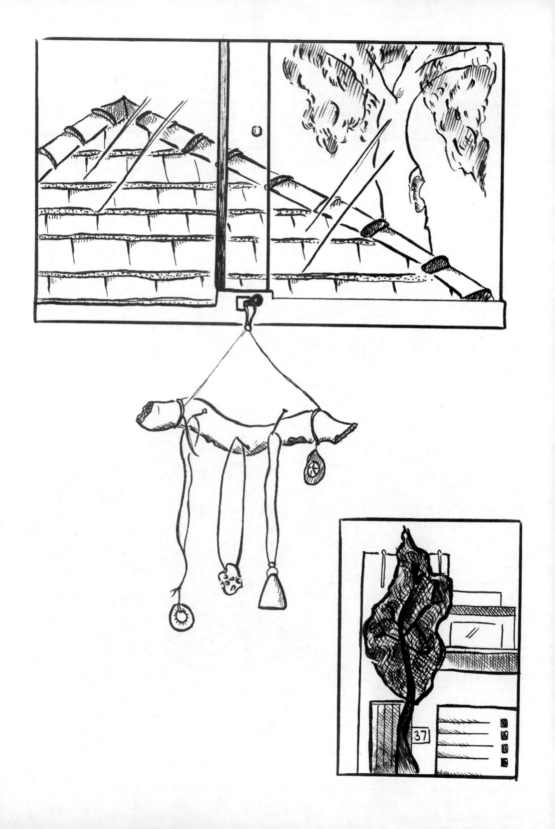

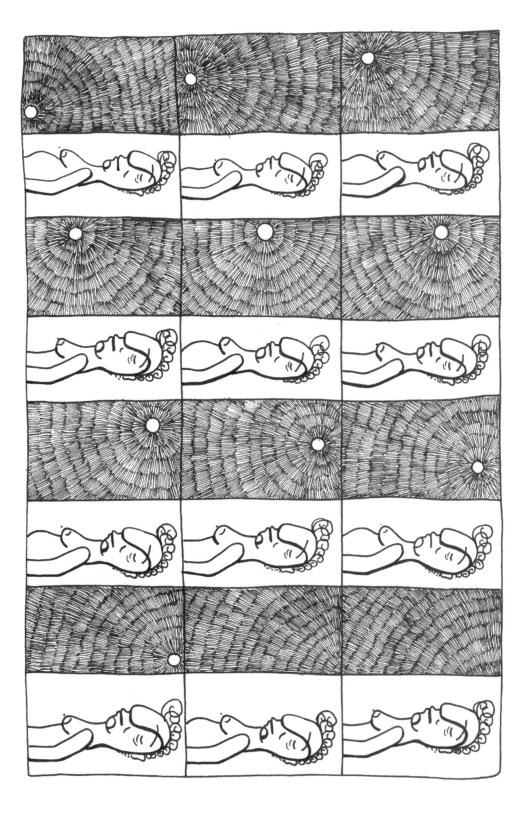

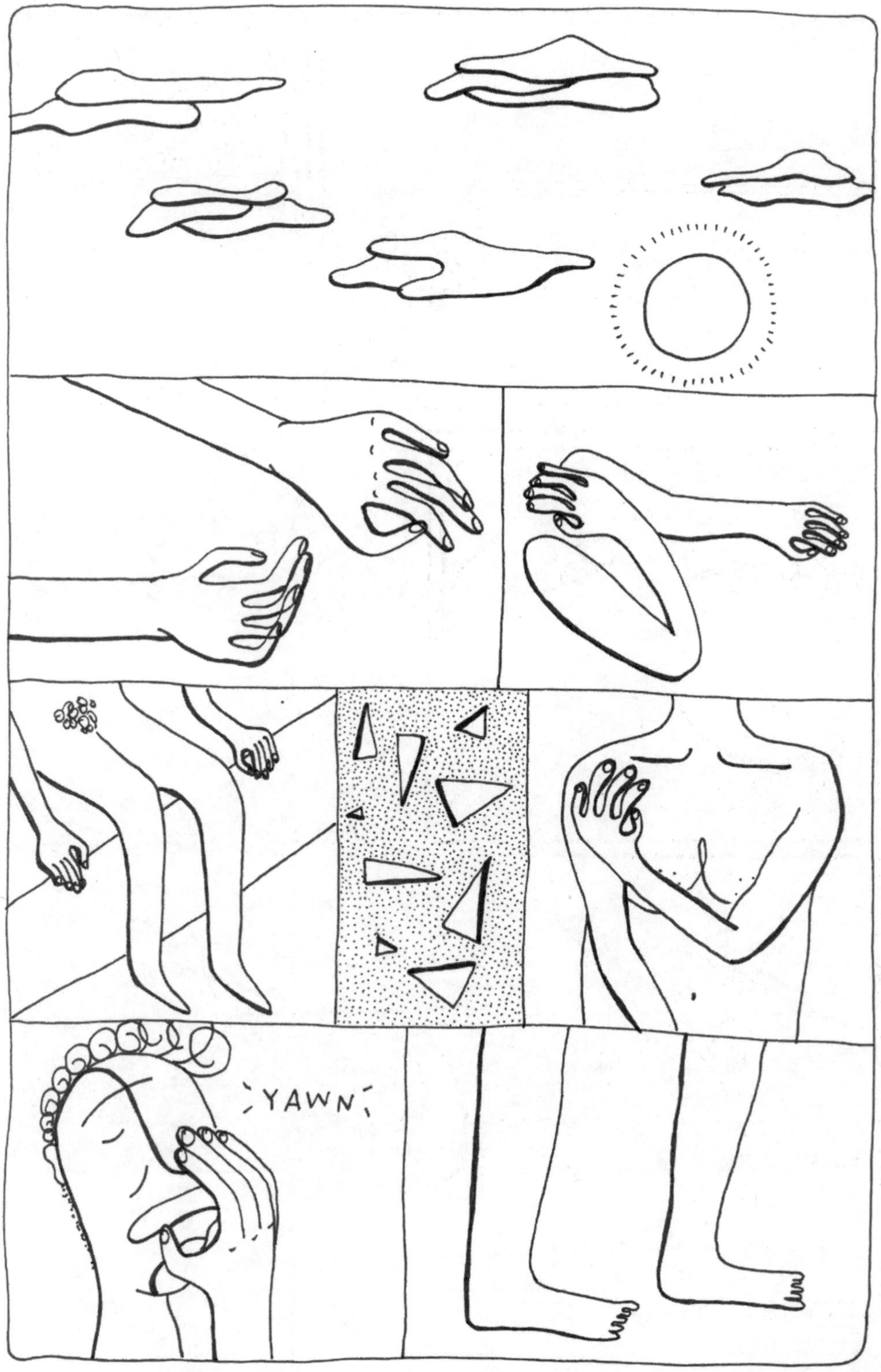
YAWN

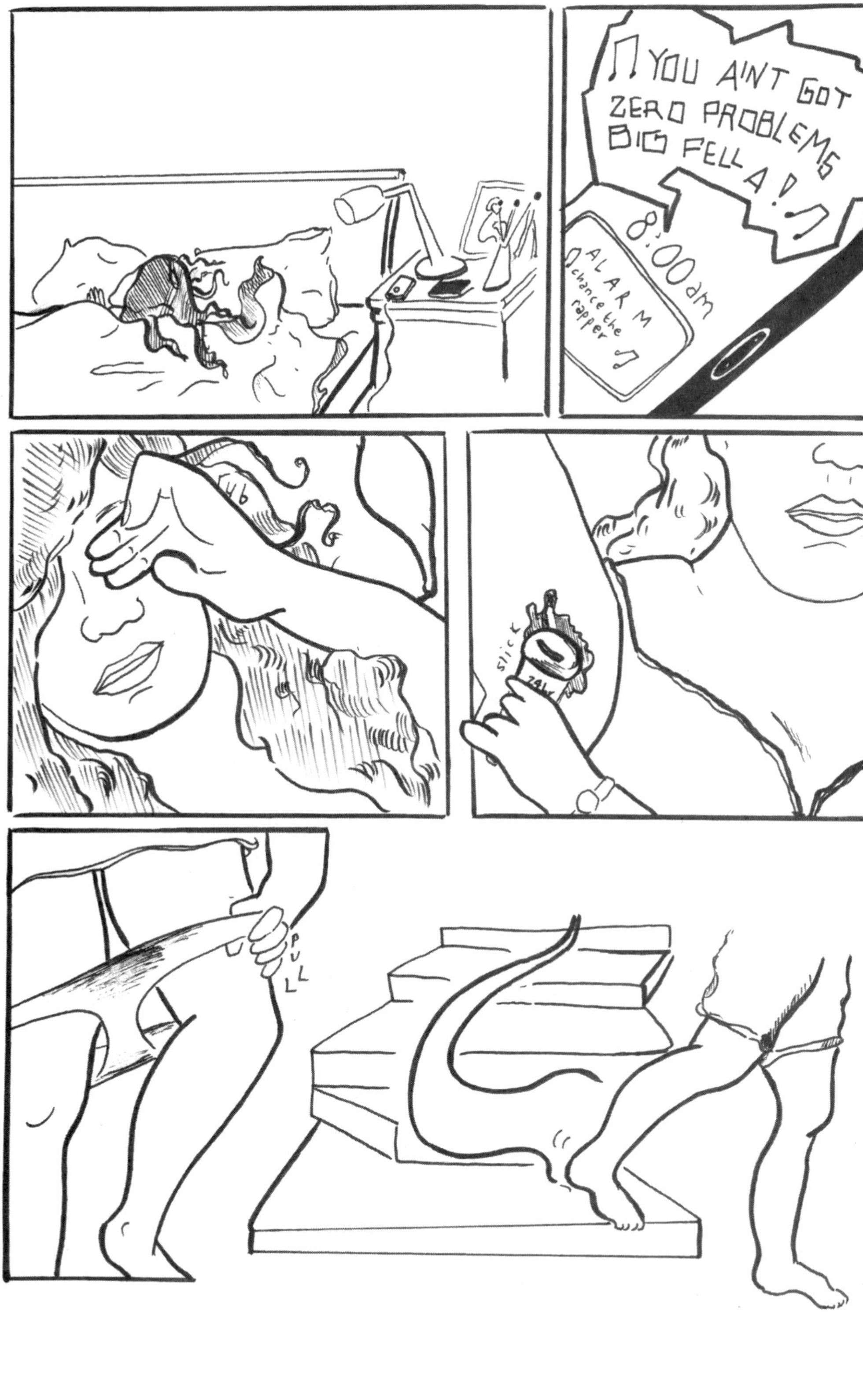
♫ YOU AIN'T GOT ZERO PROBLEMS BIG FELLA! ♫
8:00am
ALARM
♫chance the rapper ♫
rub
slick
24k
PULL

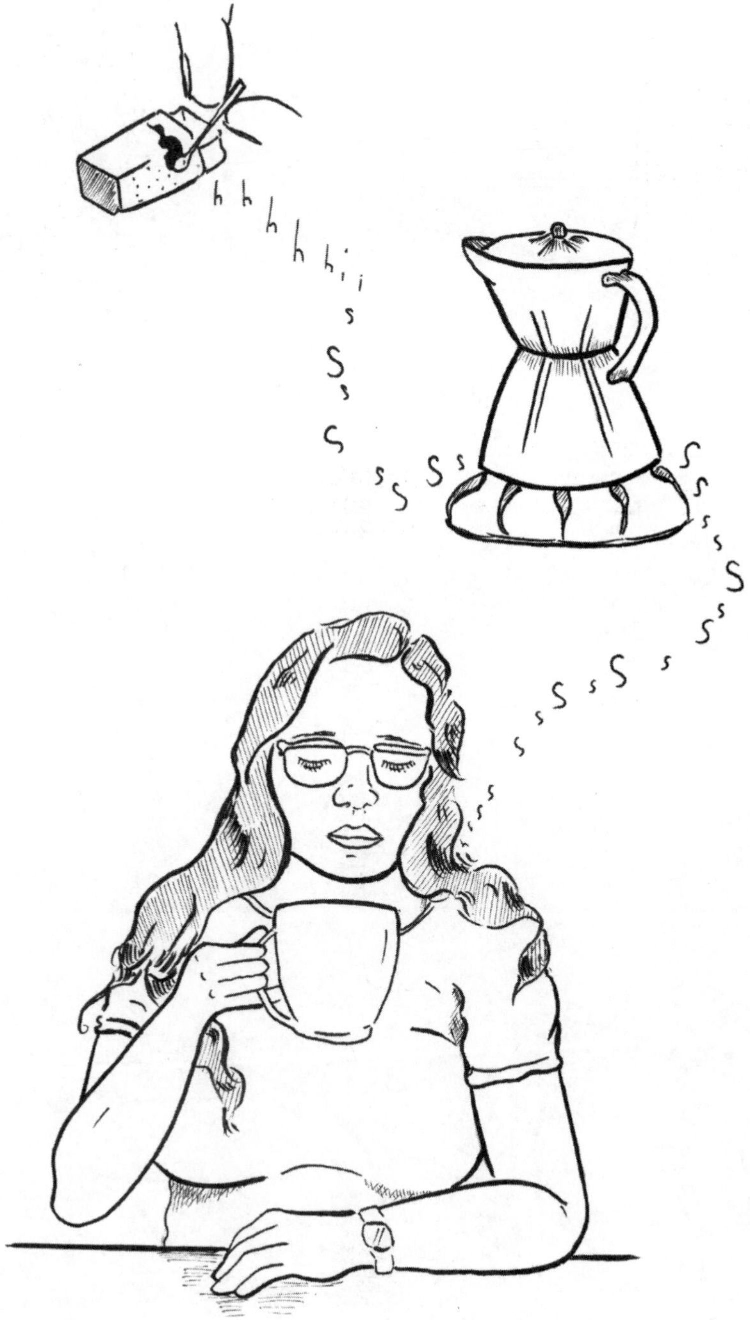

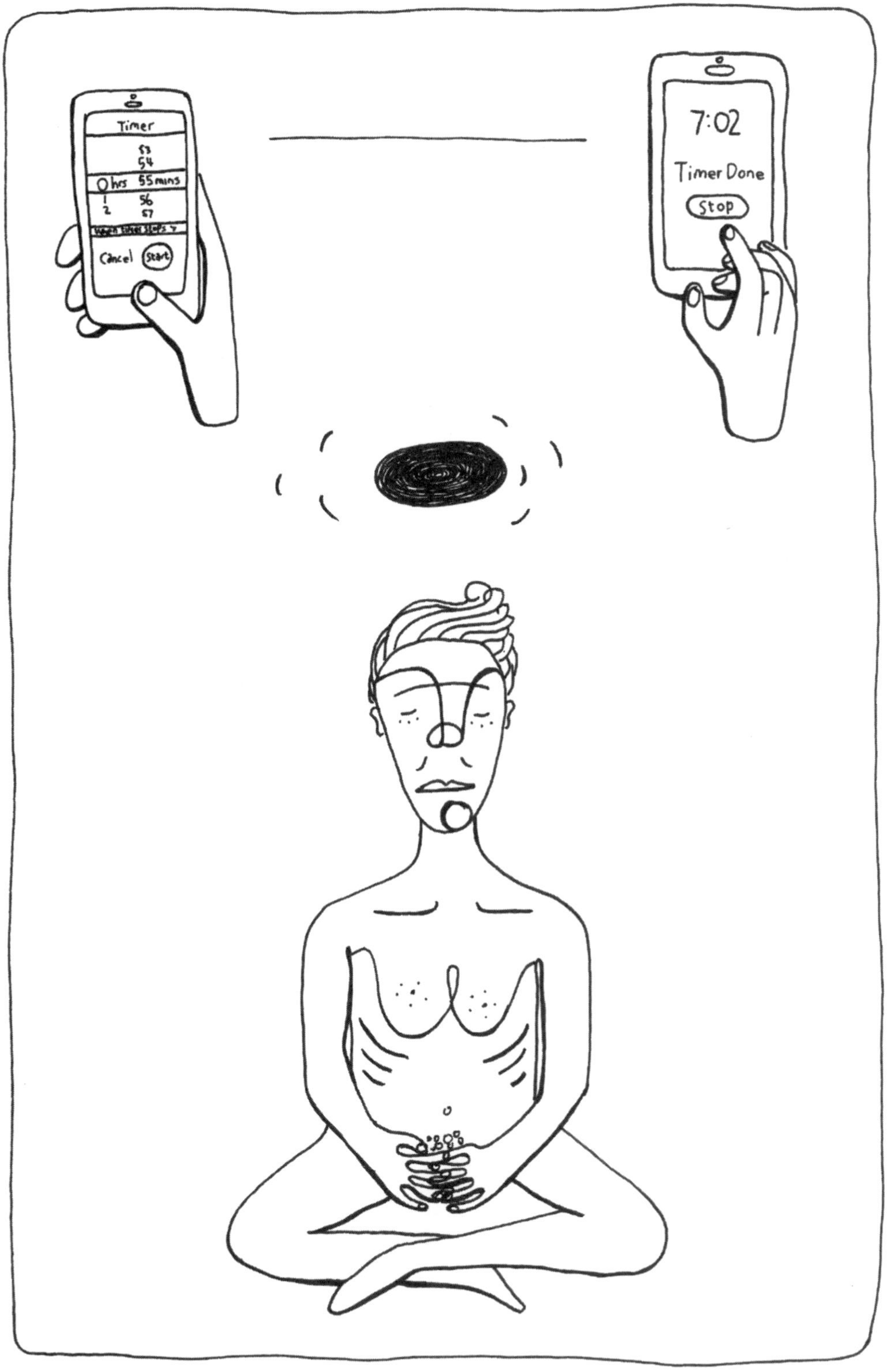
Timer
53
54
0 hrs 55 mins
1 56
2 57
Cancel
Start
7:02
Timer Done
Stop

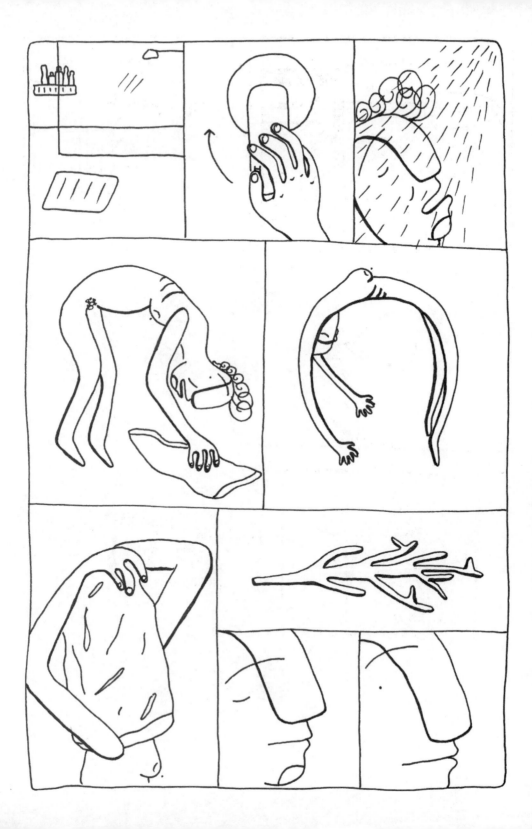

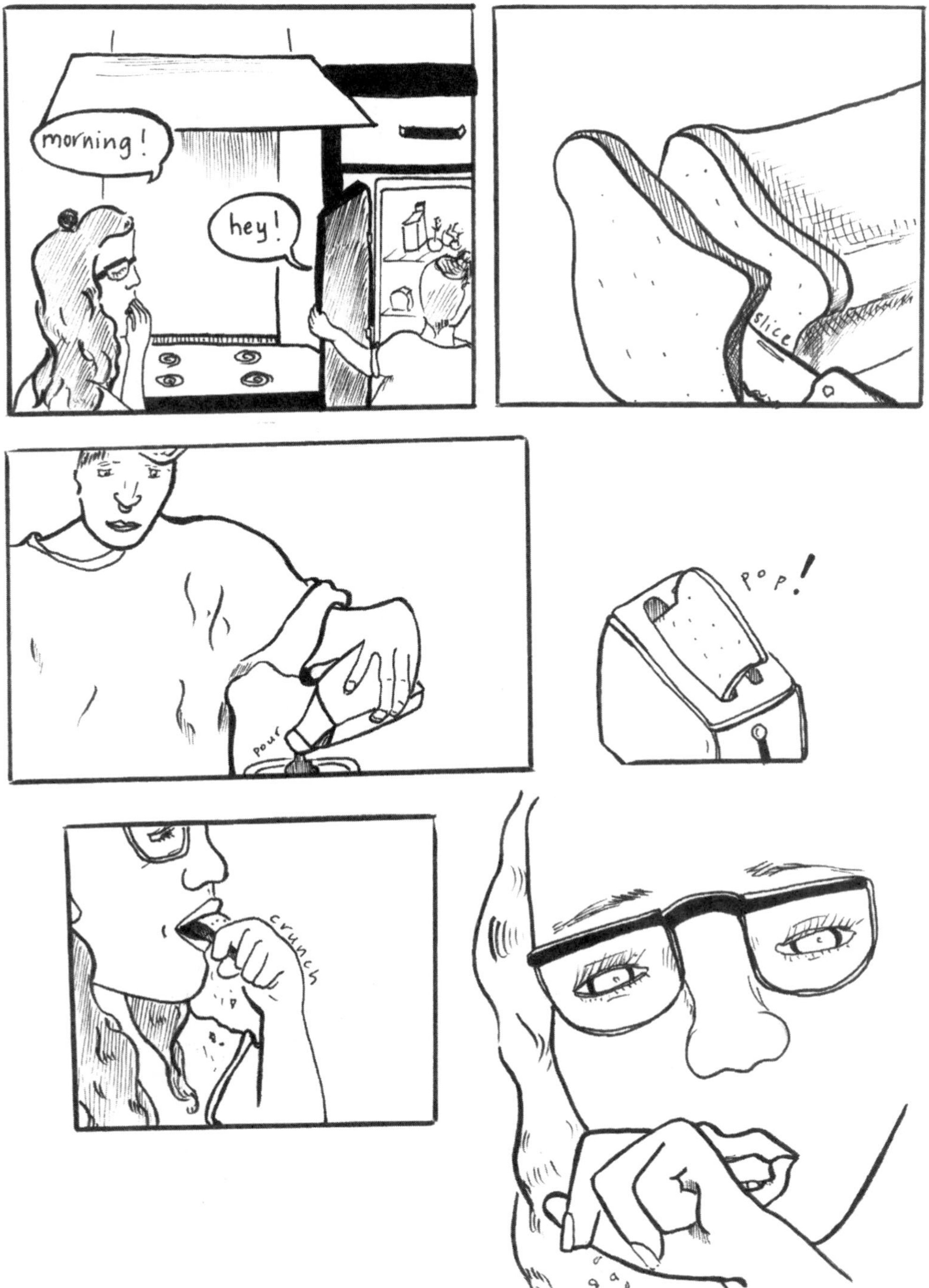
morning!
hey!
slice
pour
pop!
crunch

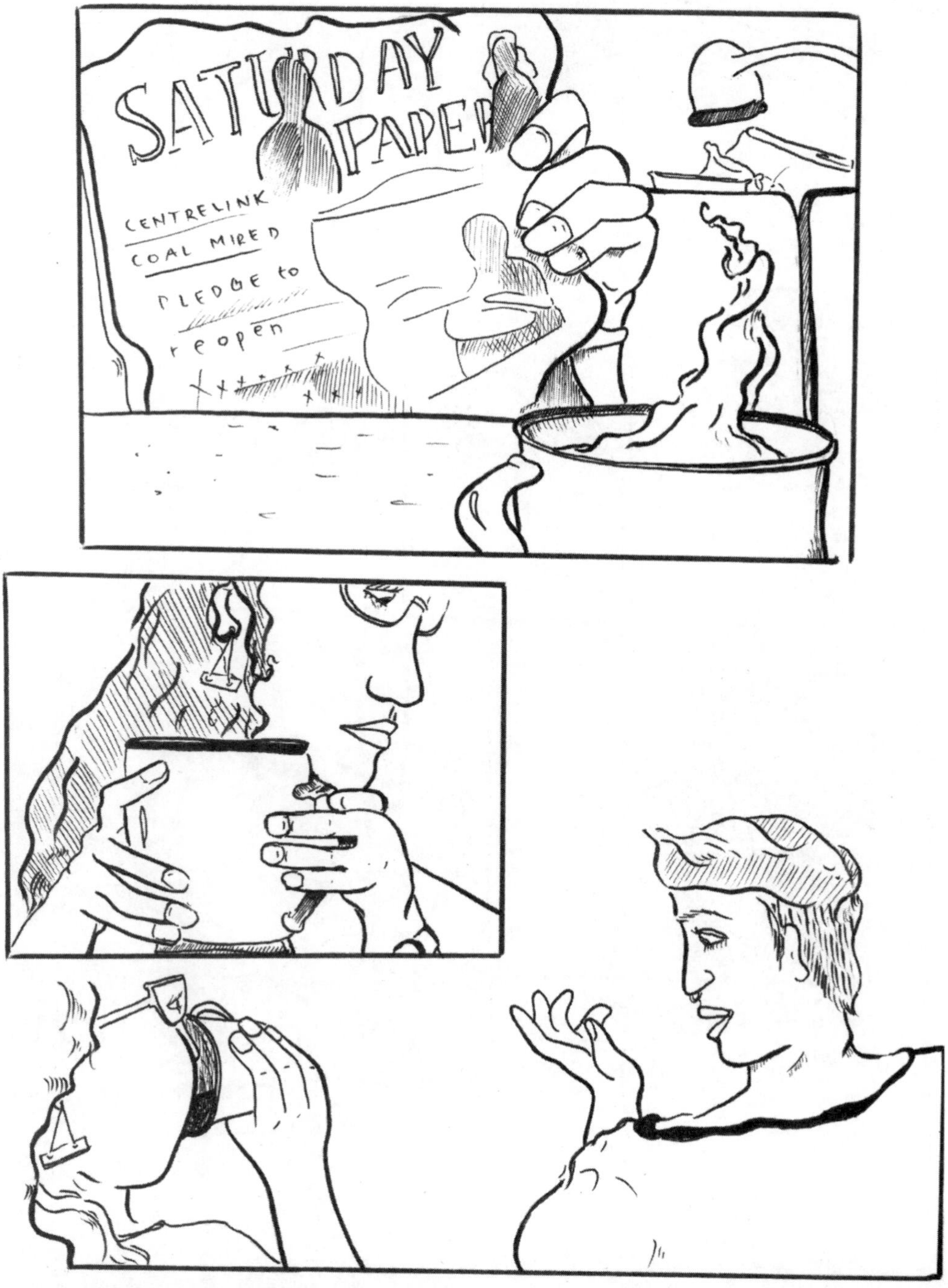
SATURDAY PAPER
CENTRELINK
COAL MIRED
PLEDGE to
reopen

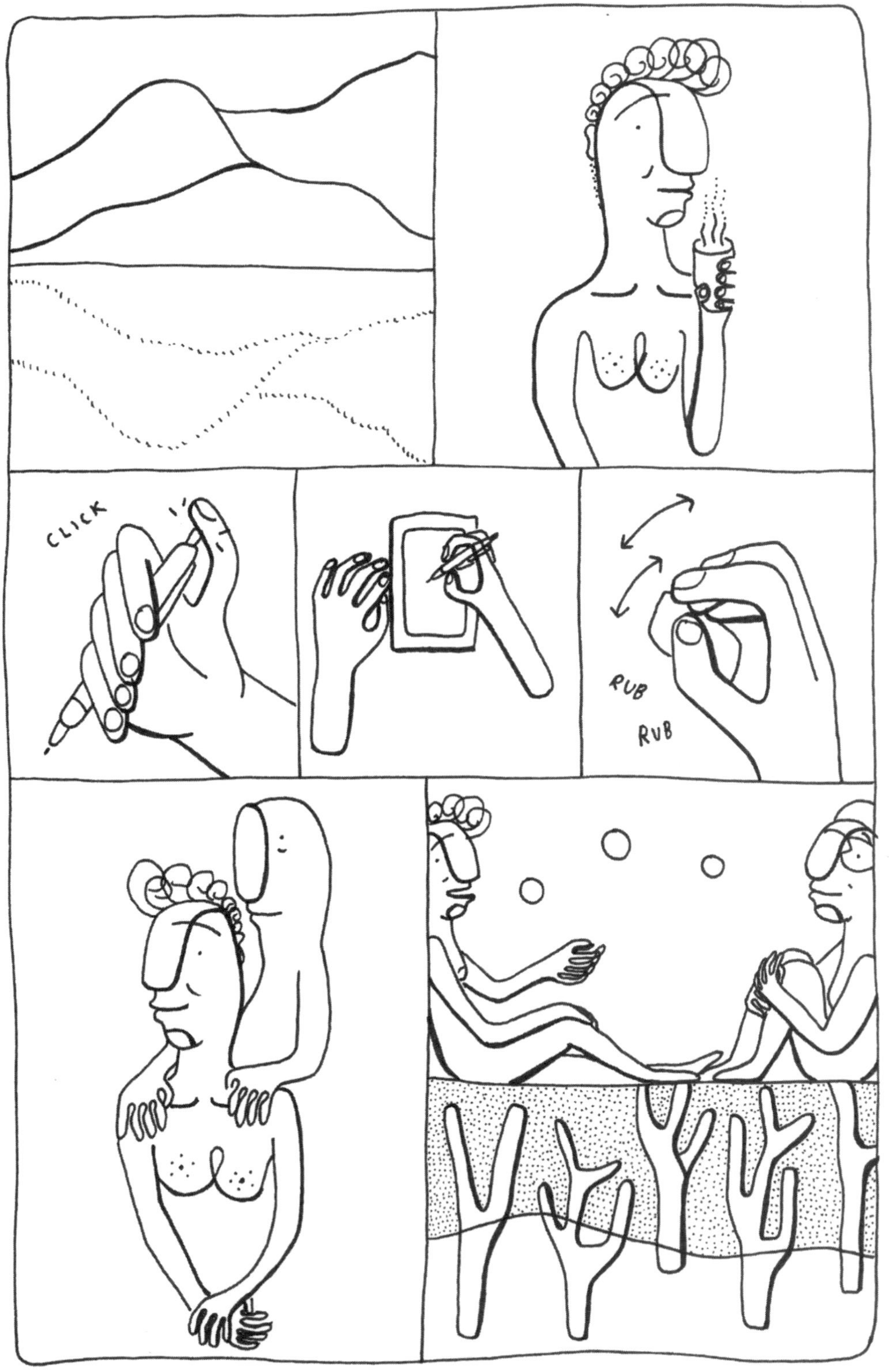
CLICK
RUB
RUB

THROUGHOUT OUR BOOK WE HAVE DRAWN ON OTHER GREAT THINKERS AND ARTISTS WHOSE WORKS HAVE NO DOUBT INSPIRED, INFORMED AND ENABLED OURS TO COME INTO BEING.

IN ORDER OF APPEARANCE THEY ARE

PARRISH, TOMMI. "I WAS JUST TRYING TO BE ALIVE." 2014. ONLINE. TOMMIPG.TUMBLR.COM.

CVETKOVICH, ANN. "DEPRESSION, A PUBLIC FEELING." DURHAM: DUKE UNIVERSITY PRESS, 2012. PRINT.

CLAYCOMB, EVA. "IT'S OK TO BE SAD" IN BREAKFAST ZINE AUSTIN: MONOFONUS PRESS, 2015. PRINT.

ERLICHMAN, SHIRA. "ODE TO LITHIUM #140: NATURAL." WOMEN'S STUDIES QUARTERLY, 44.3 & 4 (2016). pp 260-261. ONLINE. SHIRAE.COM.

CASSEL, ERIC J. "THE NATURE OF SUFFERING AND THE GOALS OF MEDICINE." NEW YORK: OXFORD UNIVERSITY PRESS, 1991. PRINT.

LITTLE BEAR, LEROY. "JAGGED WORLDVIEWS COLLIDING," IN RECLAIMING INDIGENOUS VOICE & VISION, ED. BATTISTE, MARIE. TORONTO/ VANCOUVER UNIVERSITY OF BRITISH COLUMBIA, 2000. pp 77-85. PRINT.

HO, DAVID Y. F. & RAINBOW T. H. HO. "MEASURING SPIRITUALITY AND SPIRITUAL EMPTINESS." REVIEW OF GENERAL PSYCHOLOGY, 11.1 (2007). pp 62-74. PRINT.

BIRD-ROSE, DEBORAH. "HIDDEN HISTORIES." ISLAND MAGAZINE, 52 (1992). pp 14-19. PRINT.

STARK, MICHAEL J & MICHAEL C. WASHBURN. "EGO, EGOCENTRICITY AND SELF-TRANSCENDENCE." PHILOSOPHY EAST AND WEST. 27.3 (1977). pp 265-283.

CROGGON, ALISON. "NAMING THE DAMAGE." OVERLAND (12 MAY 2015). ONLINE.

GRANT, STAN. "TALKING TO MY COUNTRY." MELBOURNE: HARPER COLLINS, 2016. PRINT.

TO STRUGGLE WITH THE TEXTURES OF OUR MENTAL LANDSCAPE CAN FEEL LIKE THE MOST BRUTALISING, LONELY THING. WHAT CHIPKIN AND TAVASSOLI HAVE GIFTED US IS ONE-OF-A-KIND: THE LENS OF KINSHIP. THROUGH THEIR DUAL PERSPECTIVES, WE EAVESDROP ON A TENDER CONVERSATION: HOW CAN I BE THERE FOR YOU? AND HOW CAN I NOT PUSH YOU AWAY? WHILE MOST MEDIA FOCUSES ON THE SO-CALLED FAILURES OR SUCCESSES OF MENTALLY ILL PEOPLE WHO REGAIN NORMALCY, THESE ARTISTS KEEP THEIR FOCUS ON RELATIONSHIP. WE WITNESS QUESTIONS OF HEALTH AND THE REALITIES OF ILLNESS AS TRAVERSED THROUGH THAT MOST PRECIOUS, PRIVATE KINGDOM: HOMIEDOM. THE DEPTH AND NUANCE OF THESE PAGES IS TREASURE IN THE PALM.

—— SHIRA ERLICHMAN (WRITER, VISUAL ARTIST, PRODUCER)

EYES TOO DRY IS A TRULY BEAUTIFUL AND UNIQUE GRAPHIC DEPICTION OF A STORY THAT MANY OF US HAVE EXPERIENCED, BUT MAY NOT HAVE FOUND A WAY TO SPEAK ABOUT. YES, IT'S A SPECIFIC STORY OF TWO YOUNG QUEER WOMEN TRYING TO KEEP THEIR FRIENDSHIP ALIVE THROUGH THE ORDEAL OF DEPRESSION, BUT ITS THEMES OF FEAR AND FRUSTRATION AND SADNESS AND IMMENSE LOVE AND SUPPORT ALL EXISTING IN ONE RELATIONSHIP IS UNIVERSAL. I HAVE NEVER SEEN MENTAL ILLNESS DEPICTED IN THIS WAY, AND THE ILLUSTRATIONS CONVEY THE EMOTIONAL AND PHYSICAL TOLL OF DEPRESSION MORE POWERFULLY THAN ANYTHING I'VE SEEN BEFORE. THIS IS AN IMPORTANT BOOK ABOUT A TOPIC THAT STILL HOLDS SO MUCH STIGMA, AND THE MORE PEOPLE THAT READ IT THE BETTER.

—— REBECCA SHAW (WRITER, SBS COMEDY)

THIS BOOK IS A BEAUTIFUL MEDITATION ON INTIMACY, STRUGGLE, LISTLESSNESS, AND ACHING EMPATHY. ALICE AND TAVA'S INTERCHANGING CHAPTERS WEAVE PAINFULLY, TENDERLY FAMILIAR ENVIRONMENTS. MUCH LIKE THE RELATIONSHIP DEPICTED, THIS STORY CRACKS OPEN, PULLS YOU IN AND HOLDS YOU THROUGH THAT PROCESS. READING THIS FEELS LIKE A BRAVE CONVERSATION WITH AN OLD FRIEND.

—— LEE LAI (VISUAL ARTIST)

AS AN ACADEMIC WHO WORKS ACROSS THE FIELDS OF CREATIVE WRITING, COMICS, AND GRAPHIC MEDICINE, I WAS THRILLED AND INSPIRED BY THE TWO UNIQUE VOICES IN THIS BOOK, WHICH SPEAK TO EACH OTHER NOT ONLY IN WORDS, BUT IN THOSE OTHER LINES PARTICULAR TO THE MEDIUM OF COMICS: THE CURVE OF A HAND AROUND A CUP OF SOUP; THE BROKEN EDGE OF A PANEL BORDER; THE BALLOON OF AIR AROUND SPEECH; THE INKY BLACKNESS OF THE HOLES INTO WHICH WE SOMETIMES SINK. AS A PERSON WHO GREW UP WITH IMMEDIATE FAMILY MEMBERS SUFFERING THROUGH DEPRESSION AND OTHER MENTAL ILLNESSES, THIS BOOK OFFERS A PORTRAIT OF TENDERNESS, FRIENDSHIP, CARING AND LOVE THAT IS EXPRESSED NOT JUST WITH HONESTY AND COMPASSION, BUT WITH PRACTICAL, CLEAR AND SPECIFIC WAYS OF NAVIGATING COMPLEX EMOTIONAL TERRITORY. THIS BOOK HELPED ME, WITHOUT TELLING ME WHAT IT WAS DOING. I COULDN'T BE MORE ADMIRING OF THE ACHIEVEMENT OF THESE TWO YOUNG ARTISTS.

—— DR. ELIZABETH MACFARLANE (PROFESSOR AT UNIVERSITY OF MELBOURNE, PUBLISHER OF TWELVE PANELS PRESS)

[EYES TOO DRY] IS A UNIQUE, BEAUTIFUL AND HEARTRENDING DEPICTION OF TRUE LOVE AND FRIENDSHIP AND THE 'HEAVINESS OF BEING' THAT WE ALL ENCOUNTER AT TIMES IN OUR LIVES. BRAVO!

—— ASSOCIATE PROFESSOR, SALLY AYOUB
DIRECTOR OF UNDERGRADUATE MEDICAL EDUCATION, FACULTY OF MEDICINE, NURSING AND HEALTH SCIENCES, MONASH UNIVERSITY)

RECALLING THE EMOTIONAL INTIMACY AND HONESTY OF ALISON BECHDEL'S FUN HOME, IT SIMILARLY THRUMS WITH HOPE, FOCUSED AS IT IS ON QUEER FRIENDSHIP AND THE THERAPEUTIC RESULTS OF CREATING COMICS [...] A DEEPLY ENGAGING EMOTIONAL VOYAGE THAT WILL APPEAL TO ANYONE WHO HAS EVER EXPERIENCED MENTAL ILL HEALTH, EITHER PERSONALLY OR IN THEIR EXTENDED CIRCLE OF FAMILY AND FRIENDS.

—— SBS AUSTRALIA

AS AN ACADEMIC IN THE HEALTH SCIENCES FIELD, I HAVE EXPERIENCED REPEATED FRUSTRATION WITH RESPECT TO TYPICAL FORMS OF ACADEMIC CURRENCY [...] AND THE FACT THAT THEY TEND TO REACH ONLY A VERY LIMITED AUDIENCE, PRIMARILY OTHER ACADEMICS. WHILE THIS IS IMPORTANT, THERE ARE MANY OTHER STAKEHOLDERS [...] WHO NEED TO BE AWARE OF THE LIVED EXPERIENCE AND SOCIAL CONTEXT WITHIN WHICH MENTAL HEALTH AND ILLNESS IS EXPERIENCED. [EYES TOO DRY] IS A PRIME EXAMPLE OF USING VISUAL, EMBODIED WAYS OF SHARING THE VERY PERSONAL EXPERIENCE OF MENTAL HEALTH ISSUES. SUCH KNOWLEDGE TRANSLATION IS POWERFUL AND HAS THE GREAT POTENTIAL TO REACH A WIDE VARIETY OF AUDIENCES.

— KATHERINE BOYDELL (PROFESSOR OF MENTAL HEALTH, BLACK DOG INSTITUTE)

THIS MEMOIR IS SO HONEST AND BEAUTIFUL IN ITS STORYTELLING. EYES TOO DRY ISN'T AFRAID TO TALK OPENLY ABOUT DEPRESSION, PEOPLE SUPPORTING PEOPLE WITH DEPRESSION AND THE STIGMA BEHIND IT ALL. IT HAS FAST BECOME ONE OF MY FAVOURITE GRAPHIC NOVELS.

— VLADA EDIRIPPULIGE (JUNKY COMICS)

EYES TOO DRY IS COMICS-MAKING AS PROCESSING. IT'S SO LIVE AND SO RAW. [...] IT'S INCREDIBLY COMPELLING. I READ IT POWERING THROUGH THE PAGES. I REALLY RECOMMEND THIS AS A CHRONICLE, OF THESE TWO PEOPLE, BUT ALSO AS A USE OF THE FORM. AS ARCHAEOLOGY; AS DIGGING; AS NAMING — NAMING STUFF THAT IS SO HARD TO COME TO TERMS WITH. [THE STUFF THAT] EXISTS AND OBTRUDES UPON YOUR WHOLE LIFE. I THINK IT'S A REMARKABLE ACHIEVEMENT. A REMARKABLE UNDERTAKING.

— BERNARD CALEO (COMICS ARTIST, EDITOR, PERFORMER)
                    REVIEW ON RRR SMART ARTS RADIO

EYES TOO DRY IS A TIME CAPSULE, AN INTIMATE PORTRAIT OF TWO FRIENDS, AND A VITALLY POWERFUL CONVERSATION ABOUT WHAT IT'S LIKE TO HAVE 'HEAVY FEELINGS.' [...] IN THE END, IT IS AN EXTRAORDINARY WORK ABOUT DEALING WITH DEPRESSION, HELPING PEOPLE WHO SUFFER IT, AND THE EFFECTS IT CAN HAVE ON EVERYONE. BUT IT'S ALSO A CELEBRATION OF FRIENDSHIP AND A TESTAMENT TO THE THERAPEUTIC POWER OF ART AND CREATIVITY.

— VICE.COM